# A Guide to Bird Finding in Washington

by

Terence R. Wahl

and

Dennis R. Paulson

Illustrations by

Linda M. Feltner

1991 edition
revised 1994

published by

T. R. Wahl

Bellingham, Washington


Printed in the USA by

**3212 E. Hwy 30
Kearney, NE 68847
800-650-7888**

# CONTENTS

Since this book was first published there have been many changes in Washington habitats, land use and associated birds, and we attempt to update these here with corrections, some changes in site descriptions and road designations.

English or "common" names and the order in which species occur within the lists follow the latest decisions of the American Ornithologists' Union (1983 and supplements).

As interest in birds and communication among birders have increased the function of the original authors has become more editorial as, increasingly, many people have contributed to the guide. We thank them - without them we would have been unable to include many areas in which we have limited experience. These individuals (whose initials are given following site descriptions) include: Thais Bock (TB), Bill Boyes (BB), Wilson Cady (WC), Art Campbell (AC), Joan

Carson (JC), Fred Chancey (FC), Mark Conwell (MC), Jack Davis (JDa), Mike Denny (MD), Jim Duemmel (JD), Bob and Pat Evans (B&PE), Ron Friesz (RFr), Robert Furrer (RF), Eleanor Gandy (EG), Gary Garrison (GG), Warren Hall (WH), David Herr (DHe), Glen and Wanda Hoge (G&WH), Eugene Hunn (EH), David Hutchinson (DH), Bert Jahn (BJ), Norman Lavers (NL), Richard Lindstrom (RL), Phil Mattocks (PM), Anthony Mendoza (AM), Martin Muller (MM), Roger Muskat (RM), Jack Nesbit (JN), David Pearson (DPe), Evelyn Peaslee (EP), Rusty and Jeanette Rathfelder (R&JR), Alan Richards (AR), Frank Richardson (FR), Tom Schooley (TSc), Jeff Skriletz (JS), Dory Smith (DSm), Ernie Spragg (ES), Mary Stapp (MS), Andy Stepniewski (AS), Ted Stiles (TS), David Stirling (DS), Harold Stout (HS), Rob Thorn (RT), Verna Timm (VT), Mike Toochin (MT), Bill Tweit (BT), George Walter (GW), Bart Whelton (BWh), Jeff Wisman (JW), Bob Woodley (BW), Keith & Jan Wiggers (K&JW) and the authors (TW, DP).

## BIRDING POSSIBILITIES IN WASHINGTON

Great altitudinal variation in the state is easily accessible by road, and in a single day it is possible for a birder to cover several "life zones," each with its characteristic species of plants and animals. Several site descriptions include routes that cover a change of up to 6,000 feet in elevation, from sea level to timberline. Even with limited time, one can drive from Seattle to Yakima over Chinook Pass and see virtually all the state's terrestrial habitats. An equally interesting drive that omits the higher elevations is the one from Seattle to Vantage over Snoqualmie Pass. Even limiting this

drive to one day, it is possible to see a great many of the birds of each of the life zones if stops are made at a few localities on each side of the mountains and between Ellensburg and Vantage. A one-day trip to Port Townsend and Dungeness or to Whidbey Island from Seattle provides a good introduction to western Washington terrestrial and marine habitats. A few areas in location descriptions are included on the basis of published descriptions (by Washington Department of Wildlife and the U.S. Fish and Wildlife Service) regarding the presence of certain species which are sought by birders. Further, most areas administered by state and federal agencies with suitable habitats are worth visiting. Local maps and self-guided tour information are often available. Research or natural areas - concerned primarily with baseline studies of native vegetation types - of both state and federal agencies offer good birding possibilities. And of course many city, county and state parks, national forest areas, national parks and recreation areas are good birding areas, often featuring interesting species in or near campgrounds. Some of these spots are included as location accounts, but many more have good birds.Washington has an abundance of birding habitat, with many places still unexplored by birders. Locations given here are generally well-known locally, are well covered, and are chosen not only for species variety and abundance but for accessibility. There are certainly as many more good spots not included as are given here. We are very interested in learning of other good areas with which you are familiar.

## WASHINGTON CLIMATE

The distribution of land birds in the state is governed basically by variations in temperature and rainfall and the accompanying zonation of plant distribution. Physiography controls rainfall patterns and is therefore very important in the distribution of organisms. The prevailing winds come from the southwest, from the Pacific Ocean, where they have picked up a great quantity of moisture. As the winds strike the western slopes of the Olympic Mountains, the air rises, cools, and loses much of its moisture on the mountainsides. The highest rainfall in the state occurs in this area, which receives fifteen times as much rainfall annually as the driest parts of eastern Washington. Northeast of the Olympics is a marked rain shadow, an area receiving no more precipitation than the dry forests in the eastern part of the state. As the air moves across Puget Sound more moisture is picked up and much of this water is dropped on the western slopes of the Cascade Mountains, again a region of very high rainfall. Farther to the east, the rainfall decreases rapidly to a minimum at lower elevations in the Columbia River basin, then increases again in the mountains of the northeastern and southeastern corners of the state. The temperature gradient is much more pronounced altitudinally than from north to south in Washington. With an elevation range of over 14,000 feet, temperatures both in midwinter and midsummer vary greatly from sea level to the mountain tops. Daily maxima of over 100°F are common in the desert, while snow remains the year round on the higher peaks.

The seasons are well-marked, especially east of the Cascades. Precipitation is heavier in the winter and spring, summers generally being dry in all regions. In western Washington winters are very wet, with overcast skies and light rain an almost constant condition in some years. This is interspersed with short periods of northeasterly winds which bring dry and cold air from the interior, resulting in clear skies and unsurpassed views of mountains. Snowfall in the lowlands usually occurs at these times, when cold interior air meets moist coastal air. Above a thousand feet in elevation, snow remains on the ground all winter, lasting at the 5,000 foot level into July or even August. Summers west of the Cascades are warm with the amount of rainfall variable from year to year; some summers are entirely dry and quite warm, others are cool and rainy. East of the mountains, winters are cold, and snow may stay on the ground throughout colder winters, even at the lowest elevations. In warmer winters, many ponds in the Columbia Basin remain open, and snow cover melts in a few days. Summers are very dry and hot in eastern Washington. The desert areas remain green into June, but by July the general impression is one of death, many of the organisms having finished their annual life cycles and gone into a dormant state. Much of the vegetation is dry, and even birds are not particularly in evidence, except around water.

## WASHINGTON HABITATS

This section explains the symbols used in the list of birds occurring regularly in the state.

**SW** - open salt water. This includes the straits, bays, and estuaries and the open sea to 200 miles offshore. Despite its often homogenous appearance there is great variability in this habitat due to depth, bottom configuration and substrate, currents and effects of tides on the water column and its animals. Thus all open salt water isn't equal when it comes to finding birds.

**RS** - rocky shore. Characteristic of the northern outer coast, this habitat is widespread inland also. Much of the shoreline is near-vertical, with little habitat for shorebirds except for those species that forage on the rocks exposed by low tide. The northern half of the Olympic Peninsula has the most productive rocky intertidal areas, but rock jetties projecting from sandy beach areas along the southern coast support similar bird populations and may be the most dependable places to find them.

**SS** - sandy shore, mud flats, salt marsh. South of Grays Harbor almost all of the ocean shoreline is flat and sandy, and similar conditions prevail in many other areas. Mud flats in bays are included here, and have more birds than the exposed, coarse sand ocean beaches themselves.

**FW** - freshwater, marsh and shore. These freshwater habitats are widespread, even in some parts of the desert where large natural and artificial lakes are scattered throughout.

Some of them, especially those with large shallow regions, are excellent for birds; those with no littoral (shallow) zone are poor in general, although they may attract waterfowl in migration. Most ponds in the state are somewhat alkaline and support dense growths of cattails and bulrushes, and many of the species that forage in the open water nest in these beds of vegetation. Acid bog ponds are widespread in the wetter regions, but these are usually not productive of birds.

**WC** - wet coniferous forest. This habitat is one of the dominant ones in the state, being found from the coast to the upper east slopes of the Cascades, and along the northern and northeastern borders of the state. It is the habitat most people associate mentally with the Pacific Northwest. Originally these forests were characterized by huge trees, and the forest interior was dark and humid, with heavy epiphyte growth and a relatively open understory. With logging, the coniferous forests have been opened up and now much of Washington is forested with second growth, some of it impressive enough in its own right. Only a few remnants of lowland primary forest exist, but larger areas of mountain forest remain in a primeval state. Three species of trees characterize lowland coniferous forests of western Washington - Douglas fir, western hemlock, and western red cedar. In coastal areas Sitka spruce becomes important and on the coast itself is often the only species. Higher in the mountains these species are supplemented by and in some areas replaced by silver and noble firs. With still greater elevation the lowland species drop out, and the dominant trees are alpine fir, yellow cedar, lodgepole pine and mountain hemlock. The avifauna changes accordingly with elevation, although a fair number of species occur from the coast to the tree line in these forests. Often the undergrowth is lush, consisting primarily of shrubs of the heath and rose families, ferns and lilies.

**DC** - dry coniferous forest. This forested region extends as a belt around the desert and grasslands of the Columbia basin. It is most extensive on the middle eastern slopes of the Cascades and in the Spokane area. The dominant, and in many areas the only, tree species is ponderosa pine. In wetter valleys the Douglas fir is associated with it, as are grand firs, western larches and other species that may also grow in the wet forests. At higher elevations Engelmann spruce is added to the list. In the pine zone the understory is open, with relatively few shrubs (roses, serviceberries and mock orange for example) but with a great variety of herbaceous species. In typical form this is a much drier and more open habitat than the preceding one, but the two interdigitate in a complex manner, especially in valleys, where ponderosa pines grow commonly with species from the wet forest.

**BF** - broadleaf forest. There are patches of this habitat throughout the wetter parts of the state. These are never as extensive as the coniferous forests. In western Washington red alder is the dominant species, usually accompanied by bigleaf maple and vine maple and often by black cottonwood, and all may also grow in mixed stands with conifers. East of the Cascades, bigleaf and vine maples are replaced by Rocky Mountain maple, red alder by two smaller species, and cottonwood occurs widely with its relative, quaking aspen, usually in moister areas. In eastern Washington broadleaf areas occur as islands in pine forests. The extensive stands of Garry oak in south-central and "Tacoma-prairie" regions of the state are also included in this category type.

**RW** - riparian woodland. This habitat, more characteristic of eastern Washington, borders streams and lakes, next to either coniferous forest or desert or grassland. Tree species are similar to those in broadleaf forests, with cottonwoods and willows especially prominent in desert riparian growth.

**DG** - dry grassland. Very large areas of eastern Washington once supported several species of native bunchgrasses and their many characteristic plants and animals. This region proved excellent for growing wheat, however, and much of it has disappeared. In many still unfarmed areas introduced cheatgrass has outcompeted the native grasses and drastically transformed the nature of the vegetation. Now there are only relict patches of this habitat, and they can be expected to decrease further as little is protected. The grassland lies above the sagebrush desert through much of the state, in a belt around the Columbia basin, too cold for many of the desert species and too dry to support trees. Most of the herbaceous plant species are the same as those present in the ponderosa pine zone, and the two habitats are very similar except for the very important absence of the trees.

**WM** - wet meadow. This is primarily an alpine habitat, since most areas that are sufficiently moist to support a meadow in the lowlands succeed into forest rapidly. Around the borders of desert lakes, in very boggy areas in the coniferous forest zone, and as a result of agriculture, there are sufficient meadows in the lowlands to serve as avian habitats. Above tree line in the wetter regions (the Olympics and the crest and west side of the Cascades) herbaceous growth is lush, with grasses, sedges and forbs of many species, the latter erupting in a mid-summer floral display unexcelled anywhere.

**SD** - sagebrush desert. Very large areas of this vegetation type are associated with the Columbia River basin and the lower slopes of the mountains around it. A single shrub, big sagebrush, dominates this habitat, although other shrubs (rabbitbrush, greasewood, bitterbrush) may be locally important, and many herbaceous species, especially grasses, are common. Bunchgrass and/or cheatgrass fill the spaces between the shrubs. This is the driest and hottest habitat of the state, and it supports a biota with southern affinities.

**ST** - shrubby thicket. This habitat includes all shrubby habitats either in or out of coniferous forest or broadleaf forest, and certain species of birds are characteristic of it. Many species of angiosperm shrubs and small, young trees occur, usually in dense stands.

**PG** - parks and gardens. This urban habitat is present in cities, towns and settlements all over the state. It includes patches of native vegetation (for example, Douglas fir forest in Seattle, sagebrush in Richland) often much modified by humans, and this is inhabited by a diverse assemblage of bird species.

**FL** - farmland. Washington contains large areas of pasture and agricultural land, often inhabited by species of native grasslands, although many of the latter are not able to switch to the simpler habitats produced by human endeavor. For example, extensive wheat fields are used by only one species, the Horned Lark, out of many that existed in the original grassland. Well-irrigated cropland attracts birds of wet meadows that might otherwise be lacking in many areas, for example Killdeer and several blackbirds and sparrows.

## HAZARDS IN THE FIELD

There is only one poisonous snake in the state, the Western Rattlesnake, and it occurs only east of the Cascades below about 2500 feet elevation chiefly in desert and rocky areas. Black widows are found in the east, as are scorpions, but neither is likely to be encountered. Even poisonous plants are scarce in western Washington, where poison oak is locally distributed. Poison ivy is common on rocky hillsides in the ponderosa pine zone east of the Cascade summits. Ticks are found, primarily in eastern Washington, in forested and sagebrush areas. Biting insects are nothing like they are in the Florida Everglades or the Alaska taiga, but sometimes mosquitos and biting flies can be very bothersome, especially in the mountains. A good insect repellant is usually adequate. In the back country, water from streams may not be safe for drinking, because of the spotty occurrence of giardia. While forest fires are not a likely hazard, the fire season can cause forest closures and inconvenience. A final hazard might be log trucks if you're on logging roads at the wrong time (usually week days) or not keeping up with the fast pace set by these behemoths on Olympic Peninsula highways. Caution and not stopping on roadways will avoid problems. Local inquiries about conditions of unpaved mountain and back-country roads in early spring are advisable.

Birding in some areas of Washington has recently brought us problems experienced previously in other parts of North America where both larger human populations and intense birding pressure have existed for years. Some locations noted in this book are on or adjoin private property, and have been visited in the past by many birders. Please respect private property, pay attention to signs, and do not do anything that might jeopardize future use by others. Contact property owners ahead of time before visiting bird feeders. Please do not take large groups into fragile habitats unless the area is public and facilities there (trails, etc.) can take it.

Special pleas: Tramping in marshes can have minimal effects if done infrequently by a few; repeated "stomps" are something else. Please be very careful not to disturb threatened or rare species. Their status may result from disturbance in the first place - don't make it worse through photographic efforts, etc. Use tape recorders with discretion. Don't use playbacks on the same bird more than once or twice; don't play tapes in an area where other people are doing the same thing. It's relatively easy to find another place and call up one's own birds. Please consider others - property owners, others enjoying birds and the animals themselves and their habitats.

These lists include the species recorded regularly and are intended to reflect the likelihood of the species' being seen in the proper region, habitat and season. Species names and order correspond to the Sixth edition of the A.O.U. **Checklist of North American Birds** (1983) and subsequent supplements (**Auk** 101:348, **Auk** 102:680-686). Because field guides and other sources retain previous names, a footnote following the Occurrence checklist and the Casuals list gives former English or "common" names. Placement of species on regular or casual lists here is based on status given in Mattocks, Hunn and Wahl (1976). A checklist of the birds of Washington State, with recent changes annotated, **Western Birds** 7(1):1-24, 1984 and subsequent information about the occurrence of species through 1990, as accepted by the Washington Bird Records Committee. Check-list of Washington Birds, revised.

**Washington Birds** 1:1-5. Our list represents a compromise between a necessarily generalized regular status which does not include casual occurrences of many species in unusual regions, habitats and seasons, and the need to point out very localized species or differences between western and eastern parts of the state.

The first checklist is particularly intended to be used with the bird finding locality descriptions (Pp. 39-155). Occurrence codes given on the next page are used in both checklist and locality descriptions.

In species with subspecies or color morphs easily recognizable in the field, footnotes indicate which forms occur in Washington.

A listing of species known to have occurred casually in the state follows the first checklist.

Use the codes below to determine general abundance, distribution and habitat preference of species occurring regularly (seen every year) in the state. The symbol (#) indicates a notation for that species in the SPECIES NOTATIONS section following.

ORIGIN: Introduced species - (I)

BREEDING: * - nests regularly   *R - nests rarely

REGIONS  (left set of columns on list of birds)
   O - offshore; out of sight of land
   C - coast; includes all coast and estuarine areas
   W - west of Cascades in lowlands (to 3000'elevation)
   M - mountains (over 3000')
   E - east of Cascades in lowlands (to 3000')

SEASONALITY (in columns under REGIONS)
   P - permanent resident; present all year; abundance may vary seasonally
   S - summer visitor only (includes spring and fall)
   W - winter visitor only (includes spring and fall)
   M - migrant only (spring and fall)
   F - fall migrant only (may be rarely seen in spring)

HABITATS (right set of columns)
   SW - open salt water
   RS - rocky shore
   SS - sandy shore, mud flats, salt marsh
   FW - fresh water, including marsh and shore
   WC - wet coniferous forest
   DC - dry coniferous forest
   BF - broadleaf forest
   RW - riparian woodland (along watercourses)
   DG - dry grassland
   WM - wet meadow (includes alpine meadow)
   SD - sagebrush desert
   ST - shrubby thickets (in or out of forest)
   PG - parks and gardens (cities)
   FL - farmland

ABUNDANCE (in columns under HABITATS)
   C - common; often seen or heard in appropriate habitats
   U - uncommon; usually present but not seen or heard
      on every visit to appropriate habitats
   R - rare; present in appropriate habitats only in
      small numbers and seldom seen or heard; this designation
      is not applied to common species in seldom-used habitats

Capital letter - breeding habitat; lower case letter -  non-breeding habitat

| | REGIONS | | | | | HABITATS | | | | | | | | | | | | | |
|---|---|---|---|---|---|---|---|---|---|---|---|---|---|---|---|---|---|---|---|
| | O | C | W | M | E | SW | RS | SS | FW | WC | DC | BF | RW | DG | WM | SD | ST | PG | FL |
| **GAVIIDAE** | | | | | | | | | | | | | | | | | | | |
| Red-throated Loon # | - | W | - | - | - | c | - | - | - | - | - | - | - | - | - | - | - | - | - |
| Pacific Loon # | - | W | - | - | F | c | - | - | r | - | - | - | - | - | - | - | - | - | - |
| Common Loon *R # | - | W | W | S | P | c | - | - | U | - | - | - | - | - | - | - | - | - | - |
| Yellow-billed Loon | - | W | - | - | - | r | - | - | - | - | - | - | - | - | - | - | - | - | - |
| **PODICIPEDIDAE** | | | | | | | | | | | | | | | | | | | |
| Pied-billed Grebe * | - | W | P | - | S | u | - | - | C | - | - | - | - | - | - | - | - | - | - |
| Horned Grebe *R | - | W | M | - | P | c | - | - | U | - | - | - | - | - | - | - | - | - | - |
| Red-necked Grebe * | - | W | - | - | S | c | - | - | U | - | - | - | - | - | - | - | - | - | - |
| Eared Grebe * | - | W | M | - | S | u | - | - | C | - | - | - | - | - | - | - | - | - | - |
| Western Grebe * # | - | W | M | - | P | c | - | - | C | - | - | - | - | - | - | - | - | - | - |
| Clark's Grebe * # | - | - | - | - | S | - | - | - | U | - | - | - | - | - | - | - | - | - | - |
| **DIOMEDEIDAE** | | | | | | | | | | | | | | | | | | | |
| Black-footed Albatross # | P | - | - | - | - | c | - | - | - | - | - | - | - | - | - | - | - | - | - |
| Laysan Albatross | W | - | - | - | - | r | - | - | - | - | - | - | - | - | - | - | - | - | - |
| **PROCELLARIIDAE** | | | | | | | | | | | | | | | | | | | |
| Northern Fulmar # | P | - | - | - | - | c | - | - | - | - | - | - | - | - | - | - | - | - | - |
| Pink-footed Shearwater # | S | - | - | - | - | c | - | - | - | - | - | - | - | - | - | - | - | - | - |
| Flesh-footed Shearwater # | S | - | - | - | - | u | - | - | - | - | - | - | - | - | - | - | - | - | - |
| Buller's Shearwater | F | - | - | - | - | c | - | - | - | - | - | - | - | - | - | - | - | - | - |
| Sooty Shearwater # | S | S | - | - | - | c | - | - | - | - | - | - | - | - | - | - | - | - | - |
| Short-tailed Shearwater # | F | - | - | - | - | u | - | - | - | - | - | - | - | - | - | - | - | - | - |
| **HYDROBATIDAE** | | | | | | | | | | | | | | | | | | | |
| Fork-tailed Storm-Petrel *# | S | - | - | - | - | C | - | - | - | - | - | - | - | - | - | - | - | - | - |
| Leach's Storm-Petrel *# | S | - | - | - | - | C | - | - | - | - | - | - | - | - | - | - | - | - | - |
| **PELECANIDAE** | | | | | | | | | | | | | | | | | | | |
| American White Pelican # | - | M | - | - | S | r | - | - | R | - | - | - | - | - | - | - | - | - | - |
| Brown Pelican # | - | F | - | - | - | c | u | u | - | - | - | - | - | - | - | - | - | - | - |
| **PHALACROCORACIDAE** | | | | | | | | | | | | | | | | | | | |
| Double-crested Cormorant *# | - | P | - | - | S | C | C | - | U | - | - | - | - | - | - | - | - | - | - |
| Brandt's Cormorant * # | - | P | - | - | - | C | C | - | - | - | - | - | - | - | - | - | - | - | - |
| Pelagic Cormorant * | - | P | - | - | - | C | C | - | - | - | - | - | - | - | - | - | - | - | - |
| **ARDEIDAE** | | | | | | | | | | | | | | | | | | | |
| American Bittern * | - | P | P | - | S | - | - | - | U | - | - | - | - | - | - | - | - | - | - |
| Great Blue Heron * | - | P | P | - | P | - | C | C | C | - | - | - | - | - | - | - | - | - | u |
| Great Egret * | - | F | F | - | S | - | - | r | R | - | - | - | - | - | - | - | - | - | - |
| Cattle Egret # | - | - | F | - | F | - | - | - | - | - | - | - | - | - | - | - | - | - | r |
| Green Heron *# | - | - | S | - | - | - | - | - | U | - | - | - | - | - | - | - | - | - | - |
| Black-crowned Night-Heron *# | - | - | P | - | S | - | - | - | C | - | - | - | - | - | - | - | - | - | - |
| **ANATIDAE** | | | | | | | | | | | | | | | | | | | |
| Tundra Swan # | - | W | M | - | M | c | - | - | c | - | - | - | - | - | - | - | - | - | u |
| Trumpeter Swan * | - | W | W | - | - | u | - | - | u | - | - | - | - | - | - | - | - | - | u |
| Greater White-fronted Goose # | - | M | M | - | M | u | - | - | r | - | - | - | - | - | - | - | - | - | - |
| Snow Goose #1 | - | W | - | - | M | c | - | - | r | - | - | - | - | - | - | - | - | - | c |
| Ross' Goose | - | - | W | - | W | r | - | - | r | - | - | - | - | - | - | - | - | - | - |
| Brant #2 | - | W | - | - | - | c | - | - | - | - | - | - | - | - | - | - | - | - | - |
| Canada Goose * | - | P | P | - | P | c | - | - | C | - | - | - | - | - | - | - | - | - | c |
| Wood Duck * | - | - | S | - | S | - | - | - | C | - | - | - | - | - | - | - | - | - | - |
| Green-winged Teal *3 | - | W | W | - | R | c | - | - | C | - | - | - | - | - | - | - | - | - | c |
| American Black Duck *(l)# | - | - | P | - | - | - | - | - | R | - | - | - | - | - | - | - | - | - | - |
| Mallard * | - | P | P | - | P | c | - | - | C | - | - | - | - | - | - | - | - | - | c |
| Northern Pintail * | - | W | W | - | P | c | - | c | C | - | - | - | - | - | - | - | - | - | c |

| | O | C | W | M | E | SW | RS | SS | FW | WC | DC | BF | RW | DG | WM | SD | ST | PG | FL |
|---|---|---|---|---|---|----|----|----|----|----|----|----|----|----|----|----|----|----|----|
| Blue-winged Teal * | - | M | S | - | S | r | - | - | C | - | - | - | - | - | - | - | - | - | - |
| Cinnamon Teal * | - | M | S | - | S | r | - | - | C | - | - | - | - | - | - | - | - | - | - |
| Northern Shoveler *# | - | W | W | - | P | c | - | - | C | - | - | - | - | - | - | - | - | - | - |
| Gadwall *# | - | W | P | - | P | u | - | - | C | - | - | - | - | - | - | - | - | - | u |
| Eurasian Wigeon | - | W | W | - | M | u | - | - | u | - | - | - | - | - | - | - | - | - | u |
| American Wigeon *# | - | W | W | - | P | c | - | - | C | - | - | - | - | - | - | - | - | - | c |
| Canvasback *# | - | W | W | - | P | c | - | - | U | - | - | - | - | - | - | - | - | - | - |
| Redhead *# | - | - | W | - | P | - | - | - | C | - | - | - | - | - | - | - | - | - | - |
| Ring-necked Duck *# | - | - | W | - | P | - | - | - | C | - | - | - | - | - | - | - | - | - | - |
| Tufted Duck | - | - | W | - | - | - | - | - | r | - | - | - | - | - | - | - | - | - | - |
| Greater Scaup | - | W | W | - | W | c | - | - | u | - | - | - | - | - | - | - | - | - | - |
| Lesser Scaup *# | - | W | W | - | P | c | - | - | C | - | - | - | - | - | - | - | - | - | - |
| Harlequin Duck * | - | W | - | S | - | c | c | - | U | - | - | - | - | - | - | - | - | - | - |
| Oldsquaw # | - | W | - | - | M | c | - | - | r | - | - | - | - | - | - | - | - | - | - |
| Black Scoter # | - | W | - | - | - | u | - | - | - | - | - | - | - | - | - | - | - | - | - |
| Surf Scoter # | - | W | M | - | M | c | - | - | r | - | - | - | - | - | - | - | - | - | - |
| White-winged Scoter # | - | W | M | - | M | c | - | - | r | - | - | - | - | - | - | - | - | - | - |
| Common Goldeneye *R# | - | W | W | - | W | c | - | - | c | - | - | - | - | - | - | - | - | - | - |
| Barrow's Goldeneye * | - | W | W | S | P | c | - | - | U | - | - | - | - | - | - | - | - | - | - |
| Bufflehead *R# | - | W | W | - | P | c | - | - | c | - | - | - | - | - | - | - | - | - | - |
| Hooded Merganser * | - | W | P | - | P | u | - | - | U | - | - | - | - | - | - | - | - | - | - |
| Common Merganser * | - | W | P | S | P | c | - | - | C | - | - | - | - | - | - | - | - | - | - |
| Red-breasted Merganser | - | W | M | - | M | c | - | - | r | - | - | - | - | - | - | - | - | - | - |
| Ruddy Duck *# | - | W | W | - | P | c | - | - | C | - | - | - | - | - | - | - | - | - | - |
| **CATHARTIDAE** | | | | | | | | | | | | | | | | | | | |
| Turkey Vulture * | - | - | S | M | S | - | - | - | - | U | U | U | U | U | - | U | - | - | - |
| **ACCIPITRIDAE** | | | | | | | | | | | | | | | | | | | |
| Osprey * | - | S | S | - | S | U | - | U | U | U | U | - | U | - | - | - | - | - | - |
| White-tailed Kite *# | - | - | P | - | - | - | - | - | - | - | - | - | r | - | R | - | - | - | r |
| Bald Eagle * | - | P | P | M | W | C | C | C | C | - | - | - | - | - | - | - | - | - | - |
| Northern Harrier * | - | - | P | M | P | - | - | - | c | - | - | - | c | C | c | - | - | - | c |
| Sharp-shinned Hawk * | - | - | P | P | P | - | - | - | U | U | u | u | - | - | - | - | - | u | - |
| Cooper's Hawk * | - | - | P | P | P | - | - | - | u | u | U | U | - | - | - | - | - | u | - |
| Northern Goshawk * | - | - | P | P | P | - | - | - | U | U | - | - | - | - | - | - | - | - | - |
| Swainson's Hawk *# | - | - | - | M | S | - | - | - | - | - | - | - | U | - | U | - | - | - | U |
| Red-tailed Hawk *4 | - | - | P | P | P | - | - | - | U | C | C | C | C | C | C | - | - | - | C |
| Ferruginous Hawk * | - | - | - | - | S | - | - | - | - | - | - | - | R | - | R | - | - | - | - |
| Rough-legged Hawk | - | - | W | M | W | - | - | - | - | - | - | - | c | c | c | - | - | - | c |
| Golden Eagle *# | - | - | - | S | P | - | - | - | - | - | U | - | - | U | U | U | - | - | - |
| **FALCONIDAE** | | | | | | | | | | | | | | | | | | | |
| American Kestrel * | - | - | P | S | P | - | - | - | - | - | C | U | C | c | - | C | - | - | c |
| Merlin * | - | P | P | - | W | - | - | u | - | U | u | u | - | - | - | - | - | u | u |
| Peregrine Falcon *# | - | P | P | - | W | - | - | R | - | R | - | - | - | - | - | - | - | - | r |
| Gyrfalcon | - | W | W | - | W | - | - | r | - | - | - | - | - | r | r | - | - | - | - |
| Prairie Falcon *# | - | - | - | - | P | - | - | - | - | - | R | - | - | R | - | R | - | - | r |
| **PHASIANIDAE** | | | | | | | | | | | | | | | | | | | |
| Gray Partridge (I)*# | - | - | - | - | P | - | - | - | - | - | - | - | - | U | - | - | - | - | U |
| Chukar (I)* | - | - | - | - | P | - | - | - | - | - | - | - | - | C | - | C | - | - | - |
| Ring-necked Pheasant (I)* | - | - | P | - | P | - | - | - | - | - | - | - | - | C | - | U | - | - | C |
| Spruce Grouse *# | - | - | - | P | - | - | - | - | - | U | - | - | - | - | - | - | - | - | - |
| Blue Grouse * | - | - | P | P | P | - | - | - | - | C | C | - | - | - | - | - | - | u | - |
| White-tailed Ptarmigan * | - | - | - | P | - | - | - | - | - | - | - | - | - | - | U | - | - | - | - |
| Ruffed Grouse * | - | - | P | - | P | - | - | - | - | U | - | C | - | - | - | - | - | - | - |
| Sage Grouse *# | - | - | - | - | P | - | - | - | - | - | - | - | - | - | - | - | U | - | - |
| Sharp-tailed Grouse *# | - | - | - | - | P | - | - | - | - | - | - | - | - | - | u | U | - | - | - |
| Wild Turkey(I) *# | - | - | P | - | P | - | - | - | - | R | R | - | - | - | - | - | - | - | - |
| Northern Bobwhite (I)*# | - | - | P | - | P | - | - | - | - | - | - | - | - | - | - | - | R | - | R |
| Scaled Quail (I)*# | - | - | - | - | P | - | - | - | - | - | - | - | R | - | R | - | - | - | - |

| | O | C | W | M | E | SW | RS | SS | FW | WC | DC | BF | RW | DG | WM | SD | ST | PG | FL |
|---|---|---|---|---|---|---|---|---|---|---|---|---|---|---|---|---|---|---|---|
| California Quail (I)* | - | - | P | - | P | - | - | - | - | - | U | - | C | - | - | U | C | C | - |
| Mountain Quail *# | - | - | P | - | P | - | - | - | - | - | U | U | - | - | - | - | U | - | - |
| **RALLIDAE** | | | | | | | | | | | | | | | | | | | |
| Virginia Rail * | - | - | P | - | S | - | - | - | C | - | - | - | - | - | - | - | - | - | - |
| Sora * | - | - | S | - | S | - | - | - | C | - | - | - | - | - | - | - | - | - | - |
| American Coot * | - | W | P | - | P | c | - | - | C | - | - | - | - | - | - | - | - | - | - |
| **GRUIDAE** | | | | | | | | | | | | | | | | | | | |
| Sandhill Crane *R# | - | M | - | - | M | - | - | - | u | - | - | - | - | - | u | u | - | - | u |
| **CHARADRIIDAE** | | | | | | | | | | | | | | | | | | | |
| Black-bellied Plover | - | W | M | - | M | - | - | c | r | - | - | - | - | - | - | - | - | - | u |
| American Golden-Plover # | - | M | F | - | F | - | - | u | r | - | - | - | - | - | r | - | - | - | r |
| Pacific Golden-Plover # | - | M | - | - | - | - | - | u | - | - | - | - | - | - | - | - | - | - | - |
| Snowy Plover *# | - | S | - | - | - | - | - | U | - | - | - | - | - | - | - | - | - | - | - |
| Semipalmated Plover *R# | - | M | M | - | M | - | - | c | u | - | - | - | - | - | - | - | - | - | - |
| Killdeer * | - | P | P | S | P | - | - | u | C | - | - | - | - | - | C | - | - | - | C |
| **HAEMATOPODIDAE** | | | | | | | | | | | | | | | | | | | |
| Black Oystercatcher *# | - | P | - | - | - | - | C | - | - | - | - | - | - | - | - | - | - | - | - |
| **RECURVIROSTRIDAE** | | | | | | | | | | | | | | | | | | | |
| Black-necked Stilt *# | - | - | - | - | S | - | - | - | U | - | - | - | - | - | - | - | - | - | - |
| American Avocet * | - | M | - | - | S | - | - | r | C | - | - | - | - | - | - | - | - | - | - |
| **SCOLOPACIDAE** | | | | | | | | | | | | | | | | | | | |
| Greater Yellowlegs | - | W | M | - | M | - | - | c | c | - | - | - | - | - | - | - | - | - | - |
| Lesser Yellowlegs | - | M | M | - | M | - | - | c | c | - | - | - | - | - | - | - | - | - | - |
| Solitary Sandpiper | - | - | M | M | M | - | - | - | u | - | - | - | - | - | - | - | - | - | - |
| Willet # | - | W | - | - | M | - | - | r | r | - | - | - | - | - | - | - | - | - | - |
| Wandering Tattler # | - | M | - | - | - | - | c | - | - | - | - | - | - | - | - | - | - | - | - |
| Spotted Sandpiper * | - | M | P | S | S | - | u | c | C | - | - | - | - | - | - | - | - | - | - |
| Upland Sandpiper # | - | - | - | - | S | - | - | - | - | - | - | - | - | R | - | - | - | - | - |
| Whimbrel | - | M | - | - | M | - | - | c | r | - | - | - | - | - | - | - | - | - | u |
| Long-billed Curlew *# | - | W | - | - | S | - | - | r | r | - | - | - | - | U | - | - | - | - | u |
| Bar-tailed Godwit | - | M | - | - | - | - | - | r | - | - | - | - | - | - | - | - | - | - | - |
| Marbled Godwit # | - | W | - | - | M | - | - | u | r | - | - | - | - | - | - | - | - | - | - |
| Ruddy Turnstone # | - | M | - | - | M | - | c | c | r | - | - | - | - | - | - | - | - | - | - |
| Black Turnstone | - | W | - | - | - | - | c | u | - | - | - | - | - | - | - | - | - | - | - |
| Surfbird | - | W | - | - | - | - | c | - | - | - | - | - | - | - | - | - | - | - | - |
| Red Knot # | - | M | - | - | F | - | - | c | r | - | - | - | - | - | - | - | - | - | - |
| Sanderling | - | W | - | - | M | - | u | c | r | - | - | - | - | - | - | - | - | - | - |
| Semipalmated Sandpiper | - | M | M | - | M | - | - | r | u | - | - | - | - | - | - | - | - | - | - |
| Western Sandpiper | - | W | M | - | M | - | - | c | c | - | - | - | - | - | - | - | - | - | - |
| Least Sandpiper | - | W | M | - | M | - | - | c | c | - | - | - | - | - | - | - | - | - | - |
| Baird's Sandpiper # | - | F | F | F | M | - | - | u | u | - | - | - | - | - | - | - | - | - | - |
| Pectoral Sandpiper # | - | F | F | - | F | - | - | c | c | - | - | - | - | - | - | - | - | - | - |
| Sharp-tailed Sandpiper # | - | F | - | - | - | - | - | r | r | - | - | - | - | - | - | - | - | - | - |
| Rock Sandpiper | - | W | - | - | - | - | u | - | - | - | - | - | - | - | - | - | - | - | - |
| Dunlin | - | W | W | - | M | - | u | c | u | - | - | - | - | - | - | - | - | - | c |
| Stilt Sandpiper | - | F | F | - | F | - | - | r | r | - | - | - | - | - | - | - | - | - | - |
| Buff-breasted Sandpiper # | - | F | - | - | - | - | - | r | - | - | - | - | - | - | r | - | - | - | - |
| Ruff # | - | F | - | - | - | - | - | r | - | - | - | - | - | - | - | - | - | - | - |
| Short-billed Dowitcher | - | M | M | - | M | - | - | c | r | - | - | - | - | - | - | - | - | - | - |
| Long-billed Dowitcher | - | W | M | - | M | - | - | c | c | - | - | - | - | - | - | - | - | - | - |
| Common Snipe * | - | W | R | M | S | - | - | u | C | - | - | - | - | - | C | - | - | - | - |
| Wilson's Phalarope * | - | M | M | - | S | - | - | r | C | - | - | - | - | - | - | - | - | - | - |
| Red-necked Phalarope | M | M | M | - | M | c | - | u | u | - | - | - | - | - | - | - | - | - | - |
| Red Phalarope # | M | M | - | - | M | c | - | r | r | - | - | - | - | - | - | - | - | - | - |

## LARIDAE

| | O | C | W | M | E | SW | RS | SS | FW | WC | DC | BF | RW | DG | WM | SD | ST | PG | FL |
|---|---|---|---|---|---|---|---|---|---|---|---|---|---|---|---|---|---|---|---|
| Pomarine Jaeger # | M | - | - | - | - | c | - | - | - | - | - | - | - | - | - | - | - | - | - |
| Parasitic Jaeger # | M | M | - | - | - | c | - | - | - | - | - | - | - | - | - | - | - | - | - |
| Long-tailed Jaeger # | F | - | - | - | F | r | - | - | r | - | - | - | - | - | - | - | - | - | - |
| South Polar Skua # | M | - | - | - | - | u | - | - | - | - | - | - | - | - | - | - | - | - | - |
| Franklin's Gull # | - | F | F | - | F | r | - | r | r | - | - | - | - | - | - | - | - | - | r |
| Little Gull # | - | F | F | - | - | r | - | - | r | - | - | - | - | - | - | - | - | - | - |
| Bonaparte's Gull | - | W | M | - | M | c | - | c | c | - | - | - | - | - | - | - | - | - | - |
| Heermann's Gull # | - | S | - | - | - | c | c | c | - | - | - | - | - | - | - | - | - | - | - |
| Mew Gull # | - | W | W | - | - | c | - | c | c | - | - | - | - | - | - | - | - | - | - |
| Ring-billed Gull *# | - | P | W | - | P | c | - | u | C | - | - | - | - | - | - | - | - | - | c |
| California Gull *# | M | M | M | - | S | c | - | c | C | - | - | - | - | - | - | - | - | - | c |
| Herring Gull | W | W | W | - | W | c | - | c | c | - | - | - | - | - | - | - | - | - | - |
| Thayer's Gull | W | W | W | - | - | c | - | c | c | - | - | - | - | - | - | - | - | - | r |
| Western Gull * # 5 | P | P | - | - | - | C | C | C | - | - | - | - | - | - | - | - | - | - | - |
| Glaucous-winged Gull * 5 | P | P | W | - | W | C | C | C | c | - | - | - | - | - | - | - | - | - | c |
| Glaucous Gull | W | W | W | - | W | r | - | r | r | - | - | - | - | - | - | - | - | - | - |
| Black-legged Kittiwake | W | W | - | - | - | c | u | - | - | - | - | - | - | - | - | - | - | - | - |
| Sabine's Gull # | M | M | - | - | - | u | - | - | - | - | - | - | - | - | - | - | - | - | - |
| Caspian Tern *# | - | S | - | - | S | C | - | C | U | - | - | - | - | - | - | - | - | - | - |
| Elegant Tern # | - | F | - | - | - | r | - | r | - | - | - | - | - | - | - | - | - | - | - |
| Common Tern | - | M | M | - | M | c | - | c | u | - | - | - | - | - | - | - | - | - | - |
| Arctic Tern *R# | M | M | - | - | - | u | - | R | - | - | - | - | - | - | - | - | - | - | - |
| Forster's Tern *# | - | - | - | - | S | - | - | - | C | - | - | - | - | - | - | - | - | - | - |
| Black Tern * | - | - | M | - | S | r | - | - | C | - | - | - | - | - | - | - | - | - | - |

## ALCIDAE

| | O | C | W | M | E | SW | RS | SS | FW | WC | DC | BF | RW | DG | WM | SD | ST | PG | FL |
|---|---|---|---|---|---|---|---|---|---|---|---|---|---|---|---|---|---|---|---|
| Common Murre * | P | P | - | - | - | C | C | - | - | - | - | - | - | - | - | - | - | - | - |
| Pigeon Guillemot * | - | P | - | - | - | C | C | - | - | - | - | - | - | - | - | - | - | - | - |
| Marbled Murrelet *# | - | P | - | - | - | C | - | - | - | U | - | - | - | - | - | - | - | - | - |
| Xantus' Murrelet # | F | - | - | - | - | u | - | - | - | - | - | - | - | - | - | - | - | - | - |
| Ancient Murrelet *R# | W | W | - | - | - | u | - | - | - | - | - | - | - | - | - | - | - | - | - |
| Cassin's Auklet *# | P | S | - | - | - | C | - | - | - | - | - | - | - | - | - | - | - | - | - |
| Rhinoceros Auklet * | P | P | - | - | - | C | - | - | - | - | - | - | - | - | - | - | - | - | - |
| Tufted Puffin * | P | S | - | - | - | C | C | - | - | - | - | - | - | - | - | - | - | - | - |

## COLUMBIDAE

| | O | C | W | M | E | SW | RS | SS | FW | WC | DC | BF | RW | DG | WM | SD | ST | PG | FL |
|---|---|---|---|---|---|---|---|---|---|---|---|---|---|---|---|---|---|---|---|
| Rock Dove * | - | - | P | - | P | - | - | - | - | - | - | - | - | - | - | - | - | C | C |
| Band-tailed Pigeon *# | - | - | P | - | - | - | - | - | - | - | C | U | U | - | - | - | - | U | u |
| Mourning Dove *# | - | - | P | - | P | - | - | - | - | - | C | - | C | - | - | C | - | - | C |

## TYTONIDAE

| | O | C | W | M | E | SW | RS | SS | FW | WC | DC | BF | RW | DG | WM | SD | ST | PG | FL |
|---|---|---|---|---|---|---|---|---|---|---|---|---|---|---|---|---|---|---|---|
| Barn Owl * | - | - | P | - | P | - | - | - | - | - | U | U | - | - | U | - | - | U | U |

## STRIGIDAE

| | O | C | W | M | E | SW | RS | SS | FW | WC | DC | BF | RW | DG | WM | SD | ST | PG | FL |
|---|---|---|---|---|---|---|---|---|---|---|---|---|---|---|---|---|---|---|---|
| Flammulated Owl * # | - | - | - | S | S | - | - | - | - | - | U | - | - | - | - | - | - | - | - |
| Western Screech-Owl * | - | - | P | - | P | - | - | - | - | C | - | C | C | - | - | - | - | U | - |
| Great Horned Owl * | - | - | P | P | P | - | - | - | - | C | C | C | C | - | - | C | - | U | - |
| Snowy Owl # | - | W | W | - | W | - | - | r | - | - | - | - | - | r | r | - | - | - | r |
| Northern Pygmy-Owl * | - | - | P | P | P | - | - | - | - | C | U | U | - | - | - | - | - | - | - |
| Burrowing Owl * # | - | - | - | - | S | - | - | - | - | - | - | - | - | U | - | C | - | - | - |
| Spotted Owl * | - | - | P | P | P | - | - | - | - | - | - | R | R | - | - | - | - | - | - |
| Barred Owl *# | - | - | P | - | P | - | - | - | - | - | U | - | U | U | - | - | - | - | - |
| Great Gray Owl *R# | - | - | - | - | P | - | - | - | - | - | R | R | - | - | - | - | - | - | - |
| Long-eared Owl *# | - | - | W | - | S | - | - | - | - | - | - | - | r | U | - | - | - | - | - |
| Short-eared Owl * | - | - | P | - | P | - | - | - | - | - | - | - | - | U | C | c | - | - | C |
| Boreal Owl * | - | - | - | P | - | - | - | - | - | - | R | R | - | - | - | - | - | - | - |
| Northern Saw-whet Owl * | - | - | P | P | P | - | - | - | - | C | U | U | U | - | - | - | - | u | - |

## CAPRIMULGIDAE

| | O | C | W | M | E | SW | RS | SS | FW | WC | DC | BF | RW | DG | WM | SD | ST | PG | FL |
|---|---|---|---|---|---|---|---|---|---|---|---|---|---|---|---|---|---|---|---|
| Common Nighthawk *# | - | - | S | S | S | - | - | - | - | - | C | - | - | C | - | C | - | C | C |
| Common Poorwill *# | - | - | - | - | S | - | - | - | - | - | C | - | - | - | - | U | - | - | - |

12

| | O | C | W | M | E | SW | RS | SS | FW | WC | DC | BF | RW | DG | WM | SD | ST | PG | FL |
|---|---|---|---|---|---|---|---|---|---|---|---|---|---|---|---|---|---|---|---|
| **APODIDAE** | | | | | | | | | | | | | | | | | | | |
| Black Swift *# | - | - | S | S | - | - | - | - | - | - | - | - | - | - | - | - | - | - | * |
| Vaux's Swift *# | - | - | S | S | S | - | - | - | - | C | C | C | - | - | - | - | - | - | * |
| White-throated Swift *# | - | - | - | - | S | - | - | - | - | - | - | - | - | - | - | C | - | - | - |
| **TROCHILIDAE** | | | | | | | | | | | | | | | | | | | |
| Black-chinned Hummingbird * | - | - | - | - | S | - | - | - | - | - | - | - | U | - | - | - | - | U | - |
| Anna's Hummingbird *# | - | - | P | - | - | - | - | - | - | - | - | - | - | - | - | - | - | U | - |
| Calliope Hummingbird *# | - | - | - | S | S | - | - | - | - | C | C | - | C | - | c | - | - | - | - |
| Rufous Hummingbird * | - | - | S | S | S | - | - | - | - | C | - | C | C | - | c | - | C | C | - |
| **ALCEDINIDAE** | | | | | | | | | | | | | | | | | | | |
| Belted Kingfisher * | - | P | P | - | P | - | - | C | C | - | - | - | - | - | - | - | - | - | - |
| **PICIDAE** | | | | | | | | | | | | | | | | | | | |
| Lewis' Woodpecker *# | - | - | - | - | S | - | - | - | - | - | U | - | U | - | - | - | - | - | - |
| Acorn Woodpecker *R# | - | - | - | - | P | - | - | - | - | - | - | U | - | - | - | - | - | - | - |
| Red-naped Sapsucker * | - | - | - | S | S | - | - | - | - | C | - | C | C | - | - | - | - | u | - |
| Red-breasted Sapsucker * | - | - | S | S | - | - | - | - | - | C | - | U | U | - | - | - | - | u | - |
| Williamson's Sapsucker * | - | - | - | S | S | - | - | - | - | U | U | - | - | - | - | - | - | - | - |
| Downy Woodpecker * | - | - | P | - | P | - | - | - | - | - | - | C | C | - | - | - | U | U | - |
| Hairy Woodpecker * | - | - | P | P | P | - | - | - | - | C | C | U | - | - | - | - | - | - | - |
| White-headed Woodpecker *# | - | - | - | - | P | - | - | - | - | - | U | - | - | - | - | - | - | - | - |
| Three-toed Woodpecker * | - | - | - | P | - | - | - | - | - | R | - | - | - | - | - | - | - | - | - |
| Black-backed Woodpecker * | - | - | - | P | P | - | - | - | - | R | R | - | - | - | - | - | - | - | - |
| Northern Flicker *6 | - | - | P | P | P | - | - | - | - | C | C | C | C | - | u | u | - | C | u |
| Pileated Woodpecker * | - | - | P | P | P | - | - | - | - | U | U | - | - | - | - | - | - | - | - |
| **TYRANNIDAE** | | | | | | | | | | | | | | | | | | | |
| Olive-sided Flycatcher * | - | - | S | S | S | - | - | - | - | C | U | - | - | - | - | - | - | u | - |
| Western Wood-Pewee * | - | - | S | S | S | - | - | - | - | U | C | U | C | - | - | - | - | U | - |
| Willow Flycatcher * | - | - | S | - | S | - | - | - | - | - | C | C | - | - | - | - | - | u | - |
| Least Flycatcher *R# | - | - | S | - | S | - | - | - | - | - | R | R | - | - | - | - | - | - | - |
| Hammond's Flycatcher * | - | - | S | S | M | - | - | - | - | C | U | U | - | - | - | - | - | c | - |
| Dusky Flycatcher *# | - | - | - | S | S | - | - | - | - | - | C | - | - | - | - | - | - | u | - |
| Gray Flycatcher * | - | - | - | - | S | - | - | - | - | - | C | - | - | - | - | - | - | - | - |
| Pacific-slope Flycatcher * | - | - | S | S | - | - | - | - | - | C | - | U | U | - | - | - | - | u | - |
| Say's Phoebe *# | - | - | M | - | S | - | - | - | - | - | - | C | - | - | - | C | - | - | - |
| Ash-throated Flycatcher *# | - | - | - | - | S | - | - | - | - | - | - | R | - | - | - | - | - | - | - |
| Western Kingbird * # | - | - | S | - | S | - | - | - | - | - | - | C | U | - | U | - | - | - | C |
| Eastern Kingbird * # | - | - | S | - | S | - | - | - | - | - | - | C | - | - | - | - | - | - | C |
| **ALAUDIDAE** | | | | | | | | | | | | | | | | | | | |
| Eurasian Skylark *# | - | - | P | - | - | - | - | - | - | - | - | - | U | - | - | - | - | - | - |
| Horned Lark *# | - | - | P | S | P | - | - | u | - | - | - | - | C | - | - | C | - | - | u |
| **HIRUNDINIDAE** | | | | | | | | | | | | | | | | | | | |
| Purple Martin *# | - | - | S | - | - | - | - | - | U | - | - | - | - | - | - | - | - | U | - |
| Tree Swallow * | - | - | S | S | S | - | - | - | C | - | - | C | C | - | - | - | - | C | C |
| Violet-green Swallow * | - | - | S | S | S | - | - | - | C | C | C | C | C | - | - | - | - | C | C |
| Northern Rough-winged Swallow * | - | - | S | - | S | - | - | - | C | - | - | - | C | - | - | - | - | - | - |
| Bank Swallow *# | - | - | M | - | S | - | - | - | C | - | - | - | - | - | - | C | - | - | - |
| Cliff Swallow * | - | - | S | M | S | - | - | - | C | - | - | - | - | - | - | C | - | C | C |
| Barn Swallow * | - | - | S | M | S | - | - | - | C | - | - | - | - | - | - | - | - | C | C |
| **CORVIDAE** | | | | | | | | | | | | | | | | | | | |
| Gray Jay *# | - | - | P | P | - | - | - | - | - | C | - | - | - | - | - | - | - | * | - |
| Steller's Jay * | - | - | P | P | P | - | - | - | - | C | U | - | - | - | - | - | - | C | - |
| Blue Jay | - | - | W | - | W | - | - | - | - | - | - | r | r | - | - | - | - | r | - |
| Scrub Jay *# | - | - | P | - | - | - | - | - | - | - | U | - | - | - | - | - | - | - | - |

| | O | C | W | M | E | SW | RS | SS | FW | WC | DC | BF | RW | DG | WM | SD | ST | PG | FL |
|---|---|---|---|---|---|---|---|---|---|---|---|---|---|---|---|---|---|---|---|
| Clark's Nutcracker *# | - | - | - | P | P | - | - | - | - | C | C | - | - | - | - | - | - | - | - |
| Black-billed Magpie *# | - | - | - | - | P | - | - | - | - | - | - | - | C | - | - | C | - | - | C |
| American/Northwestern Crow *7 | - | P | P | P | P | - | C | C | C | C | - | C | C | - | - | - | - | C | C |
| Common Raven * | - | - | P | P | P | - | - | - | - | C | C | - | - | U | - | C | - | - | U |
| **PARIDAE** | | | | | | | | | | | | | | | | | | | |
| Black-capped Chickadee * | - | - | P | - | P | - | - | - | - | U | u | C | C | - | - | - | C | C | - |
| Mountain Chickadee *# | - | - | - | P | P | - | - | - | - | C | C | - | - | - | - | - | - | r | - |
| Boreal Chickadee *# | - | - | - | P | - | - | - | - | - | R | - | - | - | - | - | - | - | - | - |
| Chestnut-backed Chickadee * | - | - | P | P | P | - | - | - | - | C | - | U | - | - | - | - | - | c | - |
| Bushtit *# | - | - | P | - | - | - | - | - | - | - | - | C | C | - | - | - | C | C | - |
| **SITTIDAE** | | | | | | | | | | | | | | | | | | | |
| Red-breasted Nuthatch * | - | - | P | P | P | - | - | - | - | C | U | U | c | - | - | - | - | u | - |
| White-breasted Nuthatch * | - | - | P | - | P | - | - | - | - | - | C | C | - | - | - | - | - | u | - |
| Pygmy Nuthatch *# | - | - | - | - | P | - | - | - | - | - | C | - | - | - | - | - | - | - | - |
| **CERTHIDAE** | | | | | | | | | | | | | | | | | | | |
| Brown Creeper * | - | - | P | P | P | - | - | - | - | C | u | u | u | - | - | - | - | - | - |
| **TROGLODYTIDAE** | | | | | | | | | | | | | | | | | | | |
| Rock Wren *# | - | - | - | - | S | - | - | - | - | - | - | - | - | - | - | C | - | - | - |
| Canyon Wren *# | - | - | - | - | P | - | - | - | - | - | - | - | U | - | - | U | - | - | - |
| Bewick's Wren *# | - | - | P | - | - | - | - | - | - | - | - | C | C | - | - | - | C | C | - |
| House Wren * | - | - | S | - | S | - | - | - | - | - | C | C | C | - | - | - | C | C | - |
| Winter Wren * | - | - | P | S | P | - | - | - | - | C | - | c | - | - | - | - | - | u | - |
| Marsh Wren * | - | - | P | - | S | - | - | - | C | - | - | - | - | - | - | - | - | - | - |
| **CINCLIDAE** | | | | | | | | | | | | | | | | | | | |
| American Dipper * | - | - | P | P | P | - | - | - | C | - | - | - | - | - | - | - | - | - | - |
| **MUSCICAPIDAE** | | | | | | | | | | | | | | | | | | | |
| Golden-crowned Kinglet * | - | - | P | P | M | - | - | - | - | C | u | c | c | - | - | u | u | c | - |
| Ruby-crowned Kinglet * | - | - | W | S | W | - | - | - | - | c | C | c | c | - | - | u | u | c | - |
| Western Bluebird *# | - | - | S | - | S | - | - | - | - | - | C | - | U | U | - | - | - | - | - |
| Mountain Bluebird *# | - | - | - | S | S | - | - | - | - | U | C | - | - | U | - | U | - | - | - |
| Townsend's Solitaire * | - | - | W | S | S | - | - | - | - | U | C | - | u | - | - | u | - | u | - |
| Veery *# | - | - | - | - | S | - | - | - | - | - | - | C | C | - | - | - | - | - | - |
| Swainson's Thrush * | - | - | S | S | S | - | - | - | - | C | - | C | C | - | - | - | - | - | - |
| Hermit Thrush *# | - | - | M | S | M | - | - | - | - | C | - | - | - | - | - | - | u | c | - |
| American Robin * | - | - | P | S | P | - | - | - | - | C | C | C | C | - | - | U | - | C | c |
| Varied Thrush * | - | - | P | S | W | - | - | - | - | C | - | c | c | - | - | - | - | c | - |
| **MIMIDAE** | | | | | | | | | | | | | | | | | | | |
| Gray Catbird *# | - | - | - | - | S | - | - | - | - | - | - | - | - | C | - | - | C | - | - |
| Northern Mockingbird *R# | - | - | W | - | W | - | - | - | - | - | - | - | - | - | - | - | r | r | - |
| Sage Thrasher *# | - | - | - | - | S | - | - | - | - | - | - | - | - | - | - | C | - | - | - |
| **MOTACILLIDAE** | | | | | | | | | | | | | | | | | | | |
| American Pipit * | - | - | W | S | M | - | - | c | - | - | - | - | - | c | C | - | - | - | c |
| **BOMBYCILLIDAE** | | | | | | | | | | | | | | | | | | | |
| Bohemian Waxwing *R # | - | - | W | - | W | - | - | - | - | - | u | - | u | u | - | - | - | u | - |
| Cedar Waxwing *# | - | - | P | S | P | - | - | - | - | u | - | C | C | - | - | - | - | C | - |
| **LANIIDAE** | | | | | | | | | | | | | | | | | | | |
| Northern Shrike * | - | - | W | - | W | - | - | - | - | - | - | - | u | u | u | u | - | - | u |
| Loggerhead Shrike * # | - | - | - | - | S | - | - | - | - | - | - | - | - | U | - | U | - | - | - |
| **STURNIDAE** | | | | | | | | | | | | | | | | | | | |
| European Starling * | - | - | P | P | P | - | - | - | - | U | U | C | C | c | c | C | - | C | C |

| | O | C | W | M | E | SW | RS | SS | FW | WC | DC | BF | RW | DG | WM | SD | ST | PG | FL |
|---|---|---|---|---|---|---|---|---|---|---|---|---|---|---|---|---|---|---|---|
| **VIREONIDAE** | | | | | | | | | | | | | | | | | | | |
| Solitary Vireo * | - | - | S | S | S | - | - | - | - | C | C | U | - | - | - | - | - | u | - |
| Hutton's Vireo * | - | - | P | - | - | - | - | - | - | C | - | C | - | - | - | - | - | U | - |
| Warbling Vireo * | - | - | S | S | S | - | - | - | - | u | - | C | C | - | - | - | - | c | - |
| Red-eyed Vireo * | - | - | S | - | S | - | - | - | - | - | - | C | C | - | - | - | - | - | - |
| **EMBERIZIDAE** | | | | | | | | | | | | | | | | | | | |
| Orange-crowned Warbler * | - | - | S | S | M | - | - | - | - | - | - | C | - | - | - | - | C | C | - |
| Nashville Warbler *# | - | - | - | S | S | - | - | - | - | - | - | C | C | - | - | - | C | u | - |
| Yellow Warbler * | - | - | S | F | S | - | - | - | - | - | - | C | C | - | - | - | C | c | - |
| Yellow-rumped Warbler *# 8 | - | - | P | S | S | - | - | - | - | C | C | c | c | - | - | c | - | c | - |
| Black-throated Gray Warbler * | - | - | S | - | - | - | - | - | - | - | - | C | - | C | - | - | - | - | - |
| Townsend's Warbler *# | - | - | S | S | M | - | - | - | - | - | - | C | C | u | u | - | - | c | - |
| Hermit Warbler *# | - | - | S | S | - | - | - | - | - | - | - | C | U | - | - | - | - | - | - |
| Palm Warbler | - | - | F | - | - | - | - | - | - | - | - | - | - | - | - | - | - | r | - |
| American Redstart *# | - | - | - | - | S | - | - | - | - | - | - | C | U | - | - | - | - | - | - |
| Northern Waterthrush *# | - | - | - | - | S | - | - | R | - | - | - | R | R | - | - | - | - | - | - |
| MacGillivray's Warbler * | - | - | S | S | S | - | - | - | - | U | - | C | C | - | - | - | - | C | - |
| Common Yellowthroat * | - | - | S | - | S | - | - | - | C | - | - | - | - | - | - | - | - | c | - |
| Wilson's Warbler * | - | - | S | S | S | - | - | - | - | - | - | C | - | - | - | - | C | C | - |
| Yellow-breasted Chat *# | - | - | - | - | S | - | - | - | - | - | - | - | C | - | - | - | C | - | - |
| Western Tanager * | - | - | S | S | S | - | - | - | - | C | C | U | - | - | - | - | - | c | - |
| Black-headed Grosbeak * | - | - | S | - | S | - | - | - | - | - | - | C | C | - | - | - | - | U | - |
| Lazuli Bunting *# | - | - | - | - | S | - | - | - | - | - | - | C | - | - | - | - | C | - | - |
| Green-tailed Towhee *# | - | - | S | - | - | - | - | - | - | - | - | - | - | - | - | - | - | R | - |
| Rufous-sided Towhee * | - | - | P | S | S | - | - | - | - | - | - | C | C | - | - | - | C | C | - |
| American Tree Sparrow * | - | - | W | - | W | - | - | - | - | - | - | - | u | u | - | u | u | - | u |
| Chipping Sparrow * | - | - | S | S | S | - | - | - | U | C | C | - | - | - | - | - | - | u | - |
| Brewer's Sparrow *# | - | - | - | S | - | - | - | - | - | - | - | - | - | C | - | - | - | - | - |
| Vesper Sparrow *# | - | - | S | - | S | - | - | - | - | - | - | - | C | C | C | - | - | - | - |
| Lark Sparrow *# | - | - | - | - | S | - | - | - | U | - | U | - | - | - | C | - | - | - | - |
| Black-throated Sparrow *R # | - | - | - | - | S | - | - | - | - | - | - | - | - | R | - | - | - | - | - |
| Sage Sparrow *# | - | - | - | - | S | - | - | - | - | - | - | - | - | C | - | - | - | - | - |
| Savannah Sparrow *# | - | - | S | F | S | - | - | - | - | - | - | - | U | C | C | - | - | - | C |
| Grasshopper Sparrow * | - | - | - | - | S | - | - | - | - | - | - | - | - | C | - | - | - | - | - |
| Fox Sparrow *# | - | - | W | S | M | - | - | - | - | - | - | c | c | - | - | - | U | - | - |
| Song Sparrow * | - | - | P | S | P | - | - | - | - | - | - | C | C | - | - | - | C | C | - |
| Lincoln's Sparrow * | - | - | W | S | M | - | - | - | - | - | - | - | - | - | - | - | C | - | - |
| Swamp Sparrow | - | - | W | - | W | - | - | - | - | - | - | - | r | - | - | - | r | - | - |
| White-throated Sparrow | - | - | W | - | W | - | - | - | - | - | - | - | r | - | - | - | r | r | - |
| Golden-crowned Sparrow *R | - | - | W | F | M | - | - | - | - | - | - | - | c | - | - | - | c | c | u |
| White-crowned Sparrow * | - | - | P | S | W | - | - | - | - | - | - | - | c | - | - | c | C | C | u |
| Harris' Sparrow | - | - | W | - | W | - | - | - | - | - | - | - | r | - | - | - | r | r | - |
| Dark-eyed Junco *9 | - | - | P | S | P | - | - | - | C | U | c | c | - | - | - | - | c | c | - |
| Lapland Longspur # | - | W | W | - | W | - | - | u | - | - | - | - | u | - | - | - | - | - | u |
| Snow Bunting # | - | W | W | - | W | - | - | u | - | - | - | - | u | - | - | - | - | - | u |
| Bobolink *# | - | - | - | - | S | - | - | - | - | - | - | - | - | - | U | - | - | - | - |
| Red-winged Blackbird * | - | - | P | - | P | - | - | C | - | - | - | - | - | - | - | - | - | u | c |
| Western Meadowlark * | - | - | P | - | P | - | - | - | - | - | - | - | C | C | C | - | - | - | C |
| Yellow-headed Blackbird *# | - | - | M | - | S | - | - | C | - | - | - | - | - | - | - | - | - | - | c |
| Brewer's Blackbird * | - | - | P | - | P | - | - | - | - | - | - | - | C | C | - | - | - | C | C |
| Brown-headed Cowbird *# | - | - | S | S | S | - | - | - | - | C | C | C | C | - | - | C | - | C | C |
| Northern Oriole *10 | - | - | S | - | S | - | - | - | - | - | - | C | C | - | - | - | - | C | - |
| **FRINGILLIDAE** | | | | | | | | | | | | | | | | | | | |
| Gray-crowned Rosy Finch *# | - | - | - | S | W | - | - | - | - | - | - | - | - | u | C | - | - | - | - |
| Pine Grosbeak * | - | - | W | P | W | - | - | - | - | U | U | - | - | - | - | - | - | r | - |
| Purple Finch *# | - | - | P | - | P | - | - | - | - | C | - | C | C | - | - | - | - | c | - |
| Cassin's Finch *# | - | - | S | S | S | - | - | - | - | C | - | C | - | - | - | - | - | C | - |
| House Finch * | - | - | P | - | P | - | - | - | - | - | - | - | - | C | - | - | - | C | - |
| Red Crossbill * | - | - | P | P | P | - | - | - | - | C | C | - | - | - | - | - | - | - | - |
| White-winged Crossbill *# | - | - | W | P | W | - | - | - | - | r | r | - | - | - | - | - | - | - | - |

| | O | C | W | M | E | SW | RS | SS | FW | WC | DC | BF | RW | DG | WM | SD | ST | PG | FL |
|---|---|---|---|---|---|---|---|---|---|---|---|---|---|---|---|---|---|---|---|
| Common Redpoll | - | - | W | - | W | - | - | - | - | - | - | - | u | u | - | u | - | - | u |
| Pine Siskin * | - | - | P | S | P | - | - | - | - | C | c | c | c | - | - | - | - | c | - |
| Lesser Goldfinch *R # | - | - | - | - | P | - | - | - | - | - | - | R | - | - | - | R | - | - | - |
| American Goldfinch * | - | - | P | - | P | - | - | - | - | - | - | C | C | - | - | - | - | C | C |
| Evening Grosbeak * | - | - | P | S | P | - | - | - | - | C | U | c | - | - | - | - | - | c | - |
| PASSERIDAE | | | | | | | | | | | | | | | | | | | |
| House Sparrow * | - | - | P | - | P | - | - | - | - | - | - | - | - | - | - | - | - | C | C |

1. There are a few records of the "Blue Goose".

2. "Black" Brant is regular, but the "Atlantic" has been recorded W.

3. The Eurasian subspecies occurs rarely in winter W.

4. The "Western" Red-tailed is a common resident; "Harlan's" occurs rarely in winter both W and E.

5. Western and Glaucous-winged gulls commonly intergrade in Washington and individual birds may appear different from either "species" and may be misidentified as other, less-common species.

6. "Red-shafted" is common resident; the "Yellow-shafted" is uncommon in winter throughout the state. "Hybrids" between the two common in winter.

7. The two crows are combined; they are probably a single species.

8. The "Myrtle" subspecies is a migrant W and E and winters commonly on the coast. "Audubon's" is common, breeding W and M; a few winter E.

9. The "Oregon" is the subspecies predominant in Washington; the "Slate-colored" is uncommon in winter, W and E.

10. "Bullock's" is the common subspecies; "Baltimore" is a casual migrant.

Red-throated Loon - recorded in winter East. A few summer West.

Pacific Loon - previously considered a race of Arctic Loon which is not recorded in Washington.

Common Loon - local in summer West; nests in few locations on both sides of the mountains. Nest sites should be reported.

Western Grebe - some birds spend summer in coastal and inland marine waters. Main winter populations in large embayments: Bellingham/Samish, Boundary, Skagit, Port Susan bays and smaller flocks in southern Puget Sound.

Clark's Grebe - few winter records West: more likely with decreasing latitude.

Black-footed Albatross - few in winter, when species is nesting in mid-subtropical Pacific.

Northern Fulmar - also recorded in inland marine waters (Strait of Juan de Fuca and Strait of Georgia) in winter and often as beached birds in winter on outer coast.

Pink-footed Shearwater - recorded in winter.

Flesh-footed Shearwater - almost always seen near shrimp trawlers.

Sooty Shearwater - small numbers offshore in winter; records for inland marine waters, particularly in fall.

Short-tailed Shearwater - variable year-to-year; recorded in inland marine waters, mostly in early winter.

Fork-tailed Storm-Petrel - recorded in inland marine waters.

Leach's Storm-Petrel - occasional in inland marine waters. Infrequently seen on boat trips during nesting season: presumably forages far offshore.

American White Pelican - very local in summer East, where a few winter. A few reported in West each year during migration.

Brown Pelican - numbers along coast increasing since near absence in 1970s. Most abundant from Columbia River to Grays Harbor, with records N to Point Roberts.

Double-crested Cormorant - local East. Numbers increaseing. Only cormorant likely to be seen on fresh water.

Brandt's Cormorant - few nest in state; large numbers of non-breeders in summer along coast and in San Juans.

Cattle Egret - Variable in occurrence and numbers. Most appear to succumb to cold during severe winters in northern western Washington.

Green Heron - occasional in winter; also recorded East.

Black-crowned Night-Heron - local East; rare West, where very local breeder.

Tundra Swan - care required when distinguishing from Trumpeter Swan: when latter first reappeared in state there was a habitat separation, with Tundras on salt water, Trumpeters on fresh. With growing numbers of latter, flocks have mixed.

Greater White-fronted Goose - primarily outer coast in migration; recorded in winter West.

Snow Goose - most winter at Skagit River delta.

Brant - recorded East. Winter chiefly at Padilla Bay, Lummi Bay and Dungeness. Widespread - practically wherever there is eelgrass (Zostera) - during spring migration.

Canada Goose - now widespread and abundant, particularly in winter and including urban habitats. Populations now almost at "pest" level and other neighboring, breeding waterfowl may have declined.

Wood Duck - uncommon to rare in winter West, appears to be increasing.

American Black Duck - introduced population at Everett; previous records of wild migrants.Blue-winged Teal - nests locally West.

Northern Shoveler - nests locally West.

Gadwall - nests locally west.

American Wigeon - nests locally West.

Canvasback - local in winter West.

Redhead - rare in winter West.

Ring-necked Duck - rare breeder West.

Lesser Scaup - nests locally West.

Oldsquaw - most common in deeper waters than other ducks: flocks of hundreds have been observed off Point Roberts, Bellingham Bay and other areas.

Black Scoter - local concentrations in winter.

Surf Scoter - large non-breeding flocks often summer at Penn Cove, Drayton Harbor and other heavily-used winter locations.

White-winged Scoter - as Surf Scoter in summer.

Common Goldeneye - rare breeder West.

Bufflehead - rare breeder East and West.

Ruddy Duck - nests locally West.

White-tailed Kite - local in SW areas, north to Grays Harbor; has bred near Raymond. Non-breeding records elsewhere West.

Swainson's Hawk - recorded West.

Ferruginous Hawk - local in East; recorded West.

Golden Eagle - local resident West, as in San Juan Islands; winter records West.

Peregrine Falcon - most birds appear to be of race *Anatum*.

Prairie Falcon  - rare in winter West.

Gray Partridge - very local West (Whatcom, Skagit counties at least until mid-1970s).

Spruce Grouse - most in northeast.

Sage Grouse - habitat reduction apparently affecting distribution.

Sharp-tailed Grouse - habitat loss.

Wild Turkey - local; most readily found on San Juan Island.

Northern Bobwhite - local.

Scaled Quail - very local.

Mountain Quail - local, most in southeast; very local West.

Sandhill Crane - breeds at Conboy Lake; winters in numbers near Vancouver, scattered winter records elsewhere.

American Golden-Plover - recorded in spring East.

Pacific Golden-Plover - recorded in winter West.

Snowy Plover - Very limited nesting distribution; recorded in winter on Coast.

Semipalmated Plover - has nested at Grays Harbor; winters rarely on coast.

Black Oystercatcher - rocky areas on outer coast and northern inland marine waters. Pairs during nesting season, often concentrating localized flocks (up to 40 birds) in winter.

Black-necked Stilt - local East; rare migrant West and Coast.

Willet - regular occurrence is local; most at north side of Willapa Bay. Records north to Drayton Harbor.

Wandering Tattler - most migrate along outer coast, local in appropriate habitat elsewhere.

Upland Sandpiper - probably now extirpated as breeder in Spokane County, casual migrant West.

Long-billed Curlew - winters regularly at Willapa Bay.

Marbled Godwit - winters regularly at Willapa Bay.

Ruddy Turnstone - winters rarely on Coast.

Red Knot - winters rarely on Coast.

Baird's Sandpiper - few in spring West.

Pectoral Sandpiper - few in spring.

Sharp-tailed Sandpiper - few fall records East.

Buff-breasted Sandpiper - few fall records East.

Ruff - recorded East.

Red Phalarope - most likely offshore, possible on coast after storms.

Pomarine Jaeger - recorded also along coast and East.

Parasitic Jaeger - recorded East.

Long-tailed Jaeger - recorded Coast; also East.

South Polar Skua - rare along coast and in inside marine waters.

Franklin's Gull - few spring records East.

Little Gull - few spring and winter records.

Heermann's Gull - normal distribution along outer coast, Strait of Juan de Fuca, Admiralty Inlet and San Juans. Rare in embayments and shallow estuaries.

Mew Gull - rare in winter East.

Ring-billed Gull - breeds East and at Grays Harbor; non-breeders abundant and widespread West in summer.

California Gull - uncommon winter and summer Coast and West.

Western Gull - recorded East.

Sabine's Gull - most records offshore. Recorded East.

Caspian Tern - nests at Grays Harbor, Willapa Bay, Jetty Island (Everett) and once at Swinomish (Anacortes). Non-breeders abundant and widespread in summer.

Elegant Tern - Numbers recorded along southern outer coast since 1983 El Niño warm water event, few in inland waters.

Arctic Tern - very small nesting colony at Everett.

Forster's Tern - recorded West.

Marbled Murrelet - nesting locations in old growth forests.

Xantus' Murrelet - almost all records from offshore: unlikely to be seen from shore.

Ancient Murrelet - recorded East.

Cassin's Auklet - infrequently seen from shore; occasion in inland marine waters in winter.

Band-tailed Pigeon - rare summer Mountains and East.

Mourning Dove - much less common in winter.

Flammulated Owl - recorded West.

Snowy Owl - cyclical, occurring on unknown schedule.

Burrowing Owl - recorded (formerly bred) West.

Barred Owl - has spread all over state except Columbia Basin since first recorded in early 1970s.

Great Gray Owl - recorded winter West.

Long-eared Owl - has nested West.

Common Nighthawk - has nest on building roofs West.

Common Poorwill - recorded West.

Black Swift - nests on cliffs (often at waterfalls) in mountains, perhaps Coast.

Vaux's Swift - may use chimneys during migration and nesting season.

White-throated Swift - recorded West.

Anna's Hummingbird - recorded East.

Calliope Hummingbird - recorded West in migration, nesting in upper Skagit River.

Lewis' Woodpecker - recorded West, where formerly nested; winters locally East.

Acorn Woodpecker - recently resident at Lyle, Klickitat County.

White-headed Woodpecker - recorded West.

Least Flycatcher - sporadic summer records East and West.

Dusky Flycatcher - rare migrant West.

Say's Phoebe - rare winter and regular spring migrant West.

Ash-throated Flycatcher - local along Columbia River and in Columbia Basin.

Western Kingbird - rare nester West.

Eastern Kingbird - very local West.

Eurasian Skylark - restricted to southern San Juan Island.

Horned Lark - has decreased as nesting species in lowland West.

Purple Martin - nests in buildings and pilings over water, reestablishing via bird box projects; only very small colonies.

Bank Swallow - rare West.

Gray Jay - resident in lowlands in southwest part of the state.

Scrub Jay - Clark, Cowlitz, Skamania, Klickitat counties north to Olympia, casual records elsewhere.

Clark's Nutcracker - wanders to low elevations in winter.

Black-billed Magpie - casual in winter West.

Mountain Chickadee - variable numbers in winter West.

Boreal Chickadee - restricted to Whatcom, Okanogan and Pend Oreille counties at high elevations.

Bushtit - also resident in Kittitas and Yakima counties.

Pygmy Nuthatch - recorded West.

Rock Wren - around rocks; occurs sporadically West, primarily in San Juan Islands, Cascades.

Canyon Wren - in canyons in open or woodland edge. Recorded West.

Bewick's Wren - also locally resident in Yakima County and along Snake River.

Western Bluebird - very local West; most on Fort Lewis. Absent from much of historical range.

Mountain Bluebird - rare in winter West.

Veery - recorded in summer West. Possibly has nested.

Hermit Thrush - a few winter West.

Gray Catbird - recorded West.

Northern Mockingbird - also recorded in summer West and East; one pair bred Grant County.

Sage Thrasher - recorded West.

Bohemian Waxwing - cyclical West; may nest in northern mountains.

Cedar Waxwing - much less common in winter.

Loggerhead Shrike - rare in winter West and East.

Nashville Warbler - rare migrant and, in summer, at higher elevations West: nests near Newhalem.

Yellow-rumped Warbler - winters commonly on outer coast, locally in Columbia Basin, rarely elsewhere.

Townsend's Warbler - recorded in winter West.

Hermit Warbler - breeds primarily in southern Cascades, southeastern Olympics; hybridizes with Townsend's.

American Redstart - sporadic in small numbers in summer West, recently in Skykomish and Skagit river valleys.

Northern Waterthrush - northeastern counties; recorded in winter and as migrant West.

Yellow-breasted Chat - recorded in migration West.

Lazuli Bunting - rare in summer West, though locally common in Skagit Valley and Fort Lewis area.

Green-tailed Towhee - only in Blue Mountains, where local; recorded West.

Brewer's Sparrow - recorded West.

Vesper Sparrow - local West.

Lark Sparrow - recorded West.

Black-throated Sparrow - breeds locally in eastern Kittitas County. Recorded West.

Sage Sparrow - recorded West.

Savannah Sparrow - a few winter West.

Fox Sparrow - local breeder West.

Lapland Longspur - most common as a migrant, fewer in winter. Less frequently observed in recent years.

Bobolink - local; recorded West.

Yellow-headed Blackbird - nests locally West; winters in small numbers East.

Brown-headed Cowbird - winters in small numbers.

Gray-crowned Rosy Finch - sporadic in lowlands in winter West.

Purple Finch - east to east side of Cascades.

Cassin's Finch - winters locally East. Recorded west of Cascade crest in summer.

White-winged Crossbill - sporadic: rare most years, occasionally locally common.

Lesser Goldfinch - resident at Lyle, Klickitat County.

Short-tailed Albatross
Shy Albatross
Mottled Petrel
Solander's Petrel
Murphy's Petrel
Manx Shearwater
Wilson's Storm-Petrel
Red-billed Tropicbird
Blue-footed Booby
Magnificent Frigatebird
Snowy Egret
Little Blue Heron
White-faced Ibis
Fulvous Whistling-Duck
Mute Swan
Emperor Goose
Falcated Teal
Garganey
King Eider
Steller's Eider
Smew
Red-shouldered Hawk
Broad-winged Hawk
Yellow Rail
Piping Plover
Mountain Plover
Eurasian Dotterel
Bristle-thighed Curlew
Gray-tailed Tattler
Hudsonian Godwit
Great Knot
White-rumped Sandpiper
Curlew Sandpiper
Laughing Gull
Common Black-headed Gull
Slaty-backed Gull
Red-legged Kittiwake
Ivory Gull
Least Tern
Thick-billed Murre
Kittlitz' Murrelet
Parakeet Auklet
Horned Puffin
White-winged Dove
Black-billed Cuckoo
Yellow-billed Cuckoo
Northern Hawk Owl
Allen's Hummingbird
Yellow-bellied Sapsucker

Black Phoebe
Eastern Phoebe
Vermillion Flycatcher
Tropical Kingbird
Scissor-tailed Flycatcher
Pinyon Jay
Blue-gray Gnatcatcher
Gray-cheeked Thrush
Siberian Accentor
Yellow Wagtail
White Wagtail
Black-backed Wagtail
Red-throated Pipit
White-eyed Vireo
Philadelphia Vireo
Blue-winged Warbler
Tennessee Warbler
Northern Parula
Chestnut-sided Warbler
Magnolia Warbler
Cape May Warbler
Black-throated Blue Warbler
Black-throated Green Warbler
Blackburnian Warbler
Prairie Warbler
Blackpoll Warbler
Black-and-white Warbler
Prothonotary Warbler
Ovenbird
Kentucky Warbler
Hooded Warbler
Rose-breasted Grosbeak
Indigo Bunting
Dickcissel
Clay-colored Sparrow
Lark Bunting
LeConte's Sparrow
Sharp-tailed Sparrow
Chestnut-collared Longspur
Rustic Bunting
McKay's Bunting
Rusty Blackbird
Great-tailed Grackle
Common Grackle
Orchard Oriole
Hooded Oriole
Scott's Oriole
Brambling

Reports of any species on this list or not included in this book need thorough documentation and verification by photography if possible. REPORT SIGHTINGS AS SOON AS POSSIBLE to other local observers and to the Washington Bird Records Committee or the Washington Rare Bird Alert (see p. 165).

The bar graphs which follow represent approximate periods of occurrence of the regularly occurring species of the state. These approximations are based on our experience with most species, augmented by published records. Bear in mind that there is year-to-year variation in both abundance and arrival and departure times, so that a bar that begins in mid-May, for example, simply means "usually arrives during the third week in May." Each month is divided into fourths for this purpose. Abundances of some species are quite variable from year to year, and these species are marked with an asterisk (*). "W" indicates occurrence west of the Cascades crest, an "E" indicates occurrence east of the crest and "WE" signifies similar occurrence in both regions.

We have used only three categories of abundance, which could be called "fairly common to common" (thick bar ■■ ), "rare to uncommon" (thin bar ■ ), and "very rare or absent" (blank space). A thick bar indicates periods when there is a reasonably good to excellent chance of finding the species in the appropriate habitat and region, and a thin bar indicates periods when there is a fair chance of finding it. Thus a thin bar represents either the occurrence of a rare or hard-to-find species or a period when a common species is considerably less common. Our judgments have been subjective, and other observers with different criteria for abundance could modify these charts. Virtually all species, with the obvious exception of residents, have occurred at times not indicated on the chart, but we consider these times during which the species is quite unlikely to be seen. See the preceeding section on SPECIES NOTES regarding localized distribution of a number of species.

Neither published records nor our own field records are entirely adequate to cover all "average" arrivals and departures of bird species in Washington, and we appreciate very much the assistance that active field workers can give us in pointing out revisions necessary in this section.

| | | J | F | M | A | M | J | J | A | S | O | N | D |
|---|---|---|---|---|---|---|---|---|---|---|---|---|---|
| Red-throated Loon | W | | | | | | | | | | | | |
| Pacific Loon | W | | | | | | | | | | | | |
| | E | | | | | | | | | | | | |
| Common Loon | W | | | | | | | | | | | | |
| | E | | | | | | | | | | | | |
| Yellow-billed Loon | W | | | | | | | | | | | | |
| Pied-billed Grebe | WE | | | | | | | | | | | | |
| Horned Grebe | W | | | | | | | | | | | | |
| | E | | | | | | | | | | | | |
| Red-necked Grebe | W | | | | | | | | | | | | |
| | E | | | | | | | | | | | | |
| Eared Grebe | W | | | | | | | | | | | | |
| | E | | | | | | | | | | | | |
| Western Grebe | W | | | | | | | | | | | | |
| | E | | | | | | | | | | | | |
| Clark's Grebe | W | | | | | | | | | | | | |
| | E | | | | | | | | | | | | |
| Black-footed Albatross | W | | | | | | | | | | | | |
| Laysan Albatross | W | | | | | | | | | | | | |
| Northern Fulmar * | W | | | | | | | | | | | | |
| Pink-footed Shearwater | W | | | | | | | | | | | | |
| Flesh-footed Shearwater | W | | | | | | | | | | | | |
| Buller's Shearwater * | W | | | | | | | | | | | | |
| Sooty Shearwater | W | | | | | | | | | | | | |
| Short-tailed Shearwater * | W | | | | | | | | | | | | |
| Fork-tailed Storm-Petrel | W | | | | | | | | | | | | |
| Leach's Storm-Petrel | W | | | | | | | | | | | | |
| American White Pelican | E | | | | | | | | | | | | |
| Brown Pelican | W | | | | | | | | | | | | |
| Double-crested Cormorant | W | | | | | | | | | | | | |
| | E | | | | | | | | | | | | |
| Brandt's Cormorant | W | | | | | | | | | | | | |
| Pelagic Cormorant | W | | | | | | | | | | | | |
| American Bittern | W | | | | | | | | | | | | |
| | E | | | | | | | | | | | | |

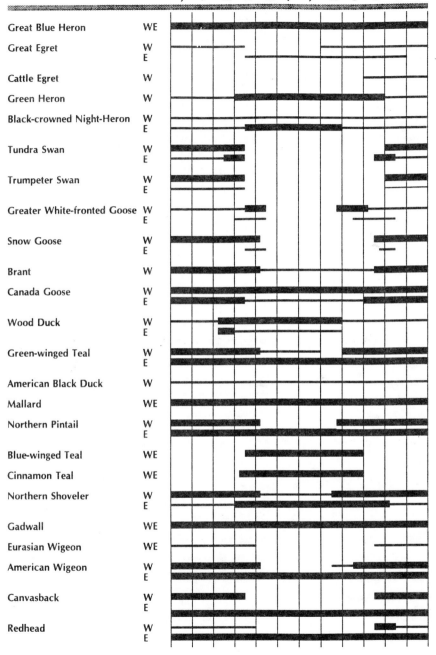

|  | | J | F | M | A | M | J | J | A | S | O | N | D |
|---|---|---|---|---|---|---|---|---|---|---|---|---|---|
| Great Blue Heron | WE | | | | | | | | | | | | |
| Great Egret | W | | | | | | | | | | | | |
| | E | | | | | | | | | | | | |
| Cattle Egret | W | | | | | | | | | | | | |
| Green Heron | W | | | | | | | | | | | | |
| Black-crowned Night-Heron | W | | | | | | | | | | | | |
| | E | | | | | | | | | | | | |
| Tundra Swan | W | | | | | | | | | | | | |
| | E | | | | | | | | | | | | |
| Trumpeter Swan | W | | | | | | | | | | | | |
| | E | | | | | | | | | | | | |
| Greater White-fronted Goose | W | | | | | | | | | | | | |
| | E | | | | | | | | | | | | |
| Snow Goose | W | | | | | | | | | | | | |
| | E | | | | | | | | | | | | |
| Brant | W | | | | | | | | | | | | |
| Canada Goose | W | | | | | | | | | | | | |
| | E | | | | | | | | | | | | |
| Wood Duck | W | | | | | | | | | | | | |
| | E | | | | | | | | | | | | |
| Green-winged Teal | W | | | | | | | | | | | | |
| | E | | | | | | | | | | | | |
| American Black Duck | W | | | | | | | | | | | | |
| Mallard | WE | | | | | | | | | | | | |
| Northern Pintail | W | | | | | | | | | | | | |
| | E | | | | | | | | | | | | |
| Blue-winged Teal | WE | | | | | | | | | | | | |
| Cinnamon Teal | WE | | | | | | | | | | | | |
| Northern Shoveler | W | | | | | | | | | | | | |
| | E | | | | | | | | | | | | |
| Gadwall | WE | | | | | | | | | | | | |
| Eurasian Wigeon | WE | | | | | | | | | | | | |
| American Wigeon | W | | | | | | | | | | | | |
| | E | | | | | | | | | | | | |
| Canvasback | W | | | | | | | | | | | | |
| | E | | | | | | | | | | | | |
| Redhead | W | | | | | | | | | | | | |
| | E | | | | | | | | | | | | |

25

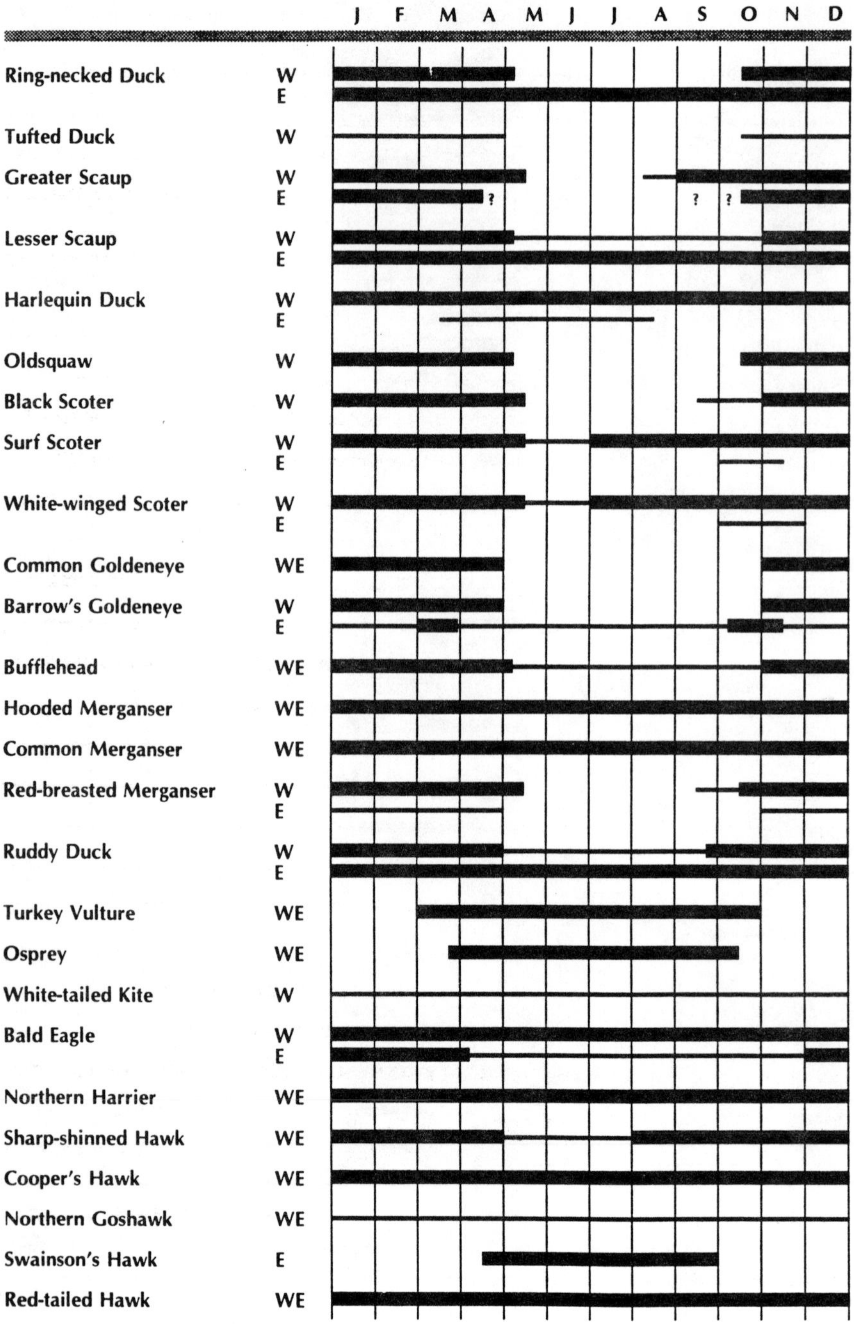
J F M A M J J A S O N D
Ring-necked Duck W E
Tufted Duck W
Greater Scaup W E
? ? ?
Lesser Scaup W E
Harlequin Duck W E
Oldsquaw W
Black Scoter W
Surf Scoter W E
White-winged Scoter W E
Common Goldeneye WE
Barrow's Goldeneye W E
Bufflehead WE
Hooded Merganser WE
Common Merganser WE
Red-breasted Merganser W E
Ruddy Duck W E
Turkey Vulture WE
Osprey WE
White-tailed Kite W
Bald Eagle W E
Northern Harrier WE
Sharp-shinned Hawk WE
Cooper's Hawk WE
Northern Goshawk WE
Swainson's Hawk E
Red-tailed Hawk WE

|  |  | J | F | M | A | M | J | J | A | S | O | N | D |
|---|---|---|---|---|---|---|---|---|---|---|---|---|---|
| Ferruginous Hawk | E | | | | | | | | | | | | |
| Rough-legged Hawk | WE | | | | | | | | | | | | |
| Golden Eagle | WE | | | | | | | | | | | | |
| American Kestrel | WE | | | | | | | | | | | | |
| Merlin | W | | | | | | | | | | | | |
| | E | | | | | | | | | | | | |
| Peregrine Falcon | WE | | | | | | | | | | | | |
| Gyrfalcon | WE | | | | | | | | | | | | |
| Prairie Falcon | E | | | | | | | | | | | | |
| Gray Partridge | E | | | | | | | | | | | | |
| Chukar | E | | | | | | | | | | | | |
| Ring-necked Pheasant | WE | | | | | | | | | | | | |
| Spruce Grouse | WE | | | | | | | | | | | | |
| Blue Grouse | WE | | | | | | | | | | | | |
| White-tailed Ptarmigan | WE | | | | | | | | | | | | |
| Ruffed Grouse | WE | | | | | | | | | | | | |
| Sage Grouse | E | | | | | | | | | | | | |
| Sharp-tailed Grouse | E | | | | | | | | | | | | |
| Wild Turkey | WE | | | | | | | | | | | | |
| Northern Bobwhite | WE | | | | | | | | | | | | |
| Scaled Quail | E | | | | | | | | | | | | |
| California Quail | WE | | | | | | | | | | | | |
| Mountain Quail | E | | | | | | | | | | | | |
| Virginia Rail | WE | | | | | | | | | | | | |
| Sora | WE | | | | | | | | | | | | |
| American Coot | WE | | | | | | | | | | | | |
| Sandhill Crane | E | | | | | | | | | | | | |
| Black-bellied Plover | W | | | | | | | | | | | | |
| | E | | | | | | | | | | | | |
| American Golden-Plover | W | | | | | | | | | | | | |
| | E | | | | | | | | | | | | |
| Pacific Golden-Plover | W | | | | | | | | | | | | |

27

|  |  | J | F | M | A | M | J | J | A | S | O | N | D |
|---|---|---|---|---|---|---|---|---|---|---|---|---|---|
| Snowy Plover | W | | | | | | | | | | | | |
| Semipalmated Plover | WE | | | | | | | | | | | | |
| Killdeer | W | | | | | | | | | | | | |
| | E | | | | | | | | | | | | |
| Black Oystercatcher | W | | | | | | | | | | | | |
| Black-necked Stilt | E | | | | | | | | | | | | |
| American Avocet | E | | | | | | | | | | | | |
| Greater Yellowlegs | W | | | | | | | | | | | | |
| | E | | | | | | | | | | | | |
| Lesser Yellowlegs | W | | | | | | | | | | | | |
| | E | | | | | | | | | | | | |
| Solitary Sandpiper | W | | | | | | | | | | | | |
| | E | | | | | | | | | | | | |
| Willet | W | | | | | | | | | | | | |
| Wandering Tattler | W | | | | | | | | | | | | |
| Spotted Sandpiper | W | | | | | | | | | | | | |
| | E | | | | | | | | | | | | |
| Upland Sandpiper | E | | | | | | ? | | | | | | |
| Whimbrel | W | | | | | | | | | | | | |
| Long-billed Curlew | W | | | | | | | | | | | | |
| | E | | | | | | | | | | | | |
| Bar-tailed Godwit | W | | | | | | | | | | | | |
| Marbled Godwit | W | | | | | | | | | | | | |
| Ruddy Turnstone | W | | | | | | | | | | | | |
| | E | | | | | | | | | | | | |
| Black Turnstone | W | | | | | | | | | | | | |
| Surfbird | W | | | | | | | | | | | | |
| Red Knot | W | | | | | | | | | | | | |
| Sanderling | W | | | | | | | | | | | | |
| Semipalmated Sandpiper | W | | | | | | | | | | | | |
| | E | | | | | | | | | | | | |
| Western Sandpiper | W | | | | | | | | | | | | |
| | E | | | | | | | | | | | | |
| Least Sandpiper | W | | | | | | | | | | | | |
| | E | | | | | | | | | | | | |
| Baird's Sandpiper | WE | | | | | | | | | | | | |

| | | J | F | M | A | M | J | J | A | S | O | N | D |
|---|---|---|---|---|---|---|---|---|---|---|---|---|---|
| Pectoral Sandpiper | W | | | | | | | | | | | | |
| | E | | | | | | | | | | | | |
| Sharp-tailed Sandpiper | W | | | | | | | | | | | | |
| Rock Sandpiper | W | | | | | | | | | | | | |
| Dunlin | W | | | | | | | | | | | | |
| | E | | | | | | | | | | | | |
| Stilt Sandpiper | WE | | | | | | | | | | | | |
| Buff-breasted Sandpiper | W | | | | | | | | | | | | |
| Ruff | W | | | | | | | | | | | | |
| Short-billed Dowitcher | W | | | | | | | | | | | | |
| | E | | | | | | | | | | | | |
| Long-billed Dowitcher | W | | | | | | | | | | | | |
| | E | | | | | | | | | | | | |
| Common Snipe | WE | | | | | | | | | | | | |
| Wilson's Phalarope | W | | | | | | | | | | | | |
| | E | | | | | | | | | | | | |
| Red-necked Phalarope | W | | | | | | | | | | | | |
| | E | | | | | | | | | | | | |
| Red Phalarope | W | | | | | | | | | | | | |
| Pomarine Jaeger | W | | | | | | | | | | | | |
| Parasitic Jaeger | W | | | | | | | | | | | | |
| Long-tailed Jaeger | W | | | | | | | | | | | | |
| South Polar Skua | W | | | | | | | | | | | | |
| Franklin's Gull | W | | | | | | | | | | | | |
| | E | | | | | | | | | | | | |
| Little Gull | W | | | | | | | | | | | | |
| Bonaparte's Gull | W | | | | | | | | | | | | |
| | E | | | | | | | | | | | | |
| Heermann's Gull | W | | | | | | | | | | | | |
| Mew Gull | W | | | | | | | | | | | | |
| | E | | | | | | | | | | | | |
| Ring-billed Gull | WE | | | | | | | | | | | | |
| California Gull | W | | | | | | | | | | | | |
| | E | | | | | | | | | | | | |
| Herring Gull | W | | | | | | | | | | | | |
| | E | | | | | | | | | | | | |

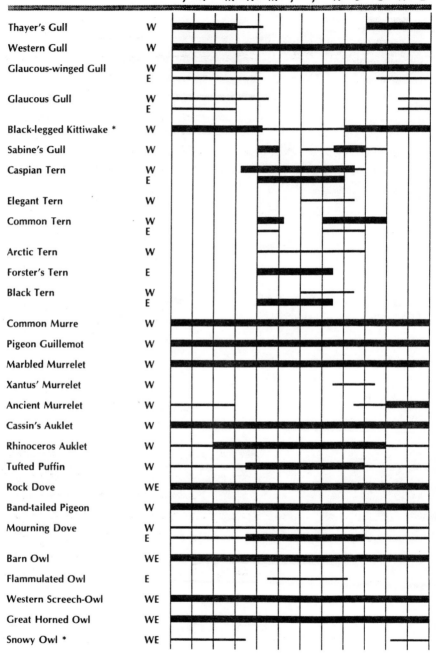

|  | | J | F | M | A | M | J | J | A | S | O | N | D |
|---|---|---|---|---|---|---|---|---|---|---|---|---|---|
| Thayer's Gull | W | | | | | | | | | | | | |
| Western Gull | W | | | | | | | | | | | | |
| Glaucous-winged Gull | W E | | | | | | | | | | | | |
| Glaucous Gull | W E | | | | | | | | | | | | |
| Black-legged Kittiwake * | W | | | | | | | | | | | | |
| Sabine's Gull | W | | | | | | | | | | | | |
| Caspian Tern | W E | | | | | | | | | | | | |
| Elegant Tern | W | | | | | | | | | | | | |
| Common Tern | W E | | | | | | | | | | | | |
| Arctic Tern | W | | | | | | | | | | | | |
| Forster's Tern | E | | | | | | | | | | | | |
| Black Tern | W E | | | | | | | | | | | | |
| Common Murre | W | | | | | | | | | | | | |
| Pigeon Guillemot | W | | | | | | | | | | | | |
| Marbled Murrelet | W | | | | | | | | | | | | |
| Xantus' Murrelet | W | | | | | | | | | | | | |
| Ancient Murrelet | W | | | | | | | | | | | | |
| Cassin's Auklet | W | | | | | | | | | | | | |
| Rhinoceros Auklet | W | | | | | | | | | | | | |
| Tufted Puffin | W | | | | | | | | | | | | |
| Rock Dove | WE | | | | | | | | | | | | |
| Band-tailed Pigeon | W | | | | | | | | | | | | |
| Mourning Dove | W E | | | | | | | | | | | | |
| Barn Owl | WE | | | | | | | | | | | | |
| Flammulated Owl | E | | | | | | | | | | | | |
| Western Screech-Owl | WE | | | | | | | | | | | | |
| Great Horned Owl | WE | | | | | | | | | | | | |
| Snowy Owl * | WE | | | | | | | | | | | | |

|  | J | F | M | A | M | J | J | A | S | O | N | D |
|---|---|---|---|---|---|---|---|---|---|---|---|---|
| Great Gray Owl | W | ? | | | | | | | | | | |
| | E | | | | | | | | | | | |
| Northern Pygmy-Owl | WE | | | | | | | | | | | |
| Burrowing Owl | E | | | | | | | | | | | |
| Spotted Owl | WE | | | | | | | | | | | |
| Barred Owl | WE | | | | | | | | | | | |
| Long-eared Owl | W | | | | | | | | | | | |
| | E | | | | | | | | | | | |
| Short-eared Owl | WE | | | | | | | | | | | |
| Boreal Owl | E | | | | | | | | | | | |
| Northern Saw-whet Owl | WE | | | | | | | | | | | |
| Common Nighthawk | W | | | | | | | | | | | |
| | E | | | | | | | | | | | |
| Common Poorwill | E | | | | | | | | | | | |
| Black Swift | W | | | | | | | | | | | |
| | E | | | | | | | | | | | |
| Vaux's Swift | W | | | | | | | | | | | |
| | E | | | | | | | | | | | |
| White-throated Swift | E | | | | | | | | | | | |
| Black-chinned Hummingbird | E | | | | | | | | | | | |
| Anna's Hummingbird | W | | | | | | | | | | | |
| Calliope Hummingbird | E | | | | | | | | | | | |
| Rufous Hummingbird | W | | | | | | | | | | | |
| | E | | | | | | | | | | | |
| Belted Kingfisher | WE | | | | | | | | | | | |
| Lewis' Woodpecker | E | | | | | | | | | | | |
| Red-naped Sapsucker | E | | | | | | | | | | | |
| Red-breasted Sapsucker | W | | | | | | | | | | | |
| Williamson's Sapsucker | E | | | | | | | | | | | |
| Downy Woodpecker | WE | | | | | | | | | | | |
| Hairy Woodpecker | WE | | | | | | | | | | | |
| White-headed Woodpecker | E | | | | | | | | | | | |
| Three-toed Woodpecker | WE | | | | | | | | | | | |
| Black-backed Woodpecker | WE | | | | | | | | | | | |

31

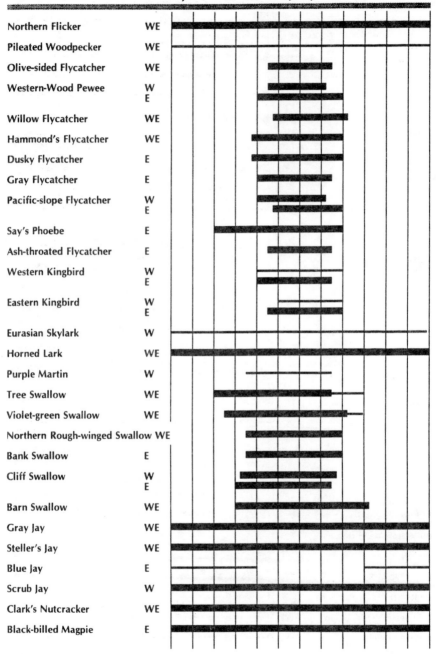

| | | J | F | M | A | M | J | J | A | S | O | N | D |
|---|---|---|---|---|---|---|---|---|---|---|---|---|---|
| Northern Flicker | WE | | | | | | | | | | | | |
| Pileated Woodpecker | WE | | | | | | | | | | | | |
| Olive-sided Flycatcher | WE | | | | | | | | | | | | |
| Western-Wood Pewee | W E | | | | | | | | | | | | |
| Willow Flycatcher | WE | | | | | | | | | | | | |
| Hammond's Flycatcher | WE | | | | | | | | | | | | |
| Dusky Flycatcher | E | | | | | | | | | | | | |
| Gray Flycatcher | E | | | | | | | | | | | | |
| Pacific-slope Flycatcher | W E | | | | | | | | | | | | |
| Say's Phoebe | E | | | | | | | | | | | | |
| Ash-throated Flycatcher | E | | | | | | | | | | | | |
| Western Kingbird | W E | | | | | | | | | | | | |
| Eastern Kingbird | W E | | | | | | | | | | | | |
| Eurasian Skylark | W | | | | | | | | | | | | |
| Horned Lark | WE | | | | | | | | | | | | |
| Purple Martin | W | | | | | | | | | | | | |
| Tree Swallow | WE | | | | | | | | | | | | |
| Violet-green Swallow | WE | | | | | | | | | | | | |
| Northern Rough-winged Swallow | WE | | | | | | | | | | | | |
| Bank Swallow | E | | | | | | | | | | | | |
| Cliff Swallow | W E | | | | | | | | | | | | |
| Barn Swallow | WE | | | | | | | | | | | | |
| Gray Jay | WE | | | | | | | | | | | | |
| Steller's Jay | WE | | | | | | | | | | | | |
| Blue Jay | E | | | | | | | | | | | | |
| Scrub Jay | W | | | | | | | | | | | | |
| Clark's Nutcracker | WE | | | | | | | | | | | | |
| Black-billed Magpie | E | | | | | | | | | | | | |

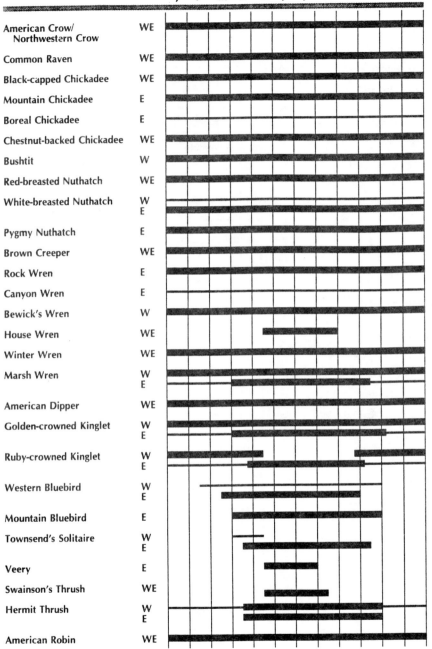

|  | | J | F | M | A | M | J | J | A | S | O | N | D |
|---|---|---|---|---|---|---|---|---|---|---|---|---|---|
| American Crow/ Northwestern Crow | WE | | | | | | | | | | | | |
| Common Raven | WE | | | | | | | | | | | | |
| Black-capped Chickadee | WE | | | | | | | | | | | | |
| Mountain Chickadee | E | | | | | | | | | | | | |
| Boreal Chickadee | E | | | | | | | | | | | | |
| Chestnut-backed Chickadee | WE | | | | | | | | | | | | |
| Bushtit | W | | | | | | | | | | | | |
| Red-breasted Nuthatch | WE | | | | | | | | | | | | |
| White-breasted Nuthatch | W E | | | | | | | | | | | | |
| Pygmy Nuthatch | E | | | | | | | | | | | | |
| Brown Creeper | WE | | | | | | | | | | | | |
| Rock Wren | E | | | | | | | | | | | | |
| Canyon Wren | E | | | | | | | | | | | | |
| Bewick's Wren | W | | | | | | | | | | | | |
| House Wren | WE | | | | | | | | | | | | |
| Winter Wren | WE | | | | | | | | | | | | |
| Marsh Wren | W E | | | | | | | | | | | | |
| American Dipper | WE | | | | | | | | | | | | |
| Golden-crowned Kinglet | W E | | | | | | | | | | | | |
| Ruby-crowned Kinglet | W E | | | | | | | | | | | | |
| Western Bluebird | W E | | | | | | | | | | | | |
| Mountain Bluebird | E | | | | | | | | | | | | |
| Townsend's Solitaire | W E | | | | | | | | | | | | |
| Veery | E | | | | | | | | | | | | |
| Swainson's Thrush | WE | | | | | | | | | | | | |
| Hermit Thrush | W E | | | | | | | | | | | | |
| American Robin | WE | | | | | | | | | | | | |

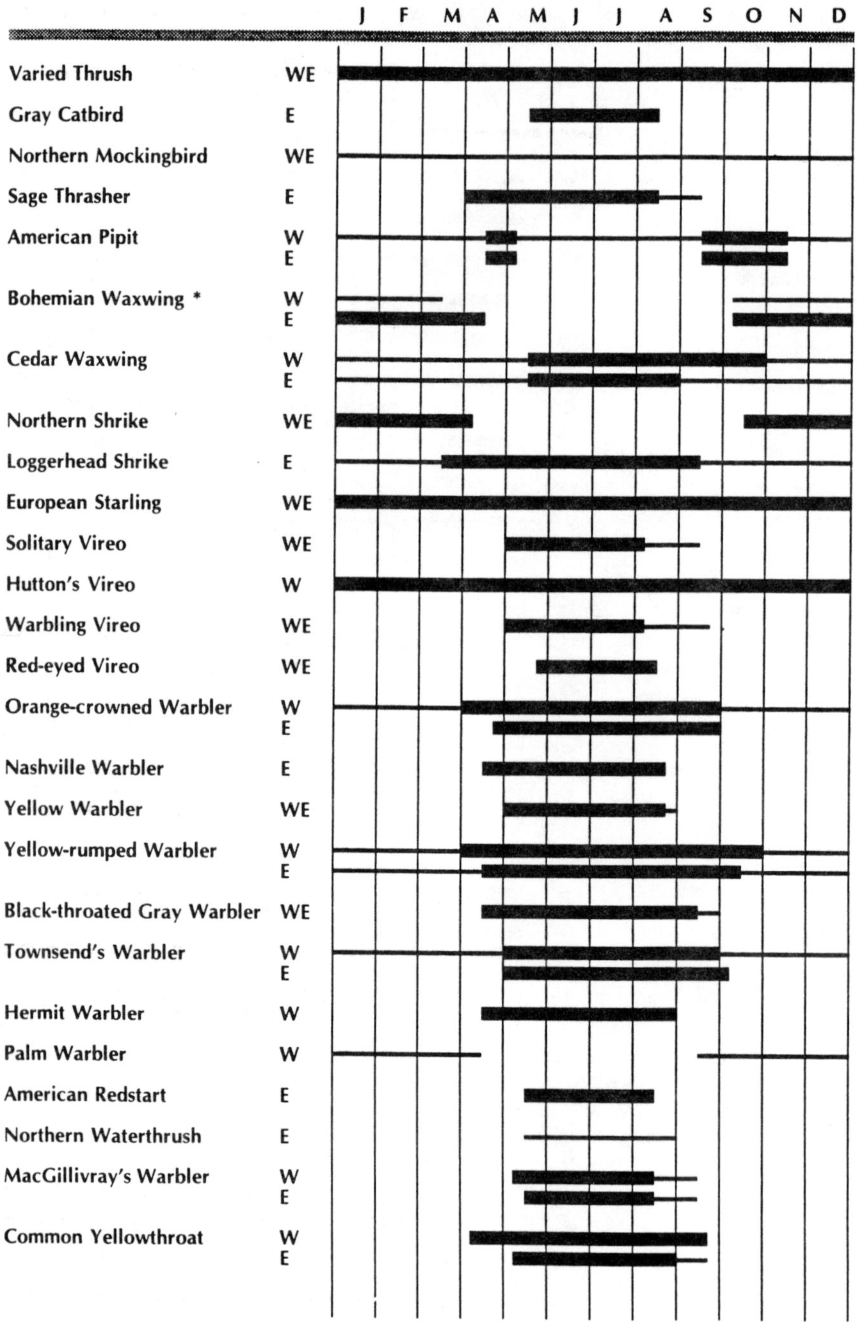

|  |  | J | F | M | A | M | J | J | A | S | O | N | D |
|---|---|---|---|---|---|---|---|---|---|---|---|---|---|

**Varied Thrush** — WE

**Gray Catbird** — E

**Northern Mockingbird** — WE

**Sage Thrasher** — E

**American Pipit** — W / E

**Bohemian Waxwing \*** — W / E

**Cedar Waxwing** — W / E

**Northern Shrike** — WE

**Loggerhead Shrike** — E

**European Starling** — WE

**Solitary Vireo** — WE

**Hutton's Vireo** — W

**Warbling Vireo** — WE

**Red-eyed Vireo** — WE

**Orange-crowned Warbler** — W / E

**Nashville Warbler** — E

**Yellow Warbler** — WE

**Yellow-rumped Warbler** — W / E

**Black-throated Gray Warbler** — WE

**Townsend's Warbler** — W / E

**Hermit Warbler** — W

**Palm Warbler** — W

**American Redstart** — E

**Northern Waterthrush** — E

**MacGillivray's Warbler** — W / E

**Common Yellowthroat** — W / E

34

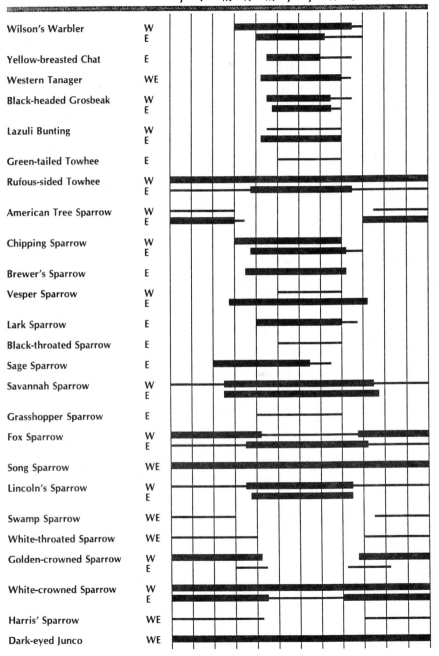

|  |  | J | F | M | A | M | J | J | A | S | O | N | D |
|---|---|---|---|---|---|---|---|---|---|---|---|---|---|
| Wilson's Warbler | W |  |  |  |  |  |  |  |  |  |  |  |  |
|  | E |  |  |  |  |  |  |  |  |  |  |  |  |
| Yellow-breasted Chat | E |  |  |  |  |  |  |  |  |  |  |  |  |
| Western Tanager | WE |  |  |  |  |  |  |  |  |  |  |  |  |
| Black-headed Grosbeak | W |  |  |  |  |  |  |  |  |  |  |  |  |
|  | E |  |  |  |  |  |  |  |  |  |  |  |  |
| Lazuli Bunting | W |  |  |  |  |  |  |  |  |  |  |  |  |
|  | E |  |  |  |  |  |  |  |  |  |  |  |  |
| Green-tailed Towhee | E |  |  |  |  |  |  |  |  |  |  |  |  |
| Rufous-sided Towhee | W |  |  |  |  |  |  |  |  |  |  |  |  |
|  | E |  |  |  |  |  |  |  |  |  |  |  |  |
| American Tree Sparrow | W |  |  |  |  |  |  |  |  |  |  |  |  |
|  | E |  |  |  |  |  |  |  |  |  |  |  |  |
| Chipping Sparrow | W |  |  |  |  |  |  |  |  |  |  |  |  |
|  | E |  |  |  |  |  |  |  |  |  |  |  |  |
| Brewer's Sparrow | E |  |  |  |  |  |  |  |  |  |  |  |  |
| Vesper Sparrow | W |  |  |  |  |  |  |  |  |  |  |  |  |
|  | E |  |  |  |  |  |  |  |  |  |  |  |  |
| Lark Sparrow | E |  |  |  |  |  |  |  |  |  |  |  |  |
| Black-throated Sparrow | E |  |  |  |  |  |  |  |  |  |  |  |  |
| Sage Sparrow | E |  |  |  |  |  |  |  |  |  |  |  |  |
| Savannah Sparrow | W |  |  |  |  |  |  |  |  |  |  |  |  |
|  | E |  |  |  |  |  |  |  |  |  |  |  |  |
| Grasshopper Sparrow | E |  |  |  |  |  |  |  |  |  |  |  |  |
| Fox Sparrow | W |  |  |  |  |  |  |  |  |  |  |  |  |
|  | E |  |  |  |  |  |  |  |  |  |  |  |  |
| Song Sparrow | WE |  |  |  |  |  |  |  |  |  |  |  |  |
| Lincoln's Sparrow | W |  |  |  |  |  |  |  |  |  |  |  |  |
|  | E |  |  |  |  |  |  |  |  |  |  |  |  |
| Swamp Sparrow | WE |  |  |  |  |  |  |  |  |  |  |  |  |
| White-throated Sparrow | WE |  |  |  |  |  |  |  |  |  |  |  |  |
| Golden-crowned Sparrow | W |  |  |  |  |  |  |  |  |  |  |  |  |
|  | E |  |  |  |  |  |  |  |  |  |  |  |  |
| White-crowned Sparrow | W |  |  |  |  |  |  |  |  |  |  |  |  |
|  | E |  |  |  |  |  |  |  |  |  |  |  |  |
| Harris' Sparrow | WE |  |  |  |  |  |  |  |  |  |  |  |  |
| Dark-eyed Junco | WE |  |  |  |  |  |  |  |  |  |  |  |  |

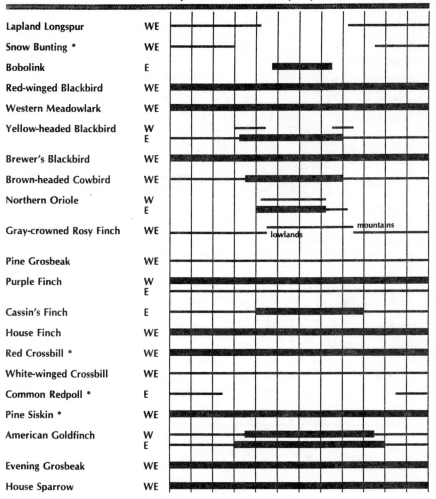

|                        |      | J | F | M | A | M | J | J | A | S | O | N | D |
|------------------------|------|---|---|---|---|---|---|---|---|---|---|---|---|
| Lapland Longspur       | WE   |   |   |   |   |   |   |   |   |   |   |   |   |
| Snow Bunting *         | WE   |   |   |   |   |   |   |   |   |   |   |   |   |
| Bobolink               | E    |   |   |   |   |   |   |   |   |   |   |   |   |
| Red-winged Blackbird   | WE   |   |   |   |   |   |   |   |   |   |   |   |   |
| Western Meadowlark     | WE   |   |   |   |   |   |   |   |   |   |   |   |   |
| Yellow-headed Blackbird| W    |   |   |   |   |   |   |   |   |   |   |   |   |
|                        | E    |   |   |   |   |   |   |   |   |   |   |   |   |
| Brewer's Blackbird     | WE   |   |   |   |   |   |   |   |   |   |   |   |   |
| Brown-headed Cowbird   | WE   |   |   |   |   |   |   |   |   |   |   |   |   |
| Northern Oriole        | W    |   |   |   |   |   |   |   |   |   |   |   |   |
|                        | E    |   |   |   |   |   |   |   |   |   |   |   |   |
| Gray-crowned Rosy Finch| WE   |   |   |   |   |   |   |   |   |   |   |   |   |
| Pine Grosbeak          | WE   |   |   |   |   |   |   |   |   |   |   |   |   |
| Purple Finch           | W    |   |   |   |   |   |   |   |   |   |   |   |   |
|                        | E    |   |   |   |   |   |   |   |   |   |   |   |   |
| Cassin's Finch         | E    |   |   |   |   |   |   |   |   |   |   |   |   |
| House Finch            | WE   |   |   |   |   |   |   |   |   |   |   |   |   |
| Red Crossbill *        | WE   |   |   |   |   |   |   |   |   |   |   |   |   |
| White-winged Crossbill | WE   |   |   |   |   |   |   |   |   |   |   |   |   |
| Common Redpoll *       | E    |   |   |   |   |   |   |   |   |   |   |   |   |
| Pine Siskin *          | WE   |   |   |   |   |   |   |   |   |   |   |   |   |
| American Goldfinch     | W    |   |   |   |   |   |   |   |   |   |   |   |   |
|                        | E    |   |   |   |   |   |   |   |   |   |   |   |   |
| Evening Grosbeak       | WE   |   |   |   |   |   |   |   |   |   |   |   |   |
| House Sparrow          | WE   |   |   |   |   |   |   |   |   |   |   |   |   |

This guide is used with standard state road maps and should be supplemented with county road maps, Forest Service maps, and local maps like state parks and wildlife areas. Two important supplements are the Washington State Interstate Guide, a map published by the state Department of Transportation which gives freeway exit numbers (often unavailable on other road maps), and the widely-used DeLorme Washington Atlas and Gazetteer.

Each birding area is numbered, corresponding to its regional map. Localities may be considered a "birding unit", and may include several locations and diverse habitats which are visited during a birding trip. For each area we have included information about the best season (S), elevation (E), and main habitat types (H). Habitat types correspond with those given in the bird checklist section. Directions for locating the area and some of the sites within it are given, along with some description of the area and what might be expected. In no case have we made an attempt to give a complete species list but have instead listed some of the characteristic species and some of the rarities that might

be sought. The state is divided into nine regions as shown on the following map, and the accounts within these regional sections are arranged generally from west to east and/or north to south. Following recent birder custom we have included the DeLorme atlas ("DLA" on site descriptions) map page number(s) and coordinates for the locality.

In addition to codes corresponding to those used in the checklist section, several abbreviations are also used, including those for main compass directions (N, S, E, W): CG - campground; GS - guard station (U.S. Forest Service); NF - National Forest (U.S. Forest Service); NWR - National Wildlife Refuge (U.S. Fish and Wildlife Service); SP - State Park; STP - sewage treatment pond; US - U.S. Highway; WA - State Highway; and WRA - Wildlife Recreation Area (Washington Dept. of Wildlife).

In the sections that follow, we have organized the descriptions of the birding areas generally into geographic regions based on county boundaries, modified in a few cases to reflect travel route realities.

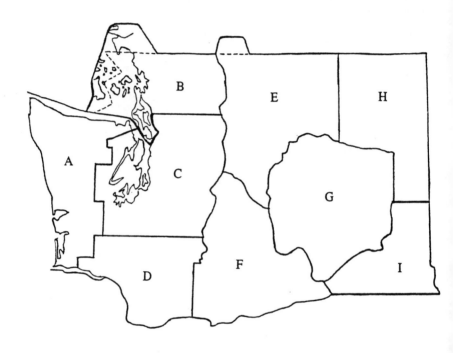

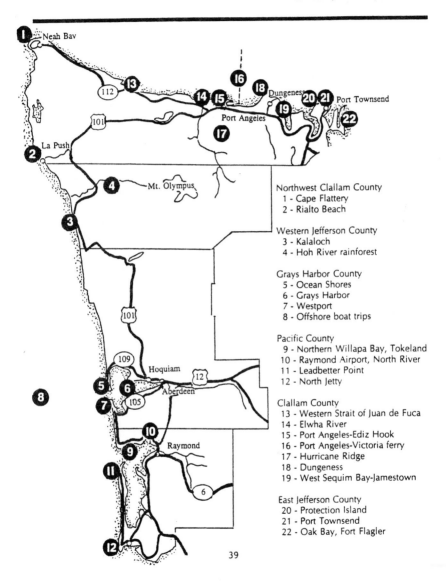

Northwest Clallam County
1 - Cape Flattery
2 - Rialto Beach

Western Jefferson County
3 - Kalaloch
4 - Hoh River rainforest

Grays Harbor County
5 - Ocean Shores
6 - Grays Harbor
7 - Westport
8 - Offshore boat trips

Pacific County
9 - Northern Willapa Bay, Tokeland
10 - Raymond Airport, North River
11 - Leadbetter Point
12 - North Jetty

Clallam County
13 - Western Strait of Juan de Fuca
14 - Elwha River
15 - Port Angeles-Ediz Hook
16 - Port Angeles-Victoria ferry
17 - Hurricane Ridge
18 - Dungeness
19 - West Sequim Bay-Jamestown

East Jefferson County
20 - Protection Island
21 - Port Townsend
22 - Oak Bay, Fort Flagler

39

S: all year  E: 0-1000'
H: SW RS WC ST
Maps: DLA 90:A-B 3

# Cape Flattery

A - 1

Go SW from Neah Bay (see Neah Bay, A - 14) toward **Mukkaw Bay,** with the Waatch River on your left. Where a bridge crosses it, you can proceed to the left and down to Mukkaw Bay, During migration one may see most of the shore birds of the rocky shore as well as those of open sandy beach habitats like Whimbrel and Sanderling. Harlequin Ducks are common in the surge channels around the rocks, and loons, grebes, scoters and alcids swim in the surf. Great Blue Herons, Common Mergansers, Bald Eagles and Ospreys and Peregrines are possible. The spruce forests and thickets have Rufous Hummingbirds, Hairy Woodpeckers, flickers, Steller's Jays, crows, Chestnut-backed Chickadees, Red-breasted Nuthatches, Brown Creepers, Winter Wrens, Golden-crowned Kinglets, Swainson's and Varied thrushes, Orange-crowned, Townsend's and Wilson's Warblers, White-crowned Sparrows and Purple Finches. During the summer, Black and Vaux' swifts wheel overhead, especially during stormy weather.

Return to and cross the Waatch River bridge, turn left. At about 5.5-6 miles park at a pull-off on the left side marked **"Cape Trails"**. It is about 0.3 mile downhill over roots and muddy spots to the cliffs at Cape Flattery. Seabird watching may be excellent - a spotting scope is essential. Pelagic Cormorants, Black Oystercatchers, Glaucous-winged Gulls, Common Murres, Pigeon Guiillemots and Tufted Puffins can be seen

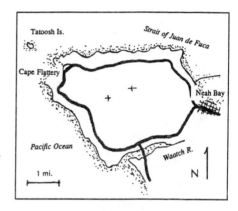

coming and going during spring and summer to the seabird colony on **Tatoosh Island** about 0.5 mile offshore. Leach's and Fork-tailed storm-petrels and Cassin's Auklets visit nests during darkness and are seldom seen during the day. During migrations and winter many other species may be seen. The Falcon Research Group has monitored migrations here and recorded many hundreds of raptors and Sandhill Cranes passing the Cape and crossing the Strait of Juan de Fuca in the spring. During spring also, gray whales often pass under the Cape Flattery cliffs, allowing you to look directly down on them as they move north along the coast. (DP, TW)

# Rialto Beach

A - 2

S: all year   E: 0
H: SW RS SS FW WC
Maps: DLA 74:A 3

One mile N of Forks on SR 101, turn SW on the road to LaPush. At about 4 miles bear left and at 10.5 miles turn right at signs to Rialto Beach and Mora Campground. Past the campground the road ends at a parking lot. Large flocks of seabirds may be just off the south end of Rialto Beach. Gulls, ducks and shorebirds that prefer sand and mud can often be found in the slough behind the beach and at the mouth of the Quillayute River. In early summer the Quillayute Needles offshore are covered with nesting Common Murres, Pigeon Guillemots, Tufted Puffins, cormorants and gulls. In addition, non-breeding Harlequin Ducks, scoters, loons, and grebes may be numerous. Black Oystercatchers, turnstones, Surfbirds and other species that prefer rocks are sometimes more likely at one of the other ocean beaches (2nd and 3rd beaches to the S are easily reached), especially when low tides make more rocks visible from the beach.

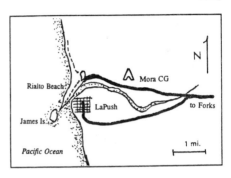

Look for Bald Eagles or Peregrines perched on trees on offshore rocks. Though birds can sometimes be scarce along the open beaches, wind-sculptured trees, sand patterns, waves, tide pools, the arches and the offshore rocks are impressive. (JD, TW)

# Kalaloch

A - 3

S: all year  E: 0
H: SW RS SS WC ST
Maps: DLA 75:C 5

The Olympic National Park ocean strip has ocean front woodlands, ocean and both sandy and and rocky shores. **Ruby Beach,** a few miles N of the Kalaloch campground, is a good place for "rock" shorebirds. The sandy beaches have wintering Dunlins and Sanderlings. Loons, grebes, cormorants, sea ducks, gulls and alcids are found in large numbers in season. Heermann's Gulls are found all along the coast in summer. **Destruction Island,** an important nesting colony for 25,000 Rhinoceros Auklets and many other seabirds, lies offshore. Most of Washington's very few sea otters reside in the kelp beds around Destruction Island. (TW)

41

# Hoh River rain forest

A - 4

What remains of Washington's vast, dark rain forest is primarily within Olympic National Park. The specialized animals found there are either secretive or hard to see, but several sought-after birds inhabit the dank forests and can be looked for along trails penetrating the area from the lowlands to alpine habitats. About 20 miles N of Kalaloch on SR 101, the Hoh River Rd goes E up the valley through the Olympic rain forest to the Hoh Ranger Station, trails, campground and interpretive center. Back-country trails to Mt. Olympus take off from this area. Bird variety is not great, but Varied Thrushes, Dippers and other animals like elk inhabit the dark forests and stream banks. Watch for Spotted Owls (and report them if noted) in dense stands of big trees, usually on a slope and near water. Other likely places for this species include the upper Quinault Valley and the Elwha Valley, on the N side of the Olympics. Olympic, North Cascades and Mount Rainier National Parks contain remaining areas of unlogged habitat. Spruce Grouse, of uncertain occurrence in the Olympics, have been reported near the Olympus shelter on the Hoh River trail. Marbled Murrelets nest in the Olympics, as well as in other old-growth forest locations in western Washington. (TW)

## GRAYS HARBOR COUNTY

Grays Harbor offers the exposed sandy shoreline of the Pacific Ocean, and protected sand/mud estuarine habitats which support huge numbers of marine birds throughout the year. Migrating and wintering shorebirds, large numbers of gulls and Caspian Terns, feeding seabirds and many passerines are found in the area.

# Ocean Shores

A - 5

The Ocean Shores area is W of Hoquiam via SR 109 and 115, and is one of Washington's best shorebird areas. Many exciting state records have come from the Ocean Shores area in recent years. Dotterel, Ruff, Bar-tailed and Hudsonian godwits, Upland and Buff-breasted sandpipers are among the highlights. From the town of Ocean Shores, two main roads go S. The west side road (Ocean Shores Blvd) leads to a sandy parking area at the SW tip of **Point Brown,** a great place to see Sooty Shearwaters, cormorants, shorebirds, gulls, and many other birds along or at the end of the rock jetty. Wandering Tattlers are common migrants and Black Turnstones, Surfbirds and Rock Sandpipers are resident from fall through spring. Brown Pelicans are present in summer. This is a good location for watching migrating loons, cormorants, alcids, ducks and geese, which sometimes pass by in huge numbers. The dunes and shortgrass flats areas east of the jetty provide habitat in fall for many species like golden-plovers, Whimbrel, possibly Buff-breasted Sandpiper, and Horned Lark and Lapland Longspur. In winter, look for Snow Buntings, Snowy Owls, hawks and other species. The eastern road (Pt. Brown Ave.) ends at the marina at the SE tip of the peninsula. Ocean Shores Blvd. and Pt. Brown Ave. connect at the S end of the peninsula via Marine View Dr. Between these two roads, on the protected S shore, is the **Oyhut Wildlife Area** marked by signs and a wire fence next to the sewage treatment plant. Check the salt marsh for many waders and shorebirds, including both species of golden-plovers, Sharp-tailed Sandpipers and Ruffs, in the fall. This and the adjoining beach are good for Marbled Godwits with flocks of 50 or more not uncommon. Buff-breasted Sandpipers have been found almost every fall S of the marsh. Snowy Plovers have been found nesting (as have Semipalmated Plovers) at the end of the long sand spit which extends E from the area. The **golf course/airport** in the center of Ocean Shores is good in the fall for golden-plovers.

**Ocean City State Park,** N along SR 115 from Ocean Shores, has campsites and good birds (especially in the swampy ponds behind the dunes between the park and highway). Bitterns and Virginia Rails nest here, and Great Egrets are possible. During

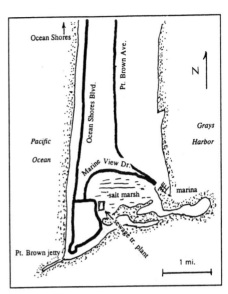

fall migrations the trees and shrubs may teem with warblers and other migrants. Some birds like "Yellow-shafted" Northern Flickers, Hermit Thrushes and "Myrtle" Yellow-rumped warblers are much more common in winter here on the coast than anywhere else in the state, and this is the state's best place to find Palm Warblers. (EH, DP, BT, TW)

---

S: all year    E: 0
H: SW SS FW WC BF RW WM ST FL
Maps: DLA 44:A 1-2

**Bowerman Basin** is one of several good locations for shorebirds in the inner Grays Harbor estuary. It's the tidal flats lying between Bowerman Field (Hoquiam Airport) and highway SR 101 on the N side of Grays Harbor. Census data in recent years have shown this to be one of the west coast's most important stops for migrating shorebirds, with huge flocks (as many as

# Grays Harbor

A - 6

500,000 Western Sandpipers) present at one time. Up to 50,000 Dunlins winter here. Many other species may also be seen, including dabbling ducks and Peregrines. Access is through Hoquiam on Hwy 109. Just to the W of the high school, turn left onto the Paulson Rd ("Airport" sign) which dead ends at a sewage treatment pond. This pond is excellent for many ducks and may have uncommon migrants such as Eared Grebe, phalaropes or Franklin's Gull. Go to the end of the road along the N side of the airport to the Bowerman mudflats.

**Aberdeen sewage treatment ponds** treat industrial wastes and are located about 1-2 miles W of the entrance to Grays Harbor College on SR 105. They lie behind high dikes on the N side of the road, and are posted with warning signs. There is great variability in the use of the various ponds both by the disposal operators and the birds, though the most consistent pond for birds appears to be at the eastern end of the complex. Park in pull-offs at the road edge, but don't block truck access. Many unusual

species for the state have been sighted here, including Hudsonian Godwit and Stilt Sandpiper. **Bottle Beach** is about 2.5 miles W of the Elk River bridge on SR 105, where the road curves to the left away from the diked fields. "Ocean Avenue" - a hard-to-see one-lane road - turns abruptly to the right, off the highway and peters out a short distance further where a large vehicle cannot turn around. Not a great beginning, but a path over a tidal creek, through Scots Broom to the beach reaches one of the best mud-flat shorebird habitats on the bay. Large numbers of Black-bellied Plovers, dowitchers and peeps mingle with less-abundant species here in migration. (DP, BT)

---

S: all year   E: 0
H: SW RS SS WC WM ST FL
Maps: DLA 58:A-B 2-3

# Westport

Westport has several good birding areas. The **South Jetty** extending out from Point Chehalis (at Westhaven State Park) at the south entrance to the harbor can be one of the best locations in the state for shearwaters, gulls, and many other species, including shorebirds of the open sandy beaches. Parasitic Jaegers may be seen here in migration, chasing the kittiwakes and Common Terns. These species also occur inside Grays Harbor itself and can be viewed by scope from the Grays Harbor **channel observation platform** near the mariners' monument at the end of the waterfront drive in Westport. The sand islands to the E have large nesting colonies of Double-crested Cormorants, Caspian Terns and gulls, and huge flocks of gulls roost there at all seasons. E of Westport's grass airstrip is the **airport saltmarsh,** reached by parking on a gravel road just S of, and outside the fence from, the Coast Guard station and walking to the beach. Sand dunes, scrub, grassy spots and ponds offer many good birding possibilities. After storms, many coastal areas are worth checking for unusual species driven ashore by strong gales. Some offshore birds may

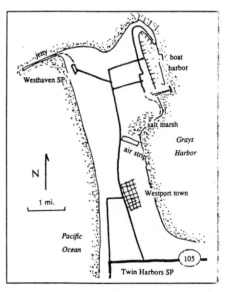

resort to the harbors, and phalaropes may be seen in rain puddles. The Westport and Pt. Brown areas are also two places in western Washington where passerine migrations are actually noticeable. Grays Harbor can be good for birds at almost any time but, like many coastal locations, may have days of fog, especially in early fall. Birders in coastal areas should also be prepared for wind and rain. The annual rainfall total in the area is among the highest in the lower 48 states. Westport has abundant motels and large campgrounds at Twin Harbors State Park, 3 miles S of Westport, or Grayland Beach SP, 4 miles S of Twin Harbors. Both have good birds. Campgrounds and motels are often full on summer weekends, so early reservations are advisable. (TW)

# Offshore boat trips

Most "offshore" species can be seen only by going out for 25-30 miles. The numbers of albatrosses, fulmars, shearwaters, storm-petrels, phalaropes, jaegers, gulls, and alcids found off Washington are great, and seeing them and marine mammals is a unique birding experience in the state.

Sooty Shearwaters and Black-legged Kittiwakes can be seen from the jetties at Westport and Ilwaco and Sooties can be seen inside Grays Harbor and Willapa Bay in the fall when flocks of hundreds of thousands stream along the coast, extending as far as the eye can see. Most of the species listed under "offshore" on the state species list, including Black-footed Albatross, Northern Fulmar, Pink-footed, Flesh-footed, Buller's and Short-tailed shearwaters, Leach's and Fork-tailed storm-petrels, Red Phalarope, Pomarine and Long-tailed jaegers, South Polar Skua, Sabine's Gull, Arctic Tern, and Cassin's Auklets are seen from shore only infreqently and a boat trip offers the best possibility for seeing them. Offshore trips also encounter other inshore species like cormorants, gulls and alcids. Boat trips off Washington are as productive as any in North America. As elsewhere, however, trips are limited by weather, which is uncertain at any season. Lumpy seas, spray and seasickness are among the delights possible. Sometimes even seeing a distant bird against the moving sea can be difficult.

Sportfishing vessels operate out of Westport, and Ilwaco, in Pacific County, but boats fishing for salmon or bottom fish or are whale-watching operate within a few miles of shore, not far enough offshore. Albacore trips are costly and unpredictable. Most birding trips take place from May into early October, with weather making trips at other seasons difficult to schedule. Information on organized birding boat trips offshore and in inside waters may be obtained through Westport Seabirds, c/o 3041 Eldridge, Bellingham WA 98225 (206)733-8255 or Seattle Audubon Society, 8028 35th Ave NE, Seattle WA 98115 (206) 523-4483. (TW)

Willapa Bay is a large, shallow estuary with high biological productivity, large populations of shorebirds and waterbirds during migrations and winter seasons, and its surrounding uplands have interesting landbird potential at all seasons.

# Northern Willapa Bay, Tokeland

S: all year    E: 0
H: SW SS WC WM ST
Maps: DLA 44:C 1-2

A - 9

The **Tokeland** turn-off is about 15 miles S of Westport, or 19 miles W of Raymond, via SR 105. This area is quite good for shorebirds, gulls, terns and waterfowl. The upland habitats here also are promising for migrants. The road to Tokeland gives a view of an extensive tidal marsh to the W - this is an excellent shorebird area, and features large species like Whimbrel, Long-billed Curlew and Marbled Godwit in migration and winter. The channel and tidal areas can be scanned from the dock at Tokeland. To the SW is the open ocean beach, while a salt marsh and protected tidal flats are to the NE. In addition to pull-offs, many of which are well-located for scanning the shallow bay, shore and marsh, other places to check include **Bruceport Park** SW of Raymond, the **Palix River channel** next to the road to Bay Center and the Willapa NWR headquarters area. Red Knots are often common around the perimeter of Willapa Bay during spring migration. (DP, TW)

# Raymond Airport, North River

S: all year    E: 0
H: SW SS FW WM ST
Maps: DLA 44:C 2

A - 10

The **Raymond Airport** is located about 3 miles W of Raymond, just off SR 105. The grassy fields and sloughs just W of Raymond usually contain large numbers of ducks during the winter. Raptors are often seen hunting over the open area, and White-tailed Kites nested at the E end of the airport property in recent years, the first verified breeding record for the state. The birds appear to be year-round residents and may be seen from near the airport buildings. The surrounding fields and brush are good for passerines all year. West of the airport, the road passes along a large area of mud flats just E of the mouth of the **North River.** Park across the road from the Dept. of Wildlife boat launch here. Several species of shorebirds may be seen here during migration, but the area is probably best known for its wintering flock of Willets, the only place in Washington where they are regularly seen. These large, showy shorebirds usually arrive in late September and stay until early April. As many as thirty individuals have been seen here at one time. (G&WH, BT)

S: all year   E: 0
H: SW SS WC WM ST
Maps: DLA 58:C-D 3

# Leadbetter Point

This is one of the outstanding birding spots on the coast. In addition to forested areas there are dunes, winding tidal channels and one of the largest remaining salicornia salt marshes on the coast. The Sand Ridge Rd. goes N from SR 101 at a blinker light just E of Seaview up the Long Beach Peninsula for about 16 miles to Oysterville where the road turns W across the peninsula. At about 0.2 miles turn N and follow the road as it changes from pavement to gravel to dirt. About 4.5 miles after turning N, you can park and walk farther N along the beach or you can drive on the road bearing straight ahead for about 0.5 mile to where it breaks out of the woods at the dunes and NWR signs. You can walk N from here for up to 2.5 miles. Shorebird migrations are impressive here - this is a regular migration stop place for Red Knots and golden-plovers as well as many more common shorebirds. Sharp-tailed Sandpipers are occasional in Sept-Oct. Many gulls, terns, waterfowl, hawks, Lapland Longspurs and other birds are found in sizable numbers in season. Snowy Plovers nest on the ocean side of the peninsula, over the dunes from the salt marsh, and parts of this area are now closed to the public to protect this rare species. Thousands of Sooty Shearwaters may be seen over the inside waters of Willapa Bay. Fall migration is the best season, followed by spring migration with big flights of Brant, Canada Geese and White-fronted Geese. Early May is the best time for White-fronts here. The upland conifer-shrub areas can be good for migrating passerines. Road-ends access to the open ocean sandy beaches at many places along the coast. In the winter flocks of Dunlins, Sanderlings and gulls forage on the outer beaches. (TW)

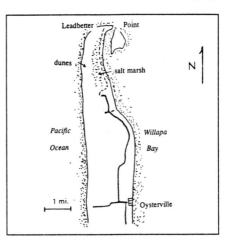

S: all year   E: 0
H: SW SS RS FW WC WM ST
Maps: DLA 58:B 1

# North Jetty

The area where the Columbia River flows into the Pacific Ocean creates sometimes-mountainous seas, offers spectacular views of cliffs and forested habitats, dunes and a wide variety of birds plus reminders and interpretation of human history of the area.

Follow signs from Ilwaco to Fort Canby State Park and from there to the North Jetty of the Columbia River. Unless weather prevents it, you can walk to the end of the jetty over a reasonably good surface (for a jetty), though erosion from storms can be severe. In season, species likely are Sooty Shearwater often occurs in spectacular flights, and Black-legged Kittiwake, numbers of which often rest on the jetty. Northern Fulmar and Pink-footed Shearwater may be seen occasionally. Heermann's Gulls, Parasitic Jaegers, loons, alcids, cormorants, sea ducks, and migrating land birds are seen from the jetty. Wandering Tattlers are regular in spring and fall; Surfbirds, Look for Black Turnstones and Rock Sandpipers from fall

through spring. This is one of the best places in the state to see Brown Pelicans. Even on pleasant days it can be windy on Washington's jetties - dress for wind and spray. Spotting scopes are highly desirable. Morning is best because of light conditions. At the Fort Canby area you can also walk along the long, sandy beach, over the dunes, or in typical coastal habitats of salal thickets, madrona, conifers and freshwater ponds. During spring and fall migration all habitats here can have many birds. Brandt's and Pelagic cormorants, Glaucous-winged Gulls and Pigeon Guillemots nest on the cliffs below the Cape Disappointment interpretive center. Stay inside the fence along the top of the cliff! (TW)

S: July-May   E: 0-100'
H: SW RS SS WC ST
Maps: DLA 90-93

# Western Strait of Juan de Fuca

A - 13

A drive W from Port Angeles on winding, slow-driving SR 112 of about 70 miles to Neah Bay offers many opportunities to see seabirds and shoreline birds between birding spots at Port Angeles and Cape Flattery. Stops here will feature loons, grebes, cormorants, diving ducks, Bald Eagles, Black Oystercatchers, rock shorebirds, phalaropes, many species of gulls, terns and alcids. Mew Gulls, Heermann's Gulls and Marbled Murrelets are common in season. Gray whales may be seen along this shoreline, and Dall's porpoises are possible in deep water offshore.

**Crescent Bay-Tongue Point.** From Port Angeles, follow SR 101 and then SR 112 W about 13 miles. Turn right (N) at signs for Salt Creek Recreation Area (Clallam County Park). From the campground and picnic area along the bluff, you obtain a great view of the Strait of Juan de Fuca, and all the wintering waterfowl including Harlequin Ducks. The road through the campground goes W to Tongue Point, where there is

access to the rocky beach. Black Oystercatchers, Rock Sandpipers, Surfbirds and turnstones may be seen. Returning to the county road, you may continue W along Crescent Bay before turning S and rejoining SR 112 at Joyce.

**Twin Rivers mouth.** Pull off the highway here and scan the shoreline and nearshore areas.

**Clallam Bay.** Scan water areas from Slip Pt., and from the Coast Guard Station NE from town.

**Kydaka Point.** Just W of Lake Ozette Rd (on S side of SR 112), go N at Crown Zellerbach headquarters of Clallam Managed Forest.

**Sekiu River mouth.** Pull off the highway here, scan the water.

**Seal and Sail Rocks** offshore are the only seabird nesting islands along this shoreline and can be seen from the road. Gulls, Tufted

Puffins and Double-crested Cormorants are conspicuous here. Look for Black Oystercatchers, too.

**Neah Bay** often has interesting birds, though numbers may be low. Rock shorebirds, including Wandering Tattlers, are often seen here. From the west end of Neah Bay, check the causeway to Waadah Island. Big flocks of nonbreeding scoters spend the summer here. Worth checking in winter and migration for rarities. (See Cape Flattery A - 1, also; DSm, BT, TW)

---

# Elwha River

A - 14

S: all year    E: 0
H: SW
Map: DLA 93:C 4

Go W from Port Angeles about 4 miles on SR 101 and turn on SR 101 and turn right on SR 112 (the road to Neah Bay). Go 2.4 miles and turn right onto Place Rd. Go 2 miles, turn right onto the Elwha Dike Rd. Go about 0.1 mile to the end of the road, park at the sign. Walk out onto the dike to the mouth of the river. Gulls will be resting across the river mouth on a gravel bar or bathing in the fresh river water. Compared to Ediz Hook, birds are fairly close but a scope is highly desirable. Low tide is best. A nice feature of this spot is that light is always behind you.

This is a good spot for gulls, with large flocks including Herring, Thayer's and Glaucous gulls. Slaty-backed has been seen here. Harlequin Ducks, Yellow-billed Loon, harbor seals, California sealions and occasional harbor porpoises are possible. (JS)

---

# Port Angeles - Ediz Hook

A - 15

S: Aug-May    E: 0
H: SW RS SS
Maps: DLA 93:C-D 5

Port Angeles harbor and its accreted sheltering gravel spit - Ediz Hook - have been greatly altered by human activity, and low numbers of birds of some species reflect this. However, the area has much to interest birders. Follow SR 101 W into Port Angeles, and continue W on Front St which becomes Marine Drive through town along the waterfront. At the Port of Port Angeles Dock there is a good view of the inner harbor. Park where permitted and go out to the end of the E pier, to the right of the Administrative office, and then out to the end of the NW pier to the left of the Administrative office. Returning to Marine Drive, follow the signs to Ediz Hook. The road going through the paper mill is a public road. Immediately after passing the mill, pull off to the left by the large tanks. The only Oldsquaws likely near Port Angeles may be here. There is parking just outside the Coast Guard station gate. Access onto the Coast Guard property is restricted.

Brandt's Cormorants almost always can be seen on the log booms in front of the boat launch. Yellow-billed Loons are now seen almost annually in Port Angeles harbor. Barrow's Goldeneye and almost all other winter waterfowl are also seen here. The log storage area attracts shorebirds, including "rock" shorebirds, Black-bellied Plovers and

Whimbrels, which may also be found on the open areas of the Coast Guard runway. Large numbers of gulls roost on the log rafts, including Herring, Thayer's, Heermann's and likely rarities. This may be one of Washington's best spots for looking for rare, large gulls due its proximity to the ocean. Common Terns, and hence Parasitic Jaegers, pass through in the fall. Waters along the outside of Ediz Hook often have few birds. However, feeding flocks of Rhinoceros Auklets, and Glaucous-winged and Heermann's gulls (summer) may include Tufted Puffin, and winter flocks of Common Murres and gulls may include other interesting species. Pelagic Cormorants nest on pilings in the harbor. (JS, DSm, TW)

---

S: all year

Maps: DLA 93:A-C 5

## Port Angeles-Victoria Ferry

A - 16

The ferry "COHO" crosses the Strait of Juan de Fuca daily between Port Angeles and Victoria, capitol city of British Columbia. The 90-minute crossing can be exciting birding if you are lucky or, more likely, quite dull. Scoters, gulls and other species are seen near shore, but the deep central waters of the strait may have no birds at all. A trip during fall migration or following a storm out on the Pacific Ocean, however, may feature ocean birds such as Sooty or Short-tailed shearwaters, storm-petrels, fulmars, phalaropes, kittiwakes or Parasitic Jaegers. Again, probabilities are low, but there could also be killer whales, Dall or harbor porpoises, white-sided dolphins, possibly a Minke whale or, along the shoreline, a gray whale. Of the many possible ferry trips in Washington, this one certainly has the greatest chance for pelagic species, but it also can be disappointing. Schedules vary with the season, and reservations, schedules and fare information should be obtained from Blackball Transport Inc. (206) 622-2222.

NOTE: Ferry routes crossing Puget Sound S of Admiralty Inlet do not usually offer much in the way of birds. Likewise the tourist ships between Seattle and Victoria are not likely to be the best means to see seabirds. (TW)

---

The rugged Olympics are home to many animals and, though trails penetrate and cross the mountain range, access is quickest via an easy drive through forests to alpine meadows and snowfields at the north side of the range to Hurricane Ridge or Deer Park.

---

S: June-Sept E: 200-5700'
H: WC WM ST
Map: DLA 77:A 4, 93:D 5

## Hurricane Ridge

A - 17

Road maps and information can be obtained from the park headquarters and provide necessary directions to National Park areas. Hurricane Ridge is 17 miles S from Port

Angeles. Birding is possible at many turn-offs along the road up the mountain - Gray Jays and Red Crossbills are almost certain, Pine Grosbeaks and Gray-crowned Rosy Finches are possible. At the Hurricane Ridge lodge area, nature trails through the meadows, famous for summer wildflowers, lead to various observation points. Olympic marmots, black-tailed deer, and many birds are possible. Follow the road past the lodge to the start of the Hurricane Ridge to the Hurricane Hill Nature Trail (about 1 mile long) where there are wildflowers, mountain scenery, marmots and mountain goats, and birds like Horned Larks, Blue Grouse, swifts and mountain passerines. In seasons when grasshoppers are abundant, numbers of hawks and eagles may be seen. While birds may not be abundant in the mountains,

places like Hurricane Ridge and nearby Deer Park offer views of mountain birds. Ravens and Gray Jays at the picnic grounds often appear at the rustle of sandwich wrappings.

There is a good downhill hike through the forest on the old road from the Ridge to Whiskey Bend in the Elwha Valley for woodland flora and fauna. Camping and interesting birding at a lower elevation is possible at Heart o' the Hills campground in ONP, 5 miles S of Port Angeles on the road to Hurricane Ridge. Northern Pygmy-Owl, Steller's and Gray jays, Varied, Swainson's and Hermit thrushes, Red-breasted Sapsucker and other typical species are possible. (DSm, TW)

---

S: all year   E: 0-100'
H: SW SS FW WC DC ST FL
Maps: DLA 93:C 7-8

# Dungeness

A - 18

Dungeness can be reached from SR 101 at Sequim. Follow signs N from the first traffic light at the E edge of town (Sequim Ave). The road reaches the shore at the Three Crabs Restaurant. Check the shore and freshwater ponds to the E of the restaurant, drive back to the S and watch for the first paved road to the right (W), which follows the shore and allows access to the beach at two boat launch areas. The eastern launch area (next to the oyster company) usually has very good numbers of birds. Scan the river mouth with a telescope. The Dungeness NWR lies offshore and provides protection for many thousands of wintering ducks and geese. Unfortunately, the shore itself is not protected, and the birds tend to stay offshore during hunting season. At other times they are abundant everywhere. All the waterfowl that winter in numbers in western Washington are common here except for some quite localized species like Harlequin Ducks and Black Scoters. Harlequins may be found on

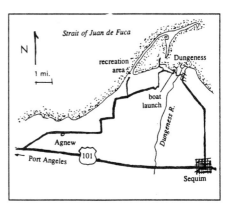

the north side of the spit near its junction with and east of Graveyard Spit (the south-running arm) and Black Scoters in the same area but on the south side of the spit. It's about a 15 minute boat trip from the launch at the Oyster House, or a 3-mile hike out the spit. Oldsquaws, Common Murres, Pigeon Guillemots, Marbled Murrelets and Rhinoceros Auklets may be seen offshore from the boat launch area in deeper water. Tundra Swans are irregular in fall and/or winter on ponds, in fields and less often on salt water. Canada Geese are resident, Brant are numerous (especially from February through April) except in summer. Eurasian Wigeon occur in the ratio of about one in one hundred American Wigeon. During the spring and fall, especially May and September, shorebirds abound on the mudflats, and rare species can be found in with the large flocks of Black-bellied Plovers, Western Sandpipers, Dunlins, dowitchers (Short-billed on the beaches, Long-billed at the freshwater ponds), and Sanderlings. At high tide, many of the flocks move to the plowed fields and grasslands behind the beach and can often be observed from the roads. Gulls and terns are abundant in season, again with a great many species possible. All the Washington loons and grebes may be observed, including the Yellow-billed Loon, which is now recorded every winter in western Washington.

The road curves around in a westerly direction and leads eventually back to Hwy

101. You can follow signs to the base of Dungeness spit in the Dungnesss Recreation Area and drive to the end of the trail through the woods and to the spit. Outside of hunting season, the DRA is a good place for birding, and includes raptors and ducks on the ponds. The spit is several miles long, and a beach hike all the way, but unusual shore birds, alcids and raptors may be seen, as well as Snow Buntings and American Pipits on the outer end of Graveyard Spit. Coming E from Port Angeles on SR 101, turn N on Kitchen Road, about 12 miles E of Port Angeles and proceed about 2 miles to Dungeness Recreation Area turnoff. Groves of fir and spruce have common birds of the wet coniferous forest, and the generally open and dry nature of the area allows species otherwise uncommon on the peninsula to breed - Mourning Dove, Western Meadowlark, Kestrel, Red-tailed Hawk and Vesper Sparrow, and in winter Rough-legged Hawk, Merlin and Short-eared Owl. Introduced Bobwhites still thrive around Sequim, along with much commoner California Quail. (DSm, DP, TW)

---

S: Aug-May    E: 0-100'
H: SW SS FW WC DC ST FL
Maps: DLA 93:C-D 8

## West Sequim Bay - Jamestown

A - 19

Sequim Bay State Park is on SR 101 on the W side of Sequim Bay. Many species may be found here (surely one of the great Crow-parks anywhere!). Almost all the wintering ducks occur, including Barrow's Goldeneye and Hooded Merganser. From the park, continue W on SR 101 for a short distance and turn right on the Old Olympic Hwy, marked "West Sequim Bay Resorts". At Pitship Point, the area near the "Silver Sands Resort" is good for waterfowl and there is a

small marsh beside the road. The road continues N then W until rejoining US 101. At the first traffic light on Hwy 101 in Sequim, turn right onto Sequim Ave. Go 1 mile to Port Williams Rd, turn E to the boat launch and a good beach and marsh walk if the tide is right (avoid hunting season). Return to Sequim Ave, go N several miles until the road curves W. Watch for the sign to Jamestown and the Sea Food Garden. Jamestown Beach is good for shorebirds at half-tide levels during spring and fall. Eagles and Peregrines use roost trees in the vicinity. This is one of the most important habitats for eelgrass-associated waterfowl - Brant and

wigeon - on the Peninsula, and other species like Red-necked and Eared grebes and many gulls occur in large numbers also. (DSm)

## Protection Island

S: May-Sept   E: 0-150'
H: SW RS SS ST
Maps: DLA 94:C-D 1

A - 20

Protection Island lies off the entrance to Discovery Bay. Access is by boat. There are spectacular numbers of birds nesting here during the summer, including hundreds of Pelagic Cormorants, many thousands of Glaucous-winged Gulls, hundreds of Pigeon Guillemots, and some Tufted Puffins and Black Oystercatchers. Over 35,000 Rhinoceros Auklets nest in burrows on the island; some may be seen during daylight around the island, but much larger numbers occur in Admiralty Inlet and other feeding areas in Rosario Strait, the Strait of Juan de

Fuca and in San Juan Channel. Many of the gulls which nest here, incidently, are intergrade Glaucous-winged X Western gulls.

This island refuge is owned by state and federal wildlife agencies and entry is strictly controlled. Visits are possible only on tours authorized by the USFWS. Visitors circling the island by boat must follow regulations which require vessels to be at least 200 yards offshore to avoid disturbance, particularly to cormorants and harbor seals. (TW)

## Port Townsend

S: all year   E: 0
H: SW RS WC ST
Maps: DLA 94:C-D 2

A - 21

The Port Townsend area is alive with birds throughout most of the year. Point Hudson, at the N edge of the town's shoreline, is a hot spot, with large numbers of birds congregating virtually at the beach, including Brant during spring migration, alcids, Harlequin Ducks, numerous gulls and small numbers of shorebirds of both sandy and rocky shores, including Black Oystercatchers.

Point Wilson is another fine locality for observing the movement of birds through Admiralty Inlet, at Fort Worden State Park. You can drive out almost to the lighthouse and walk from there to the shore where,

with spotting scope, you can watch birds passing in review for hours. (To observe from the point itself, you must request permission in advance from the Coast Guard in Port Angeles.) The tidal rips off the point have Rhinoceros Auklets, Tufted Puffins, Pigeon Guillemots, Marbled Murrelets, Glaucous-winged Gulls, and Heermann's Gulls and Pelagic Cormorants in summer. During winter, Common Murres, Ancient Murrelets, Brandt's Cormorants and many of the summer species are abundant. Cassin's Auklets, which are very unusual in the nearshore areas even on the outer coast, have been seen here in the spring. All three loons fly past (Pacifics are sometimes common), Oldsquaws and Harlequins are regular visitors, and the big migrating flocks of Bonaparte's Gulls in spring and fall may contain rarities as well as Parasitic Jaegers. Birds float past feeding in the swift currents, then fly "upstream" and float past again. Ancient Murrelets may be seen farther offshore in winter, and gray and killer whales, harbor porpoises and California and northern sea lions occur on occasion. In late fall 1986 a male Steller's Eider appeared and spent the winter. During the nesting season, the daily flights of Rhinoceros Auklets commuting between feeding grounds and Protection Island are one of the impressive avian spectacles of the state. Very few birds may be seen during slack tidal stages, so try for ebb or flood stages. Follow the coast road W of Fort Worden SP and keep bearing right to a small beach park. The area is always good for birds, with Tufted Puffins offshore in summer. (DP, TW)

---

## Oak Bay - Fort Flagler

S: September-June    E: 0
H: SW SS RS
Maps: DLA 94:D 3

A - 22

After crossing the Hood Canal Bridge to the Olympic Peninsula, immediately turn right and follow signs to Port Ludlow. After passing the Port Ludlow Resort & Marina continue on Oak Bay Rd for 7.2 miles, turn R at Portage Way and wind down the right fork to Oak Bay County Park. On one side of the road a shallow lagoon can be good for shorebirds and gulls while the rock jetty on the other side attracts oystercatchers, Harlequin Ducks and other wintering rockbirds. Back on Oak Bay Rd, go 0.4 mile to Flagler Rd Y, keep R, crossing a bridge to Indian Island (off-limits: military base) to Hadlock Lions Public Park, an old homestead where brambles and fruit trees attract passerines. Continue another 0.5 mile, turn down a steep road to a county park to view the rock jetty and channel from a different direction and check for Marbled Murrelets and other alcides - a Bald Eagle is often in the area. Before crossing the causeway to Marrowstone Island watch for ducks and shorebirds along the marshy tidal flats and sloughs. After 3.2 miles turn L to Mystery Bay County Park where, in winter, Oldsquaws and Eared Grebes are usually seen. Another 2 miles takes you into Fort Flagler SP, located at the entrance to Admiralty Inlet. Options here include, to the L, a 0.5 mile long sandspit where Harlequin Ducks congregate close to shore, 3 species of cormorants can be compared, and Black-bellied Plovers, Dunlins and oystercatchers assemble at the tip (don't disturb nesting birds in summer). Another road through the well-preserved military housing compound leads down a short but steep road to lowland fields and marshes and a point of land where Tufted Puffins, Rhinoceros Auklets and cormorants sweep by in offshore tidal rips. Another road ends at old military bunkers in a setting of a former orchard. Follow a path past sewage ponds to a long fishing pier for a view of the beach (Whimbrels in spring) and open water. (TB)

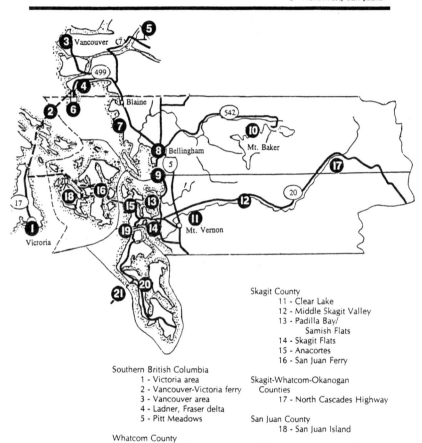

Skagit County
    11 - Clear Lake
    12 - Middle Skagit Valley
    13 - Padilla Bay/
          Samish Flats
    14 - Skagit Flats
    15 - Anacortes
    16 - San Juan Ferry

Southern British Columbia
    1 - Victoria area
    2 - Vancouver-Victoria ferry
    3 - Vancouver area
    4 - Ladner, Fraser delta
    5 - Pitt Meadows

Skagit-Whatcom-Okanogan
  Counties
    17 - North Cascades Highway

San Juan County
    18 - San Juan Island

Whatcom County
    6 - Point Roberts
    7 - Western lowlands
    8 - Bellingham
    9 - Chuckanut
    10 - Mt. Baker area

Island County
    19 - Deception Pass
    20 - Whidbey Island
    21 - Keystone Ferry
         Admiralty Inlet

From many good places for birds in southern British Columbia, we mention only a few here and suggest you obtain local birding references for more information. Washington birders usually especially want to see Skylarks, Crested Mynas and shorebirds.

## Victoria area

S: all year    E: 0
H: SW RS PG FL
Maps: B.C.; DLA 93:A 5-6

B - 1

Skylarks are found inland W from the ferry terminal at Sidney, at the Victoria Airport (those jets and planes swooping low over the ferry point the way). Cross the highway to the N side of the airport or enter via the access road S off the highway. Skylarks are also found on San Juan Island, Washington (see B-16). The many parks along the shoreline south of downtown Victoria have good seabirds, especially those associated with rocky shorelines, and should be checked. Clover Point is an outstanding spot for unusual gulls. Black-headed, Little, and Sabine's gulls have all occurred here in the same season, and Slaty-backed and Ross' gulls have also been seen here over the years! (TW)

## Vancouver-Victoria ferry

S: Aug-April

B - 2

A B.C. ferry sails every one or two hours from Tsawwassen (on the mainland near Point Roberts) and Swartz Bay (about 20 miles N of Victoria), taking about two hours for the trip. This is the main "highway" between Vancouver and Victoria. You can travel round trip as a foot passenger if you wish. This route is generally has fewer birds than the San Juans Ferry except for one 12-minute stretch that, during the October-April season at ebbing (outgoing) or flooding (incoming - second choice) tide stages, can be an exciting bird spectacle. This is Active Pass, where surging tides concentrate fish and marine organisms which may attract as many as 3000 (each!) Pacific Loons, Brandt's Cormorants, and Bonaparte's Gulls, along with hundreds of birds of other species (murres, Thayer's and Mew Gulls), dozens of Bald Eagles, and also Steller's and California sealions and killer whales. Other sections of the ferry trip can be downright boring, though a Fork-tailed Storm-Petrel and an elephant seal have been seen in the middle of Georgia Strait and Ancient Murrelets and other birds can be seen in season anywhere along the route. The shoreline at Swartz Bay often has numbers of interesting birds in winter, also. The area around the Tsawwassen terminal often has large numbers of many species of ducks, Brant, gulls (especially good looks at Thayer's in winter), Common Terns and Parasitic Jaegers, and possibly Snow Buntings on the rocks or open areas in winter. In summer Glaucous-winged Gulls nest on the breakwater to the E of the ferry terminal. (TW)

# Vancouver, B.C., area

**Stanley Park** is a unique park on a peninsula in Vancouver harbor, with marine shoreline and upland habitats. There are many places to stop and check around the shore. One good spot is Brockton Point. You can walk along the beach, from many parking areas. In the center of the park, a few hundred yards by trail off the road and marked by signs, is marshy Beaver Lake. Just inside of the Georgia St. entrance to Stanley Park is Lost Lagoon. You can walk around it by path, noting many nearly tame species at close range, including nesting Mute Swans. During migration and winter large numbers of ducks may be seen at Lost Lagoon, some are present all the time, some others roost on the lagoon only at night. Follow city map directions through downtown Vancouver, NW on Georgia St, turn right (off Highway 1 or 99 which leads over the Lion's Gate Bridge) to drive around the park.

**Iona Island.** Leave Freeway 499 at exit for "Vancouver Airport". Go W toward the airport, cross the concrete bridge over the Middle Arm of the Fraser River. About 100 yds beyond the end of the bridge, take the very first right exit at the traffic light, past Grauer (small settlement), follow the Miller Rd, turn right onto the McDonald Rd, then left on the Ferguson Rd and to its end at a sewage treatment plant in a park-like setting. Sign in at the plant office if you wish to visit ponds inside the fences. The ponds at Iona are one of the very best shorebird spots on the Pacific Coast. Birds vary with seasons and tides, but for most of the year there are birds. Many ducks also come into the ponds and can be readily scanned by telescope. There are five ponds, with water levels varying with usage by the plant. Four ponds are inside a wire fence. Though two can be seen from the road, these four can be reached through entrance to the plant. The fifth and largest pond is outside the fence,

farthest from the plant itself. This can be circled on foot, though you can usually cover it with a scope. Birding is best when high tides force shorebirds from adjacent flats into the ponds. Beyond (NW of) this last sewage pond is a long sand spit, with a cable barring entry to the service road on the spit. About 200 yds from this "gate", to the left side of the road, is a small pond amidst dunes and driftwood, just inside the beach. This can have shorebirds in it. Dowitchers, yellowlegs and peeps are abundant, and many species considered very rare on the Pacific coast have occurred on the ponds and adjacent tide flats in recent years, including the Spoonbill Sandpiper and Rufous-necked Stint. Other "rare" species that have been seen several times include Hudsonian Godwit, Ruff, and Curlew and White-rumped sandpipers. The outfall channel across the road from the plant attracts many gulls in season. When large numbers of Bonaparte's are present in fall, look for Franklin's Gulls with them. Later in the fall, look for Iceland (Kumlien's) Gulls with flocks of Thayer's Gulls here.

The farmlands, airport runway edges, salt marsh, tidal channels and the sand spit W of the sewage treatment plant are all good birding spots. Crested Mynas, though introduced, are one reason North American birders come to Vancouver. A city street map is essential. You can look for mynas N of the Oak Street bridge entering the city, between Oak and Granville St (one half mile to the W of Oak St), and N of 70th Ave. The species is reportedly dependably found along SW Marine Drive between Cambie and Main, along Kingsway near Edmonds (NW of New Westminster), and in New Westminster near 4th Ave and 6th St. One Crested Myna roost is under the Cambie St bridge near downtown Vancouver. (TW)

S: July-May   E: 0
H: SW SS FW ST FL
Map: B.C.

# Ladner-Fraser delta

B - 4

**Reifel Refuge.** Exit from Freeway to Ladner, S of Vancouver, follow signs in Ladner to "Reifel Wildfowl Refuge", go W along the dike on River Road to the bridge over the Fraser River, follow signs to the refuge. An entrance fee helps support this refuge operated by the B.C. Wildfowl Society. During fall and spring migration, winter, and to a much lesser extent in summer, the Reifel refuge is very important for waterfowl, raptors and shorebirds, as well as for passerines. A birder visiting the ponds, dikes and marshes in peak season can imagine the richness of the river delta regions of the northwest before great changes came. High tide is best for seeing shorebirds. Some of the Greater Vancouver area's most exciting birds have been recorded from this refuge, including Smew and Spotted Redshank. Sharp-tailed Sandpipers are regular in September and October. Large flocks of Snow Geese winter on the shore outside the dikes.

**Roberts Bank** is the foreshore flats facing Georgia Strait, with a huge coal loading port facility offshore. Leave BC 17 and head W on 28th Ave to its end. The shallow

intertidal habitat supports huge numbers of wintering ducks, hundreds of Tundra and Trumpeter swans, and Dunlins and Black-bellied Plovers; Merlins and Peregrines are often present. Look for many raptors along the dikes and roads and farmlands E to BC Hwy 17.

**Boundary Bay** is the general area S of the Ladner Trunk Rd and E of BC Hwy 17 which leads to Pt. Roberts and the Victoria ferry. Six roads go S from the Ladner Trunk Rd through the farmlands to the dike at the Boundary Bay shoreline. Along these roads in the winter there may be thousands of gulls roosting in fields, flocks of dabbling ducks, Red-tailed and Rough-legged hawks, Peregrines. Merlins and Gyrfalcons (check hawks atop radio towers). This area has dozens of Snowy Owls in flight years, oddities like Cattle Egrets at times, and arctic birds like Snow Buntings and Lapland Longspurs along the dikes. Buff-breasted Sandpipers have been seen at the turf farms along 64th St (Goudy Rd). A good shorebird spot is at the end of 112th St at a sewage outfall. (TW)

---

S: all year   E: 0
H: FW WM ST FL
Maps: B.C.

# Pitt Meadows

A - 5

Pitt Meadows lies at the S end of Pitt Lake, which connects via the Pitt River with the Fraser River. Good birds are present during much of the year, likely relating to its access to the interior areas of the continent via the Pitt Lake flyway. In summer, several "eastern" species nest here, and in winter species like Bohemian Waxwings are found.

Go E through Port Coquitlam on Highway 7 (Lougheed Highway); 0.2 mile E of the Pitt River bridge turn left on the Dewdney Trunk Rd. Go E 3 miles to 208th St (also called Rannie Rd). Turn left and go N 6 miles to the end of Pitt Lake and boat launch area. Walking is possible on dikes off the road or at Pitt Lake.

Start watching for birds as you leave Highway 7. A Hawk owl has wintered at the N end of the Reichenbach Rd (first left off Dewdney Trunk Rd). The wide, open farm area N of Hwy 7 is especially good for wintering raptors. Check tall trees along the river and dikes for hawks and eagles, the fields for Northern Harriers and Short-eared Owls. Distances are great and a telescope is advisable. In migration passerines are found in brush along the dikes. "Eastern"

passerines such as Eastern Kingbird and Gray Catbird have nested in local areas S and E of 208th. Farmland habitat changes to swampy brush and bogs toward the N end of 208th and offers intriguing birding possibilities at any season. The S end of Pitt Lake itself, while not usually as productive for birds as the adjacent marsh, can be scanned from the dike that separates the two. Large numbers of Trumpeter Swans are present here in winter. (TW)

S: Aug-May     E: 0
H: SW RS SS WC WM ST FL
Map: DLA 107:A 8

# Point Roberts

B - 6

The defined area of the Lower Mainland B.C. checklist area includes Washington's own Point Roberts and is heavily covered by birders. This northwest tip of Whatcom County is reached by highway through British Columbia. It is one of the best spots in the region to see many species of waterbirds. About 13.2 miles N of the U.S. border on Hwy 99 exit for "Point Roberts" or "Victoria Ferry", going W on the Ladner Trunk Rd. After 4.4 miles turn left on BC 17 and follow signs to Point Roberts. Go through Tsawwassen, B.C., and U.S. Customs. Go S about 1 mile, turn W on Gulf Rd for 0.5 mile, turn S and follow Marine Dr to the SW tip of the peninsula where there is a marine light beacon at **Lighthouse Park.** Geography, depth and currents combine to bring birds close to shore in big numbers. Parasitic Jaegers, Heermann's Gulls and terns are seen in early fall, sometimes feeding right off the beach. Ancient Murrelets occur offshore from early November on. During the winter large numbers of Pacific and other loons, sea ducks, gulls and alcids of many species can be seen by telescope from the beach. Harlequin Ducks are numerous, Oldsquaws abundant, and Black Scoters regular. Yellow-billed Loons are almost regular in winter; over the past 20 years this has proved to be the most consistent location for

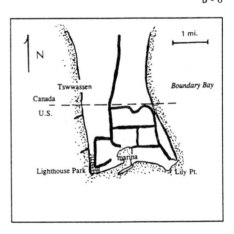

seeing this species in the state. King Eiders have been seen during several recent winters. Thayer's Gulls are regular from fall through early spring, usually in large numbers. Rhinoceros Auklets are occasional in summer and fall. Note that the stage of tide determines affects seabird activity here and at similar places like Pt. Wilson, Green Pt. (Anacortes), Active Pass and Deception Pass. Seabirds may be virtually absent during slack water periods, even during peak migration or winter seasons, yet occur in thousands only an hour or two before or after, so timing of visits with the tides is important. The marina breakwater on the shore E of the park provides "perching seabirds." Winds can be particularly cold here. Because of light direction, birding is best in the early morning. Walking the beach and checking the vegetation and open areas of the Point are worthwhile because the area is a "migrant trap" and concentrates birds in migration and winter. The uplands at Point Roberts have a dwindling number of

California Quail. Take the road along the S end of the peninsula, go E on APA Rd to a cemetary. Park off the road, at a gate. About 200 m down the trail is **Lily Point**, a high bluff overlooking Boundary Bay. The woods have many species mixed forest species, including Hutton's Vireo. The E shore of "the Point" faces Boundary Bay and has a sandy, shallow beach with lots of ducks, including Harlequins and Oldsquaws (far offshore), shorebirds and gulls. (TW)

S: all year   E: 0-200'
H: SW RS SS FW WC BF RW WM ST FL
Maps: DLA 108, 109:A-B 2-5

# Western lowlands

B - 7

**Drayton Harbor,** a large estuarine habitat, includes the waterfront at Blaine. Port fill, the tidal flats and channel at the end of the public dock are good spots. There is a county park on Semiahmoo Spit, reached by driving around Drayton Harbor from Blaine, where there is access and lots of waterbirds during winter, especially scoters and other diving ducks. The whole area is good during migrations and winter for loons, many Red-necked, Horned and Western grebes (Eared Grebes are occasional), cormorants, dabbling and diving ducks, Brant, several species of gulls, Common Terns, shorebirds, and also Pigeon Guillemots and Marbled Murrelets. Large numbers of harbor seals often haul out on the marina floats.

**Birch Bay** is reached from I-5 exit 266, W via the Grandview Rd, or S from Blaine via Harbor View or Shintaffer Rds at the S end of Drayton Harbor. A large, shallow salt bay, good in migration and winter, it is worth checking all around the shore, but the best spot is at Birch Bay SP, at the S end of the bay. A good area for Brant, Harlequins, Oldsquaws, all 3 scoters, hundreds of loons and more in season.

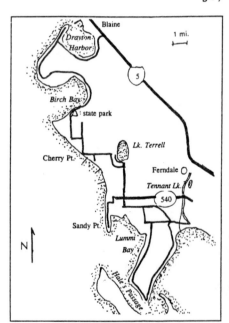

**Cherry Point** is the open shoreline area between Sandy Point and Pt. Whitehorn, at the SW point of Birch Bay. During herring spawning season in April - May very large concentrations of birds may occur here. Flocks of up to 25,000 scoters, Pacific Loons, gulls, murres and others feed on eggs and fish and form an impressive natural spectacle.

**Lake Terrell** is W from I-5 exit 260 on SR 540 (Slater Rd), then N on the Lake Terrell Rd for 3 miles. This state game WRA, with hunting in the fall, is best in early fall and spring migration for waterfowl, many passerines. Good in nesting season for ducks, marsh birds, swallows, blackbirds, marsh wrens, other song birds and some mammals. Common Loons in breeding plumage are often seen here during the nesting season.

**Tennant Lake** is W from I-5 at exit 262. Go W 0.5 mile, turn left just after the railroad underpass onto the Hovander Rd, and then right onto Neilson Rd. Go S about 0.5 mile. At the River Lay Rd you can turn in to a county historical farm park (Hovander Farm) which has good birding possibilities and access to the Nooksack River bank. Tennant Lake is beyond, at the end of the Neilson Rd, and is good for waterfowl, hawks, etc. in migration and winter, though there is hunting from mid-October through mid-January. The varied habitats in this extensive area have great potential.

**Sandy Point** is a "developed" gravel spit, good in migrations and winter. In season, loons, ducks (including Oldsquaws), Brant and many other waterbirds are seen, and the south end of the spit itself has been good for pipits and Snow Buntings, and Snowy Owls in flight years. Follow SR 540 to its end, go S along Sucia Dr to the end of the point.

**Lummi Flats** is S of SR 540 via Haxton Way or Lk Terrell Rd. Roads through this area, about 2 miles S of Haxton Way, N to 540 and E to the Ferndale Rd should be covered. This is the single best birding spot in the county. Many raptors - buteos, falcons, owls and shrikes - winter in the flats. Migrating waterfowl, shorebirds, and passerines are found throughout the various habitats. The aquaculture ponds, about 1 mile S of the intersection of Kwina Rd and Haxton Way, are visited by many waterbirds. Several hundred Trumpeter Swans have recently wintered in fields along SR 540, often commuting to the Nooksack River delta on Bellingham Bay. The entire area S of 540 is Lummi Nation.

**Hales Pass.** Follow Haxton Way around the Lummi Peninsula (it becomes Lummi Shore Dr at Fisherman's Cove and circles the W side of Bellingham Bay). At a beach access just N of the ferry dock scope the channel between the shore and Lummi Island for loons, terns, alcids and jaegers in migration. Farther S, **The Portage** connects the peninsula with tree-covered Portage Island at low tide. Numbers of scoters feed on extensive mussel beds here and many other birds are possible. Follow Lummi Shore Dr N about 4 miles, and scan the **Nooksack River delta** for Bald Eagles, Tundra and Trumpeter swans, many other waterfowl and wading bird species. At the tribal center (and Catholic Church) turn right (E) to Bellingham or go straight ahead to Haxton Way and SR 540. Wet areas along SR 540 are worth checking for waterfowl and shorebirds, hawks and blackbirds, but be sure to pull off on the shoulder.

**Wiser Lake** is about 8 miles N of Bellingham via Guide Meridian Rd, I-5 exit 256. Wiser Lake is the only non-hunting lake in the county and, especially during the hunting season, can almost be covered with birds. Surrounding housing development, however, has resulted in the lost of much shoreline and aquatic vegetation and has seriously reduced nesting habitat. Most freshwater ducks, including Redheads, may be here in winter. Park at the state game department fishing access area next to the causeway on the N side of the lake. Watch the fast and furious traffic if you attempt to scan the W end of the lake from the causeway. Gray Partridges occurred in this vicinity at least until the early 1970s. (TW)

S: all year   E: 0-600'
H: SW RS FW WC BF RW ST PG
Maps: DLA 108, 109:B-C 4-5

**Sehome Hill** city park is reached by Samish Way, I-5 exit 252, via Bill McDonald Way, and up the hill just W of Sehome High School. Good all year except mid-winter. During migration, songbirds and others families are well represented, and the extensive wooded habitat has many nesting species including Hutton's and Warbling vireos, Townsend's and Black-throated Gray warblers, two species of chickadees, Black-headed Grosbeak, Western Tanager, Pileated Woodpeckers, flycatchers and other woodland birds.

**Whatcom Falls Park,** Bayview Cemetary and Lake Whatcom are reached from I-5 via exit 253, E from downtown Bellingham via Lakeway Dr. The marshy and swampy areas along Whatcom Creek, the forest stands and edge from the cemetary to the lake have good birds. Scudder's Pond, across Electric Avenue from Bloedel Park at the end of the lake, is a refuge spot with beavers, Green Herons and nesting Hooded Mergansers. Dippers are resident at Whatcom Falls, below the fish hatchery at Whatcom Falls

Park. Look for them from the stone bridge over the creek.

**South Bellingham.** The best of several waterfront access points is reached from Alternate 99/Chuckanut Dr at a stop light at Harris Ave in the Fairhaven shopping district. Turn W, go down hill to the end of Harris Ave, cross the railroad tracks and park at Post Point Marine Park. A walk S along the tracks to a point of land with 3 trees on it will give close looks at many waterbirds in winter, as well as songbirds along the tracks (but watch for trains!). In the winter Thayer's Gulls, Oldsquaws and Harlequin Ducks are regular, and usually 3 species each of loons, grebes and cormorants are present. Common Murres, Pigeon Guillemots, Marbled Murrelets and sometimes Rhinoceros Auklets forage well offshore. Gulls feed at a sewage plant and a tidal pond across the railroad tracks from the park. Bald Eagles are seen here frequently, and river otters are resident along the shore. Good except during mid-summer. (TW)

S: all year   E: 0-1800'
H: SW RS FW WC BF ST
Maps: DLA 109:C-D 5

At **Larrabee State Park** walk downhill from the parking lot to the beach. The habitat is conifer and madrones in which you may find Hutton's Vireo, Band-tailed Pigeon and other species. From the beach and boat launch areas just N of the park you can scan the water and shore. In winter Oldsquaws and Harlequin Ducks are likely, and all 3 species of cormorants are often seen on a rock just offshore. Rock shorebirds may also

be seen here at low tide. About 0.2 mile S of the S entrance to Larrabee Park is a trail which goes downhill about 0.5 mile to **Clayton Beach,** another good bird walk.

Across from the Clayton Beach trailhead there is a road going up **Chuckanut Mountain.** Across from the Fragrance Lake trail (marked by signs) is a logging road which leads south around the hill for several miles to Lost Lake. Lots of birds are seen in spring, and Blue Grouse may be heard (if not seen). Western Screech-Owls and Barred Owls are resident in this area. Chuckanut has large, varied habitats, including timber, logged-over areas and creeks, and it is relatively accessible. Pygmy-Owls may nest here and are rather regularly reported in winter. In addition to many nesting birds -

hawks, sparrows, finches, vireos, warblers, creepers, chickadees, kinglets, woodpeckers, and Band-tailed Pigeons - other animals known to be resident here are cougar, bobcat, coyote, red fox, raccoon, porcupine, Douglas squirrel, mule deer and river otter. The area is especially good in spring and early summer. (TW)

---

S: May-Oct   E: 3000-6000'
H: FW WC RW WM
Maps: DLA 110:A-B 2-3

# Mt. Baker area

B - 10

One of the better, most accessible places for seeing White-tailed Ptarmigan and Rosy Finches is on the slopes of Mt. Baker, east of Bellingham, in the northern Cascades. A drive to about 5000' elevation and a walk up a fairly level trail leads to alpine habitats above treeline and spectacular mountain views.

**Ptarmigan Ridge.** At the Mt. Baker ski area, go uphill on a dirt road (open late July-mid October) to a parking lot at "Artists' Point". Table Mountain is on the right as you enter. A level trail leads along the side of Table Mt. After a mile the trail forks. The left fork drops through a pass on the side of Ptarmigan Ridge, crossing the ridge and then follows the other (SE) side of the ridge until the trail is lost in the glaciers and snowfields of Mt. Baker, about 4 miles from the parking lot. All along this trail White-tailed Ptarmigan, Horned Larks, American Pipits, Gray-crowned Rosy Finches, Mountain Bluebirds, swifts and Golden Eagles are possible. Pikas and hoary marmots are common, mountain goats are often seen, especially from the SE side of Ptarmigan Ridge. The marmots are quite accustomed to humans; if they suddenly start whistling all over the mountain side, search the sky for a Golden Eagle. Often the birds, especially the raptors, appear suddenly and fly by quickly. An exception is the almost always frustrating ptarmigan, which while it may allow very close approach, particularly early in the season, can be overlooked very

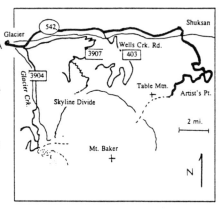

easily. Compared to most mountain trails, this one is quite level and, once the snow is gone, easy walking. Take your time and soak in the scenery. NOTE: the road going above the ski area can be snowbound all summer, forcing a much longer hike through snowfields to reach Ptarmigan Ridge.

**Glacier Creek:** Another possibility for high mountain species is to leave SR 542 at the Glacier Creek Rd, 0.5 mile past the Glacier Ranger Station, and drive 7.5 miles to the trailhead. A hike of 1 mile above this will put you on the ridges, meadows and snowfields of the western slopes of Mt. Baker. The White-tailed Ptarmigan and Gray-crowned Rosy Finch are the species especially sought in the area by birders, but many forest species are seen. Dippers inhabit creeks feeding Glacier Creek. Spotted Owls have been seen in the past along the Coleman Glacier Trail and should be watched for here as well as in other coniferous, big-tree habitats throughout

the Cascades. NOTE: inquire at the Glacier Ranger Station for trail and road conditions.

Road 3907 also leaves SR 542 at Glacier Creek, climbs to **Skyline Divide** trailhead. The trail climbs further through the alpine forest and breaks out into mountain meadows where alpine birds are often possible. The **Wells Creek Rd** leaves SR 542 near Nooksack Falls (look for Harlequins on the creek entering the Nooksack River at the falls) and winds up into high forest areas. Mountain goats may be seen on the high slopes of Barometer Mt, E of Wells Creek. (JD, GK, TW)

From estuaries, lakes and farmlands to river gorges and the crest of the Cascade Mountains at 5400', Skagit County provides a great variety of vegetation and animals, including species found few other places in western Washington. North Cascades National Park and the scenic highway encompass the most unspoiled mountain areas in the Cascade range.

S: Nov-April   E: 0
H: FW RW WM ST FL
Maps: DLA 95:A 6-7

# Clear Lake

B - 11

The Skagit Trumpeter Swan wintering population has reached over 1000 birds, a spectacular increase from about a dozen in the early 1970s. Leave I-5 exit 227 (just N of Mt. Vernon), and go E to Clear Lake. At the S end of town, go SE along the Beaver Lake Rd to **Beaver Lake** and Department of Wildlife access. This is good for many waterbirds and Bald Eagles. Redheads, Ring-necks and other ducks winter here; lots of Trumpeter Swans are possible here or on Clear Lake, just to the N. S of Beaver Lake there is extensive raptor and waterfowl habitat.

About 0.2 mile N of Clear Lake on WA 9 turn left onto the Frances Rd, go W about 1

mile to where the road parallels **DeBay Slough.** Trumpeter Swans are frequent here in winter - in recent years 300 or more have been seen in the general area. About 1.5 miles after leaving WA 9, there is a dairy farm where you might park, ask permission, take care not to let the cows out, and cautiously inspect the slough. Trumpeters, Redheads, Canvasbacks and other ducks may be seen very closely, but the swans spook easily, so try not to frighten them off. This spot can also be reached by leaving I-5 at exit 227, going E about 1.4 miles to Skagit Valley College, and turning N. The road eventually goes E and crosses the Nookachamps Slough. The dairy farm is 0.8 mile further. If the swans are not visible elsewhere, you might try Barney Lake, which lies between the Mt. Vernon-Clear Lake Rd and the Martin Rd (1 mile further S). About 0.5 mile past Skagit Valley College on College Way turn left (N) on Martin-Waugh Rd. Martin Rd curves left after about a mile and Barney Lake is visible downhill on the right. Continue a short way on Martin Rd and turn right onto Trumpeter Lane. Though you may not get too close to the lake edge, you can see if there are swans on the shallow lake. There are extensive flooded fields throughout this area in winter and waterfowl and raptors can be abundant. Along the Frances Rd at the Mud Lake Rd flocks of Whimbrels stop and feed in the fields during spring migration.

A consistent spot for Trumpeters in winter is nearby to the N. This is along the Cook Rd, between the I-5 freeway and Sedro-Woolley. There is no road shoulder: parking can be hazardous, but you may be able to stop on sideroads to check birds in the fields.You can check another farm-marsh habitat by going along US 99, N through Burlington and paralleling I-5. About 2.5 miles N of Burlington is an area known as **Butler Flats.** It is bounded on the N by the Kelleher Rd, the S by the Dahlstedt Rd and the E by the Johnson Rd. Again, hawks and winter waterfowl are the best prospects. Lazuli Buntings have nested on the hillsides to the N, along with many other more typical W Washington species. A few Gray Partridges, introduced decades ago and virtually eliminated from NW Washington by severe winters, disease, land use changes

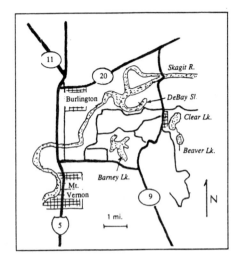

and introduced predators, may still survive in this area.

Go east through Burlington on Fairhaven St, turn S on S.Anacortes St for 1.4 miles to a large field enriched by food-processing sewage sludge, and attracts gulls and shorebirds. This is just south of a steel products company and a dairy depot with a conspicuous ice machine. This area is worth a check during migrations for Pectoral and other sandpipers, both yellowlegs, dowitchers, and snipe. (TW, EG)

65

# Middle Skagit Valley

Along the North Cascades Hwy (SR 20) there are many places to look for birds while crossing the "American Alps" enroute to the Methow Valley and the Okanogan highlands. In winter, the Skagit is one of the most important areas for Bald Eagles in the lower 48 states. Two to three hundred are seen between Concrete to Marblemount and along the tributary Sauk River. The Skagit River Bald Eagle Natural Wildlife Area is on the S side of the river, from about Rockport to Marblemount. View the eagles from mid-December to mid-February from SR 20 on the N side of the river. The

eagles are more easily seen than on the S side, and disturbance is less likely. In summer, Black and Vaux's Swifts. Northern Orioles are possible and Lazuli Buntings are regular in farm and edge habitats. Between Rockport and Newhalem the river valley narrows and scenery becomes more dramatic. Birds include Blue Grouse, Pileated Woodpeckers, Ospreys, Eastern Kingbirds, Swainson's Thrushes, Red-eyed Vireos, many warblers, including Yellow, Nashville, MacGillivray's, and Yellow-rumped, and Willow, Hammond's and Pacific-slope flycatchers. (TW)

Skagit County has two of the best estuaries for birds in Washington. The shallow embayments, sloughs and adjacent low farmlands around the bays support large numbers of waterfowl, waders, gulls, shorebirds and raptors during winter and migrations, and are also good areas for many wintering landbirds. Species like Gyrfalcon, Snowy Owl, and Trumpeter Swan winter here regularly, but may be seen only infrequently further south.

# Padilla Bay, Samish Flats

S: Aug-May    E: 0
H: SW SS FW WC ST FL
Maps: DLA 94-95:A 4-5; 108-109:D 4-5

B - 13

Samish Bay and the flats of the Samish River in the area from Edison S about 4 miles are good in winter for waterfowl, many raptors and passerines. W of Edison is **Samish Island** with several viewpoints looking over Samish and Padilla bays. The Samish flats in winter are one of the best spots in the state for Snowy Owls, Peregrines and Gyrfalcons. Roads through the farmlands and along the sloughs allow good coverage. There is a large Great Blue Heron rookery on the crown of the hill at the E end of Samish Island. Padilla and Samish bays are prime eelgrass areas and in winter and spring support many thousands of Brant. At **Bayview State Park,** 6 miles SW of Edison, Brant may be seen at close range when they come ashore to preen and "gravel up". Canvasbacks are regular here, and Yellow-billed Loons have wintered. Among the many bird possibilities of this area are big flocks of Dunlins and Black-bellied Plovers, and wintering Eurasian Wigeon (possibly North America's highest density of this species: 5% or more of some wigeon flocks in Samish and Padilla bays).

S of Bayview is more open farm habitat, crossed by a number of sloughs - the **Swinomish flats.** The area, lying N, S and W of the intersection of SR 237 (Bayview-Edison Rd) and SR 20 is also fine habitat and another area where Peregrines may winter. A mile W of the intersection there are several sloughs and the Swinomish boat channel, worth scanning especially in migration. The farmlands, especially along

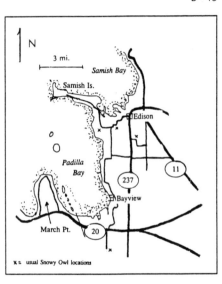

N

3 mi.

Samish Bay

Samish Is.

Edison

Padilla Bay

237

11

Bayview

March Pt.

20

x = usual Snowy Owl locations

the Bradshaw and Calhoun Roads, are preferred Snowy Owl wintering habitat. Go W on SR 20. About 0.2 mile W of the Swinomish bridge is a turn-off to **March Point.** At the old railroad stop marked "Whitmarsh", turn right. Just N of here and E of March Pt are log booms. Just beyond, on several dredge spoil islands, is a colony of Glaucous-winged Gulls in summer, and many waterbirds winter near here. Adult Caspian Terns are regular summer visitors in this area and have nested in this colony. As continue around March Point, site of two oil refineries, there are places to stop and look at the birds, Brant in particular. Just before rejoining SR 20 you drive along the Fidalgo Bay tidelands, also good in season. From March Pt you can go W to Anacortes and

ferries to the San Juan Islands and Victoria (B-16), S to DeceptionPass (B-19), Whidbey Island (B- 20) and the ferry to Port Townsend (B-21). By going E on SR 20, then S on the Best Rd you reach the Skagit flats (B-14). (TW)

---

S: all year    E: 0
H: SW SS FW RW ST FL
Maps: DLA 95:A-B 5-6

# Skagit Flats

B - 14

Leave I-5 about 5 miles S of Mount Vernon at Conway exit 221. Go NW through Conway, over the Skagit River, W on the Fir Island Rd for about 1.2 miles, turn left on **Wiley Rd,** go S about 0.7 mile to the WRA headquarters, follow signs to parking areas and trails on the dikes. The geographical features of the 12,000-acre Skagit Wildlife Area are river delta and shallow estuarine habitats. About 200 species of birds are known for this area, including swans, geese, ducks, shorebirds and raptors. Some of the many nesting species include Marsh Wren, Virginia and Sora rails, Blue-winged and Cinnamon teal, and Wood Duck. Hunting activity makes birding difficult, but winter can be good for birding - there are many raptors in the flats. Short-eared Owls, Northern Harriers, buteos and falcons hunt the area. The intertidal flats beyond the marsh are wintering habitat for up to 26,000 Snow Geese which arrive in late fall and depart for Siberia in late April. The geese, with several hundred Tundra and Trumpeter swans, are the big winter-bird spectacle of the area. W on the Fir Island Rd, about 2.5 miles W of the Wiley Rd, is the **Jensen Access,** marked by a WRA sign. Enter and park here and cautiously look over the dike - there may be thousands of Snow

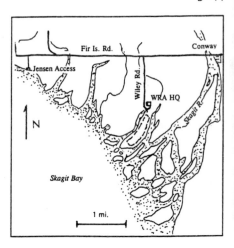

Geese on the other side. They may also be seen in the farm fields nearby. Shorebirding can be good in season, but because of extensive tidal exposure at low water, timing the incoming tide for best observation is critical. Returning to Conway, you may go S on SR 530 to Stanwood (See C-1). (EG, GG, DP, BT, TW)

Anacortes has several fine birding areas in the city itself as well as more close-by (see Padilla Bay/Samish flats for March Point information) and the ferries leaving from here are the gateway to the San Juan Islands and Vancouver Island and many interesting birds.

S: all year   E: 0
H: SW RS FW WC DC BF ST
Maps: DLA 94:A 3-4; 108:D 3-4

**Washington Park: Green Point** is one of the outstanding seabird-watching spots in the state from fall through early spring. The tidal fronts just off Green Point in Rosario Strait are foraging areas for thousands of seabirds, including Pacific Loons, Common Murres, Pigeon Guillemots, Marbled Murrelets (100 or more right off Green Pt. on occasion), all the seasonal gull species, all three cormorants and many seaducks. Bald Eagles and shorebirds are likely to be seen here. Rhinoceros Auklets are present in large numbers from July-October and Ancient Murrelets are possible in November-December. Harlequin Ducks, Black Oystercatchers and river otters frequent the shoreline, especially before human traffic starts in mid-morning. At first light during the winter hundreds of murres and Brandt's and Pelagic cormorants move up Rosario Strait to feeding areas. Hundreds of Double-crested Cormorants also fly in from night roosts on rocks offshore to shallow Fidalgo, Padilla and Samish bays east of Anacortes, and this all creates a nature spectacle of which late-rising folks are completely unaware. From downtown Anacortes follow the route to the ferry terminal, leave this at the top of the hill just before the ferry terminal turn left onto Sunset Ave with a "Washington Park" sign. Follow this to its end at the park. A one-way road circles Green Pt. and Fidalgo Head. Green Point is the grassy slope overlooking Rosario Strait. The wooded uplands of the park are very good for birds, too. Parking spaces and picnic spots are available. There's also a good campground and a boat launch. Burrows Island, S of Washington Park with a lighthouse on it, is another Anacortes park property.

**Guemes Channel,** just around the corner from Green Pt., is visible from the ferry terminal and many waterfront access points, and its eastern end can be seen from the Cap Sante Park viewpoint (go through downtown Anacortes and turn right on the only through street heading east up the hill, follow signs to the hill-top). Wintering species in Guemes Channel include Red-necked Grebes, Oldsquaws, Pigeon Guillemots, Marbled Murrelets, Brandt's and Pelagic cormorants (many of each) and others. From Cap Sante, seasonal species seen by scope include large numbers of Brant on Fidalgo Bay below and there are many passerines in the park.

**Mt. Erie,** another fine Anacortes park is reached via marked roads on its south side, near Campbell Lake. Mt. Erie has extensive and varied habitats and great bird potential. Bald Eagles may be seen along the slopes, and migrating hawks, Golden Eagles and a White-tailed Kite have been seen. (TW)

# San Juans ferry

The San Juan Islands and surrounding waters differ from adjacent regions in having a drier climate and consequently different vegetation and birds. The scenery and accessibility make visits interesting and enjoyable, though these same factors mean more humans and growth.

The ferry route from Anacortes to Sidney, B.C., through the San Juan Islands is Washington's best all-around ferry trip for seabirds. You can ride to Lopez, Shaw, Orcas or San Juan Island (good birding, especially on San Juan and Lopez) or all the way to Sidney, on Vancouver Island. The latter, an eight-hour round trip, is popular and productive. Going as a foot passenger makes it an inexpensive seabird trip, complete with a warm cabin, restrooms and hot food. Taking your car is more expensive but is essential for birding in the islands. Check Washington State Ferry schedules, or phone 1-800-542-0810 (464-6400 in Seattle). Drive to Anacortes and follow signs to the ferry terminal 4 miles W of the downtown area.

Though birds, and occasionally porpoises, may be seen anywhere along the scenic ferry route, some places are better than others. Check charts posted in the ferries for the routes, names of islands and bodies of water. One important area is just W of the Anacortes terminal where, if tidal conditions are right, thousands of murres (in winter) Rhinoceros Auklets (early fall), Heermann's Gulls and other birds may be feeding in a convergence in **Rosario Strait.** When tides are running the narrow passages, like Thatcher Pass, may have flocks of Bonapartes, Mew and Thayer's gulls, Pacific Loons or Brandt's Cormorants. Pelagic Cormorants roost and Pigeon Guillemots nest on tiny Willow Island, just to the NW of Thatcher Pass. In **Upright Channel,** before the Lopez dock, look for flocks of

Western Grebes and White-winged Scoters in winter. Look for Bald Eagles anywhere, especially in winter, and Golden Eagles are possible. From the ferry docks, as at Lopez and Shaw, many diving birds are visible, including Marbled Murrelets and Red-necked Grebes in winter. Wasp Pass, W from Orcas to San Juan Channel has many ducks, alcids, grebes, and cormorants. San Juan Channel often has few birds (Ancient Murrelets are possible in Nov-Dec, however) N of Friday Harbor. Right off Friday Harbor, however, there are often flocks of hundreds of Rhinoceros Auklets in summer, and **Friday Harbor** itself, with all its crowded floats and boat traffic and development, is one of the best seabird spots in Washington! The state's only record of Kittlitz' Murrelet, reports of Smew and Little Gull happened here, a Thick-billed Murre was seen nearby, and many other goodies have appeared right next to the ferry dock. The harbor should be scanned closely.

The northern part of **San Juan Channel** and **Speiden Channel** often have large feeding flocks of murres, Pacific Loons and Brandt's Cormorants in winter. Flocks of Bonaparte's and Mew Gulls, and Common Terns and Red-necked Phalaropes occur during migration here and in other locations. Golden Eagles and Turkey Vultures may be seen on or above Speiden Island. Haro Strait, between San Juan Island and Vancouver Island, often has very few birds in evidence, but killer whales and Dall's porpoises are more likely here than anywhere else on this ferry route. **Mandarte**

**Island** has an important nesting colony of Glaucous-winged Gulls and has the largest Double-crested Cormorant colony in Washington and British Columbia waters. From here to Sidney, bird numbers increase and can overwhelm birders in winter. Large numbers of many species, including Oldsquaws, murres, loons, and Red-necked Grebes winter along Sidney Spit, where Brant and shorebirds, Bald Eagles, Snowy Owls, and herons may be seen. From here to the ferry dock look for Yellow-billed Loons among the flocks of alcids, loons, grebes and sea ducks. The shoreline at the terminal has many more birds. Lots of exciting possibilities, but unfortunately you must disembark, even if a round-trip foot passenger, go through customs, buy a ticket and line up to get back on board! B.C.'s first Steller's Eider wintered within a short distance of the terminal. Mid-summer, before fall migration starts, can be dull. During the rest of the year, however, this ferry trip can be lots of fun and provide good looks at many species. (TW)

# North Cascades Highway

S: June-Oct  E: 500-5000'
H: FW WC DC BF RW WM ST
Maps: DLA 111:C 5-8; 112-113:C-D 1-6; 99:7

B - 17

**County Line.** The attractive riparian area downstream from Newhalem has extremely rich and interesting mixed deciduous, conifer and brush habitats containing many passerines in summer, including Red-eyed Vireo. American Redstarts were found on territory here in 1981. Gravel borrow pits became ponds adjacent to the river and support a wide variety of life. One access is on a road on the S side of the highway very near the Whatcom-Skagit county line sign. Another road leaves the highway about 1 mile W of the Goodell Creek Campground. Both these roads are for walking: gates are closed to cars. On warm summer days look for butterflies all through this area.

**Newhalem.** Across the river from Newhalem on steep hillsides and "benches" are a variety of habitats with much passerine variety. The National Park campground here has an interesting stand of lodgepole pines and other coniferous trees. Blue Grouse, Pileated Woodpeckers, Calliope Hummingbirds, and Varied, Swainson's and Hermit thrushes are found in summer in this area. Look for Calliopes atop snags next to restroom #1069 (between A and B camping loops) and along the trail W of that. On the N side of the river, Nashville Warblers and Lazuli Buntings sing from the hillside above the town of Newhalem. Nashville Warblers also occur from Newhalem E in the river gorge to Gorge Lake in summer.

The cirque at the W end of Newhalem, where Goodell Creek enters the Skagit River, is perhaps the most dependable place in western Washington for seeing Black Swifts. Hundreds may be circling overhead before dusk in June and seen from the bridges over the creek or the Skagit River. The narrow gorge up the river to Diablo Lake has interesting species in summer, including Nashville Warbler. Winter snows close the highway above Newhalem.

**Colonial Creek.** The heavily-used National Park campground on Thunder Arm has had Barred Owls and accipiters nesting near here recently. A walk S along the Thunder Creek trail features sapsuckers, MacGillivray's Warblers and species typical of the mountain passes. Veeries have been heard singing in the campground, and Lincoln's Sparrows nest at Thunder Lake, a low elevation for this species.

**Rainy Pass.** SR 20 ascends through magnificent subalpine scenery along Granite Creek to Rainy Pass. Birding is possible at highway pull-offs in many places. Clark's Nutcrackers occur along Granite Creek. Three-toed Woodpeckers have been seen along this stretch. Rock slides and road fills above Newhalem have pikas which may be heard and seen close-by. At Rainy Pass the Pacific Crest Trail crosses the highway. Pine Grosbeaks and White-winged Crossbills are often possible here. Hikes along this and other trails to Rainy Lake and Lake Ann will likely provide Gray Jays, crossbills and other mountain finches, Hairy Woodpeckers, maybe Three-toed Woodpeckers and Pygmy-Owls. Spotted Owls are definitely possible in the high country. **Washington Pass** is E of Rainy Pass and from here downhill into E

Washington there are many birds, including Clark's Nutcracker. A drive up the **Cutthroat Creek** road and hike from the road end to Cutthroat Lake has turned up Spruce Grouse (June), flocks of Bohemian Waxwings (in mid-August), and Mountain Chickadees, crossbills and more. If you're camping you might try Klipchuck Campground, about 10 miles E of Washington Pass. Nights may be cold, but the mountain birds are worth it. The vegetation changes from wet coniferous through dry coniferous and into arid grassland as you go down the E slope of the Cascades in Okanogan County. White-headed and Lewis' Woodpeckers occur here, and both kingbirds and bright Lazuli Buntings appear again as you approach Winthrop. (TW)

## SAN JUAN COUNTY

S: all year    E: 0-100'
H: SW RS SS FW WC WM ST FL
Maps: DLA 93:A 7-8; 107:C-D 7-8

# San Juan Island

B - 18

Westernmost of the San Juan Islands, San Juan is reached by ferry from Anacortes or from Sidney, B.C. The S end of the island is the most unique area for birds. Follow signs from the Friday Harbor ferry landing S about 6 miles to **American Camp** and the monument marking the site of Pickett's army encampment during the Pig War, now a National Park Service site. The area is generally between Eagle Cove, 1 mile W of the monument, and Cattle Point, about 2 miles to the E. More than other islands in the archipelago, San Juan Island itself is very rewarding for birders in virtually every area and can be covered relatively well in a weekend. The S end, including Cattle Point, is outstanding. The former hordes of introduced European rabbits made this one of the finest areas in the state for resident and migrant raptors, but the rabbit population has crashed as of this writing. Bald Eagles are still common, nevertheless, especially in winter, but they are less concentrated. Red-necked

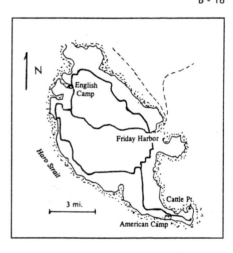

Grebes are quite numerous in winter along the ferry route, along with flocks of Pacific

Loons and all three cormorants. The San Juan climate is drier than most of western Washington; Golden Eagles are often seen, and Turkey Vultures nest in the islands. The area to the S (downhill) from the American Camp site is significant for nesting Skylarks, an obvious emigrant from nearby Victoria. Searching for nests should be avoided, as it may lead predators to nests and nestlings, but the long flight song of Skylarks is memorable in itself. Vesper Sparrows, rare in northwest Washington, have also been found in the area, singing from the monument itself.

E from American Camp is **Cattle Point** at the SE tip of the island. From here you can survey San Juan Channel, where in summer there are large numbers of Rhinoceros Auklets feeding in tidal rips. Many alcids are also present in the winter. Dall porpoises and Minke whales are occasionally seen here. Black Oystercatchers search offshore reefs, and Pacific Loons, Red-necked Grebes, Brandt's Cormorants and gulls are numerous here in season. Bird numbers here are at times staggering, especially in mid-channel (bring a spotting scope).

**False Bay,** W of American Camp via False Bay Rd, is remarkably good for shorebirds of many species and is one of the best spots in the San Juans.

The section of the **Westside Road** between San Juan County Park and the residential area on the southwestern part of San Juan Island is unique in several ways. In spring and summer Vesper Sparrows are abundant, California poppies are in bloom, and great camas, a rare local lily, is conspicuous in April and May and you may find cacti here, too. Rock Wrens are sporadically reported from this bare-looking, rocky hillside habitat. House Wrens are one of the most abundant birds nesting in this madrone-dominated woodland. Cooper's Hawks nest in the timbered gulch just north of the open hillside. Killer whales frequently pass along the shoreline in Haro Strait (a whale-watching park is here, at Lime Kiln Pt.). Perhaps moreso than elsewhere in this varied state, a surprising group of organisms coexist here!

**English Camp,** on the NW part of the island, has excellent habitat for passerines. During the winter season, walk from the parking lot to the shore, then along a bayside trail to the N to Westcott Bay, which often throngs with diving birds. Large numbers of Pacific Loons feed here, and Oldsquaws are always present in winter. Hutton's Vireo and several warblers are present in spring, and migrations should be good here. This may be one of the best spots in the state to see Turkeys (almost tame here), which are resident through much of the northwestern part of San Juan Island. Camping is possible at some private campgrounds and at San Juan (county) Park on the W side of the island. Orcas and Lopez islands have other good birding areas. (DP, TW)

Whidbey Island stretches from just west of Everett almost to Anacortes and combines many upland and shoreline habitats with exposure to swells from the Pacific and a drier climate than adjacent areas. It contains many good birding locations and is easily reached from major urban areas for day trips.

S: all year   E: 0-200'
H: SW RS FW WC ST
Maps: DLA 94:A 3-4

# Deception Pass

B - 19

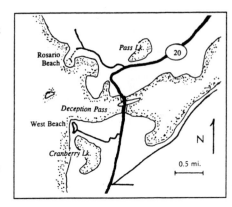

From I-5 exit 226 or 220, W on SR 20 for 7 miles, turn S toward Whidbey Island and Oak Harbor for about 5 miles. At the N entrance of Deception Pass State Park, follow the road sign to **"Rosario Beach Area"** for 0.6 mile where you take left hand fork down a steep hill, bear left through two turns and park at the end of the road. Many forest birds can be seen and heard. Walk SE about 100 yards across a grassy strip to the rocky peninsula. Short trails circle steep, high cliffs facing the Strait of Juan de Fuca. Birding is best here in fall through spring when most species of the region's loons, grebes, alcids, gulls, sea ducks and cormorants may be seen from the cliffs. During migrations the brushy parts of the peninsula may teem with migrants.

Returning to SR 20, continue S about 0.5 mile to the Deception Pass Bridge - a small parking lot is located at the S end of the bridge. Looking down from the bridge you may see feeding Pigeon Guillemots, and looking up you may see Bald Eagles as good numbers are here in winter. Drive S about 0.3 mile to the main entrance to the park, then left and then right again toward **West Beach.** The road passes freshwater Cranberry Lake, where there are often large

concentrations of birds. Also watch for river otters which are resident. Offshore from the parking lot are loons, gulls, alcids and ducks in the channel near the shore or flying past. Among regular species are Red-throated and Pacific loons and Red-necked Grebes, Marbled Murrelets and, primarily in summer, Rhinoceros Auklets. The rest of the park is dominated by coniferous forest and the big trees and edge habitats provide a good species list. (TS, TW)

S: Aug-May   E: 0-100'
H: SW RS SS FW WC ST FL
Maps: DLA 79:A-B 5; 94-95:A-D 2-5

**Cultus Bay.** From the S, follow signs from I-5 exit 189 to Mukilteo Ferry, or go S from Deception Pass at the N end of the island. Following SR 525/20 for the length of the island, there are many possibilities. Cultus Bay is 2.2 miles from the Columbia Beach ferry landing via Cultus Bay Rd S for about 5 miles. When you reach the water, continue uphill to the entrance to a private housing development, continue to the end of the road where you can look out over the Bay and Puget Sound. This is a good spot for a variety of diving birds, gulls and shorebirds.

**South Whidbey State Park.** Continue N to this heavily wooded park where there are Pileated Woodpeckers, Brown Creepers, kinglets, Varied Thrushes and other appropriate species. Continue E on this road which makes 3 right-angle turns to get back to SR 525. About 20 miles from the ferry landing or 5 miles from the junction of SR 525 and the road from South Whidbey SP, take SR 20 toward the Keystone Ferry Landing. Admiralty Inlet is on the S, and marshy Crockett's Lake is to the N. **Crockett's Lake** is good for migrating shorebirds, gulls and terns and for wintering waterbirds, waders, raptors and passerines around the marshy edge habitats. Water levels are somewhat affected by a floodgate, and numbers of shorebirds can be highly variable.

**Fort Casey State Park** is to the W and is a good spot for breeding birds and migrants. Very large numbers of gulls and Rhinoceros Auklets feed offshore in summer and fall, and Common Murres are abundant in winter. Black Oystercatchers have been seen on the jetty here. Continue N about 4 miles to rejoin SR 20. About 4 miles from this junction, SR 20 comes to a "T" and turns right. About 0.2 mile further, turn right and park at the W end of Penn Cove. **Penn Cove**, a long large bay, cuts almost across Whidbey Island from the east. Its west end

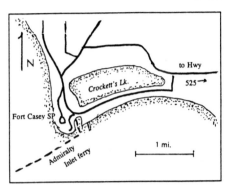

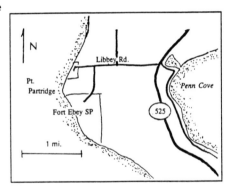

has a rocky and sandy shore that is one of most accessible examples of that shore habitat type left within the inland waters of Washington. Rock-foraging shorebirds are present much of the year: Black Turnstones and Surfbirds are common and Ruddy Turnstones, Rock Sandpipers and Wandering Tattlers are occasional. Out in Penn Cove itself, hundreds of scoters, loons, grebes and other birds may be seen. Small flocks of Eared Grebes, very local in western Washington, are seen here throughout the winter. Penn Cove has some of the largest numbers of wintering scoters in Washington, and some are present through the summer. The habitat extends from Penn Cove (E of Coupeville) northeast to include Oak and Crescent harbors and many hours could be spent inspecting bird flocks.

**Point Partridge** is due W on the Libbey Rd from the "T" on SR 20 near Penn Cove. Fuca. There is an excellent observation point at Libbey Beach County Park, looking out over the eastern Strait of Juan de Fuca. Many seabirds associated with the big kelp forest habitat of the open shoreline - Pelagic Cormorants, Red-necked and Horned grebes, Pigeon Guillemots, Harlequin Ducks - are here, and others, like murres, Red-throated, Pacific and Common loons, scoters, many gulls and Black Oystercatchers are also frequently observed. About 0.5 mile E of this small park, a road goes S to Fort Ebey State Park. This park, with good camping and

excellent coniferous and mixed woods, offers access to the driftwood beach, grassy bluffs, a spectacular view of the Olympic Mountains, ocean swells and many birds of the seashore and land habitats.

**Bos Lake** is northwest of Oak Harbor, just S of the US Naval Air Station golf course area on the West Beach Rd, W side of Whidbey Island. Just south of a strip of resort homes at Sunset Beach is an abandoned shoreside development where the storm waves won out over mere concrete. Between Smith Island, an important seabird nesting island and harbor seal haul-out, visible 5 miles offshore, large numbers of sea ducks including Oldsquaws, as well as loons, grebes, gulls and alcids forage during the winter. E of the road is a salt marsh (called Bos Lake) which can have numbers of ducks and shorebirds and which has been very good for the unusual species of the latter group on occasion. (EG, NL, BT, TW)

---

S: all year

Maps: DLA 94:C-D 2-3

## Keystone Ferry/Admiralty Inlet

B - 21

The 35-minute ferry ride from Keystone, on Whidbey Island, to Port Townsend, on the Olympic Peninsula, crosses Admiralty Inlet. This strait connects Puget Sound with the Strait of Juan de Fuca and the Pacific Ocean, and there is often much bird, mammal and ship traffic through the inlet. There are good birding possibilities at all seasons. During winter, large numbers of murres and other alcids feed here, along with many Pacific Loons, gulls and other species. Ancient Murrelets are regularly seen in Nov.-Dec. More gulls and terns, jaegers and phalaropes increase numbers during migrations. In summer this is one of the state's best areas for seeing Rhinoceros Auklets as they

commute between feeding areas and Protection Island, several miles to the W, where about 35,000 nest. Tufted Puffins may also be seen here, along with hundreds of Heermann's Gulls feeding on balls of herring in the strait in late summer and fall. Some Rhinos feed just off the beach from the landing at Fort Casey SP, but many more can be seen quite closely as they cross in front of the ferry. Feeding birds are usually much more numerous in the western one-third of the inlet, near Port Townsend, the W terminus of the Keystone ferry (see A-22). Check Washington State Ferry schedules for ferry information. Phone is 1-800-542-0810. (TW)

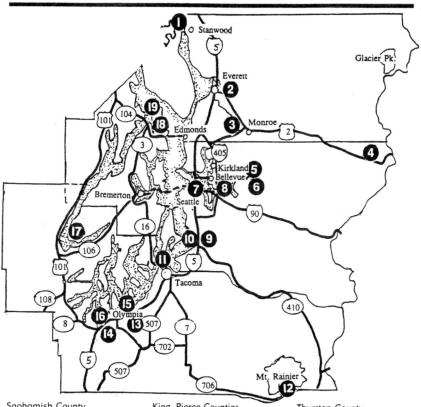

**Snohomish County**
1 - Stanwood, Camano Is.
2 - Everett, Snohomish delta
3 - Monroe, Two Rivers
4 - Stevens Pass Highway

**King County**
5 - Snoqualmie Valley loop
6 - N Fork Snoqualmie R.
7 - Seattle
8 - Lake Washington East
9 - Blue Heron Marsh

**King, Pierce Counties**
10 - Des Moines to Tacoma

**Pierce County**
11 - Pt. Defiance, The Narrows
12 - Mount Rainier National Park

**Pierce-Thurston Counties**
13 - Fort Lewis Prairies
14 - Bald Hill Lake
15 - Nisqually Delta

**Thurston County**
16 - Budd Inlet, Capitol Lk

**Mason-Jefferson Counties**
17 - Hood Canal, Great Bend

**Kitsap County**
18 - Kingston, Port Gamble
19 - Foulweather Bluff area

S: all year   E: 0
H: SW SS FW WM ST FL
Maps: DLA 94-95:B-D 4-5

# Stanwood, Camano Island

C - 1

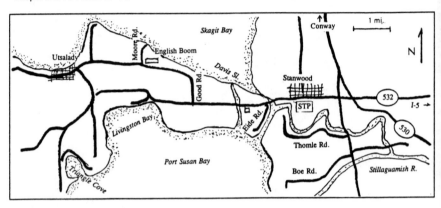

The Stillaguamish Delta around Stanwood and the nearby shorelines of Camano island provide a remarkable diversity of habitats in close proximity. The starting point for this trip is in Stanwood, reached by driving W from I-5 (exit 212) on SR 532. **Stanwood Sewage Ponds** are visible as you enter town on SR 532. Turn S on Leque Rd, park either at the gate (don't block) or continue on Leque for about 0.25 mile, park along the road behind the largest pond and clamber up onto the dike. In winter, look for shovelers, Ruddy Ducks, Canvasbacks, Lesser Scaup and Ring-necks among the large numbers of dabbling and diving ducks. Large flocks of shorebirds may be present at high tides. Hedgerows and thickets may have Tree Sparrow and other good species. Check hedgerows and blackberry thickets for wintering flocks of White-crowned and Golden-crowned sparrows - occasionally a White-throated or Harris' sparrow pops up to concerted pishing. Rare wintering passerines such as Say's Phoebe, Mountain Bluebird, Northern Waterthrush and Clay-colored and Swamp sparrows have been found in recent

years. During winter, Black-crowned Night-Herons roost during the day in downtown Stanwood, primarily in fir trees, near the intersection of 102nd Ave and 272nd St NW. Check trees at the SW corner of the intersection.

**Boe Rd/Thomle Rd.** By taking Marine View Drive S from town (the road that goes under SR 532, just E of the sewage ponds), one crosses the main part of the Stillaguamish flats. Marine View Dr is not good to stop on, but Boe Rd (236 St NW) is a good possibility; turn R onto it just before crossing over Hat Slough. The road parallels Hat Slough for 0.25 mile, passes farms and cuts straight W across the flats to dead-end at a hunting club. Check for shorebirds and gulls and raptors, including Snowy Owls in some winters. Snow Geese use this area at times. During hunting seasons birders may not be welcome on many private lands - ask permission before entering.

**South Pass/Davis Slough.** From SR 532, just after the West Pass Bridge descends onto the island, turn left onto Eide Rd. Walk along the dike for superb views of the marshes and flats of upper Port Susan Bay. After hunting season the area is alive with ducks and Snow Geese, and the flats support impressive numbers (for Puget Sound) of shorebirds during migration. The other access point is "Davis Slough Access" parking lot along SR 532 0.25 W of the high bridge (and Eide Rd). A footpath leads along Davis Slough. The brambles around the parking lot and along the tiny slough and northward across SR 532 can be good for sparrows (including Tree Sparrows).

**English Boom.** Follow SR 532 onto Camano Island and turn N on Good Rd which angles W again and turn N on Moore Rd which leads to the old log booms of English Lumber Co. This is a good vantage point on southern Skagit Bay, with a small saltmarsh to the E. Dabbling ducks and shorebirds can be abundant. The beach is cobble with a small fringe of forest right up to the shore and deeper water offshore has a flock of scoters, along with other diving ducks, loons and grebes usually present from Oct-Apr. Harbor Seals often lounge on a small offshore sandbar at low tide.

**Livingstone Bay/Triangle Cove.** These 2 bays along the SW shore of Camano offer habitat contrasts. Livingstone Bay can be surveyed from Livingstone Bay Shore Rd (a left turn off SR 532 just 0.25 mile beyond Good Rd). This wide, shallow bay is an enormous mudflat at low tide and usually has good numbers of ducks and shorebirds.The small tussocks of marsh grass invading the flats are Spartina, an East Coast marshgrass introduced at Triangle Cove and spreading slowly northward. Triangle Cove can be reached by driving further W on SR 532 and turning left on E Camano Dr at the Camano Information Center. About 2.5 miles further, turn left of Lehman Rd, turn left again onto a dirt road that cuts across the marsh at the head of the cove. The cove is very tidal and can range from a grass-covered marsh at low tide to a bay at high tide. It is very good for waterbirds, particularly ducks.

**Utsalady.** By turning right, onto N Camano Dr when SR 532 ends, you come to Utsalady, a small town on the N shore of Camano. Utsalady Bay, a sheltered bay, has a good variety of waterbirds. Just W of Utsalady watch for a righhand turn (past Utsalady Pt Rd) down to Beach Dr. A boat launch offers a great view of Saratoga Passage which is very good for seaducks and alcids. It also harbors a large flock of Western Grebes, as well as loons (Yellow-billed in some years) and other grebes. (AC, RT, BT)

---

S: all year   E: 0
H: SW SS FW RW WM ST FL
Maps: DLA 79:A 7; 95:D 7

Good winter and spring birding areas near Everett and Seattle include the Snohomish delta and the valley farmlands and marshes near the junction of the Skykomish and Snoqualmie rivers. The winding sloughs, brush and farm fields of the river delta contain numbers of birds, and the estuary (which could be covered by boat) have many waterbirds in season. Though effects of human activity are readily apparent,

# Everett, Snohomish Delta

C - 2

interesting birds occur here. One of the most interesting birding locations, the big **Everett sewage treatment lagoons,** is reached via SR 529 paralleling I-5 to the W between Marysville and Everett. From the north, take exit 198, just south of Marysville; from the south, take exit 195 (Grand Avenue) turn left and follow Walnut St to SR 529. Follow turnoff sign to Smith Island Boat Ramp, bear S and E along the slough (do not turn off at the overpass going E over I-5 or at signs for St. Regis or other industries) and continue past the boat launch and cross under the freeway, pull off at gates to the sewage ponds. The aerator ponds to the S are especially good for small gulls (Mew, Bonaparte's, Franklin's and occasional Little gulls). The settling ponds to the N have huge numbers of ducks (especially Shovelers); more during hunting season. Many uncommon migrants such as Eared Grebes, Redheads and phalaropes are being seen regularly here, and Tufted Ducks have been seen with flocks of scaup. A colony of introduced Black Ducks is a special feature here. The sewage ponds are fenced. Some of the area can be scanned from the road. Entry onto the sewage pond dikes requres a permit from the caretaker in the building just past Riverfront Langus Park sign (permit good for 2 yrs; obtained at the office, M-F 7:30 a.m.-4:30 p.m.)

The land N of the ponds reached by thebridge over I-5 is good for birds. It is owned by **Snohomish Delta Farms,** and permission for entry must be obtained at the farm noted on the map. Maintain good public relations - obtain permission for entry.

Along the Everett waterfront, the Glaucous-winged Gull colony on **Jetty Island** can be viewed by scope from Port Gardner Bay Park. Look especially for Arctic Terns here, at the southernmost recorded nesting location for the species. The terns have nested both on the island and in a fenced area on the mainland destined to become part of the navy base. Over 200 noisy California sea lions often haul out on the old beached barges on the west side of Jetty Island in the spring.

Just W of Snohomish is the **Snohomish sewage pond.** It can be reached from SR 9 just N of the Snohomish River. At present

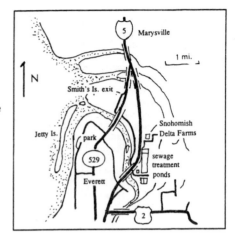

you can park on the W edge of the highway on the N side of the river and scramble down the embankment under the bridge toward the pond, which you can see from the road, or you can park at the pumping station W of SR 9 and walk around the fence. The pond itself is full of dabbling and diving ducks in migration, with variable numbers of Bonaparte's and other gulls. In the fall, there are often substantial numbers of Franklin's Gulls. Both Horned and Eared grebes are regular and can be carefully compared here. At times, flocks of small shorebirds feed on floating algal mats, and Green Herons and American Bitterns are common in the summer in surrounding grassy and shrubby marshes. Anything is possible here: it is similar to and near the Everett ponds, which not only support tremendous numbers of ducks and gulls but also regularly feature rarities and salt-water birds inland. The more wooded nature of this pond makes its borders especially good for small passerines such as warblers and sparrows. (EH, DP, TW, K&JW)

S: all year    E: 50'
H: FW RW WM ST FL
Maps: DLA 79:B 8; 80:B 1

# Monroe and Two Rivers

Drive S from Monroe on SR 203
("Monroe-Duvall Rd"). Cross the
Skykomish River, then Haskel
Slough. Turn onto **Ben Howard Rd**
on the left. This winds through
farms and forest for about 6 miles
before joining Hwy 2 at Sultan.
Good for a variety of lowland
species in spring and summer. A
cottonwood/willow grove just
before the road crosses the
Skykomish into Sultan is often
quite good for birds (one of the
state's most recent Yellow-billed
Cuckoos was here several years
ago).

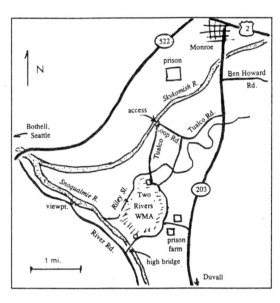

Continuing S on SR 203 turn right
onto Tualco Rd and out through
the farm fields. At about 0.5 mile
continue on ahead on **Tualco
Loop Rd** for about 0.3 mile where
it turns sharply S and a small
parking lot allows a view of the
river and shore. Farther S are
several farm fields which can be good for
gulls, raptors and blackbirds in season.

Continue on S to the northern parking lot of
**Two Rivers Wildlife Management Area.**
Area. This is probably the best chunk of
relatively little-disturbed floodplain forest left
in the region and it encompasses most of the
land within and around an old oxbow of the
Snoqualmie River. A parking lot about 0.75
mile farther S on Tualco Rd, past the prison
work-release farm also allows access to dirt
roads and footpaths and a variety of good
bird habitats, depending on the season and
trail conditions. Marshes feature bitterns and
Green Herons. The perimeter trail, with

slough on one side and fields on the other,
has good passerines, particularly wintering
songbirds like Harris, White-throated, Tree
Swamp sparrows. The western half of the
oxbow is deciduous forest (alder, willow and
bigleaf maple) and is great in spring for
many and birds including Willow and
Pacific-slope flycatchers, Warbling and Red-
eyed vireos. Wood Ducks are regular in
Riley Slough, and Ruffed Grouse are in
thickets in spring. Trails are not really
maintained during the summer and may be
closed by brush by September. We
recommended you stay out of this area
during hunting season (October-January).
(BB, RT)

S: May-Oct   E: 200-4400'
H: FW WC DC RW WM ST
Maps: DLA 80-81 A-C 1-8; 82:B-D 1-4

# Stevens Pass Highway

C - 4

Along Hwy US 2 and the Skykomish River in June, Red-eyed Vireos and Swainson's Thrushes can be heard throughout the riparian woodlands. Birders should watch for Black Swifts high overhead. On a route from the Skykomish River lowlands east over Stevens Pass there are birds corresponding to changes in altitude and vegetation. Many side trips are possible, but there are several stops where birds of special interest may be looked for along the main highway. Vaux's may also be present, so you should note size, more gliding and soaring flight of Black Swifts to be sure. (During cool, low overcast, rainy conditions in the summer, Black Swifts are often seen at low elevations along Puget Sound, feeding sometimes at eye-level - one

good thing about lousy summer weather.) Both Black and Vaux's swifts are often seen at **Deception Falls Picnic Area,** 6.2 miles E of Skykomish. Dippers may also be seen here along the stream next to the highway. At the **Stevens Pass summit** you can walk through the ski area facilities and clearcuts or along the Pacific Crest Trail (watch for muddy spots on the trail) and find species like Hermit and Varied thrushes, Townsend's Warblers and Mountain Chickadees. The **Tumwater NF campground,** just off the highway about 27 miles E of Stevens Pass, has many interesting forest species nesting in the mixed-forest area: look for American Redstarts in the big cottonwoods along the stream (see E-11). (TW)

## KING COUNTY

S: all year   E: 50'
H: FW WC RW WM ST FL
Maps: DLA 80:C-D 1-3

# Snoqualmie Valley Loop

C - 5

Areas along the Snoqualmie River offer varied birding within a short drive from the Greater Seattle area, and show that wildlife can be maintained, in spite of development and changes. Take SR 202 W from Fall City and go 2.2 miles to 308th Ave SE and turn right. Turn left at 312th Ave SE and follow the main road (called Pleasant Hill  the route). At 7.1 miles from the start, turn right at the intersection with the Tolt Hill Rd, cross the bridge over the Snoqualmie River, go left at WA 203. Just past the bridge over the Tolt River there is a county park. Continue through Carnation, turn left at the Carnation Farms Rd. Past Carnation Farms, turn right on 284th Ave NE and right on W Snoqualmie Valley Rd, then right on NE 124th, right on WA 203 and S to Fall City.

Just past the Carnation Golf Course, look for nesting Ospreys to the S of the road. At the county park at the junction of the Tolt and Snoqualmie Rivers, look for Dippers and Rough-winged Swallows. Veeries, rare W of the Cascades, have been seen here. Stop and scan Sykes Lake, just past Carnation Farms, for Hooded Mergansers and Wood Ducks. A large variety of ducks stop here throughout the year, including Cinnamon and Blue-winged teal, Eurasian Wigeon and Ringnecks. The slough N of NE 124th is good for Green Herons, American Bitterns, Wood Ducks and warblers. There are sloughs and marshy areas as well as woodlands and open farmlands. Bald Eagles may be along the river in winter and sometimes swans are seen. (B&PE)

## North Fork Snoqualmie River

C - 6

S: May-Oct   E: 100-1600'
H: FW WC RW ST FL
Maps: DLA 80:D 2-3

From Snoqualmie, N of I-90, cross the Snoqualmie River and turn right on the Reinig Rd (also may be called Ernie's Grove Rd). About 2 miles from the bridge turn left up the Lake Hancock Rd. Follow this about 18 miles to its end at a Forest Service campground. There are many logging roads in this area (gates are sometimes locked) so watch for trucks on working days. Like most of western Washington, much of this area has been logged off. The road more or less follows the river, and several popular fishing lakes are nearby. About 1.7 miles from the bridge, stop at the bend in the road to look for mountain goats on Mt. Si to the SE. Black

Swifts are quite often seen from this lower section of the road. As the road winds up into the hills scan the river for nesting Harlequin Ducks, logged areas for Blue Grouse, and coniferous stands for Gray Jays. Vaux' Swifts are common as are many passerines. This route is recommended for late spring to fall - the road can be bad in winter. A county map or local inquiry for directions to the Lake Hancock Rd or Lake Fury is recommended as it is easy to miss. Camping is possible at the Forest Service camp at the end of the county road. FS roads lead from there and are sometimes rough. (B&PE)

## Seattle

C - 7

S: all year   E: 0-100'
H: SW RS FW WC BF ST PG
Maps: DLA 79:B-D 5-7

Seattle has a number of places where birds congregate and offer good birding within a major, highly developed city. These are located in the city's many parks and include forests, marshes, lakes and saltwater shorelines. A city map will show the locations of the parks and how to reach them. The **University of Washington campus** is one of the best places for birds in the city. The **UW Arboretum** is an excellent spot for many breeding species. It is heavily planted with both native trees and exotic trees, many of them attractive to birds, particularly in migration and winter. Band-tailed Pigeons are present all year the campus. East of the UW campus is a large field bordering on Union Bay, **"Montlake Fill"**. This has become a hot spot for birds in Seattle, as it is one of the few places with open fields and freshwater ponds in the urban Seattle area. These ponds attract migrant shorebirds, usually in small numbers

but in an amazing diversity which is evident when daily checks are made. Many less common shorebirds like Solitary and Semipalmated sandpipers and Wilson's Phalaropes are now found in virtually every migration season. Northern Shrikes, American Pipits and Lapland Longspurs are regular in migration and winter; Horned Larks and Snow Buntings are occasional also. Migrants from similar habitats east of the Cascades are surprise visitors at times - American Avocet, Say's Phoebe, Loggerhead Shrike, Bobolink and Sage Sparrow are recent visitors - and sparrows are always numerous. Open-country raptors such as Northern Harriers and Short-eared Owls (and occasional Snowy Owls) also use this little patch of urban prairie. American Bitterns, Virginia Rails and Soras are summer inhabitants of the surrounding cattail marshes, and the rails may be seen in late summer feeding in the drying ponds.

Offshore in Union Bay, large numbers of the fresh-water ducks and a few salt-water ones spend the winter. Eurasian Wigeons are regular in the wigeon flocks, and Eurasian Green-winged Teal have been seen as well.

**Green Lake,** NW of the campus, is an urban opportunity for fresh-water birds. Mongrel Mallards decoy wild birds into the park, and, in addition to common waterfowl (Gadwalls are common here), you may see species within a few yards that you could not approach within a half-mile in wilder areas. White-fronted Goose, Green-winged Teal, Eurasian Wigeon and Canvasback have been rather consistently found in recent years. This is an excellent place to compare Ring-necked Duck and Greater and Lesser scaup. Close comparisons of gulls with confusing plumages are also often possible here in winter. The diving floats at the NW corner of the lake feature Glaucous-winged, Western, Herring, Thayer's, California, Ring-billed, Mew and Bonaparte's gulls. Large numbers of Bonaparte's should be checked for Little Gulls. Other species include Pied-billed Grebes, Double-crested Cormorants (roosting in spring in trees at the north end of the lake), and Bald Eagles, Green Heron and Yellow-headed Blackbird are recent "occasionals".

**Discovery Park.** At any season, this can be an exciting birding spot for out-of-town visitors as well as for patient regulars. Of the fourteen bird habitats we list for the state, this park has varying fragments of nine, scattered throughout its 530 acres - with salt water, beaches, meadows, and mixed forest being the most important. Over 50 species breed here, though usually in small numbers due to limited habitat.

Half the bird species recorded in the state have been recorded at least once in the park, and eighty species might be found on a good day during migration. Most of the park's specialty birds are relatively easy to find. Anna's Hummingbird males are abundant most of the year, except in the summer when they are moulting - listen for their insect-like "song" coming from atop a

tall tree in a clearing along the loop trail. Hutton's Vireo is also easy to find in spring if you listen for its monotonous "zwee...zwee" song. California Quail are everywhere in the underbrush. Pigeon Guilllemots nest in holes in the South Bluff near the road. Owls may surprise you at any location or season, as may a soaring Bald Eagle. Flycatchers are common around wooded areas. Barred Owls have nested for several years in the northwest corner. They might be found any place in spring or summer where there is a canopy of mature big-leaf maples - but, due to the vast preponderance of birders over owls, please do not bother them by playing tapes. Robins and chickadees often locate them for you in late summer. The most rewarding areas of the park are given below - check at the Visitor Center for a bird checklist and a map of the trails. Naturalists offer bird walks and classes for all but the expert birder. Keep to the trails as much as possible. Please report any sightings you think of interest to the staff.

Scots Broom Wilderness, densely covered with broom, salal, elderberry, trailing blackberry and many small trees, between the South Meadow and Capehart Naval Housing is one of the least disturbed places in the park. In late June, the fireweed is alive with migrant Rufous Hummingbirds, along with a few resident Anna's. Willow Flycathers "fitzbew" from small trees, Red-winged Blackbirds nest in the broom (this is one of their few upland nest sites in Washington), and the song of the Orange-crowned Warbler and an occasional Black-headed Grosbeak pervades. This sanctuary is good for sparrows, including Golden-crowned and Lincoln's in fall, and also Kestrel, Northern Harrier, Short-eared Owl and Northern Shrike. South Meadow has nesting Savannah Sparrows in summer, and Western Meadowlarks in winter. Raptors are often seen, especially in fall. In spring, the fences around the radio tower have produced migrants and rare species have been seen in the meadow. The area near the sand dune is a good spot.

North Forest is a thick belt of mixed deciduous and coniferous woodland with clearings, extending from the Visitor Center at the East Gate across the north side of the park. In winter, look for an occasional vireo or warbler in the flocks of small passerines that are common. Merlins or Accipiters are possible. Red-breasted Sapsuckers appear briefly after Christmas. Near the North Parking Lot is the Wolf Tree Nature Trail, an interpretive path used by naturalists. In summer expect Swainson's Thrush, Warbling and Solitary vireos, Black- throated Gray Warblers and Winter Wrens. A spur-trail leads from the main trail to the middle pond at the Indian Cultural Center. At the ponds there are herons, swallows, waxwings, and small numbers of ducks including Gadwalls.

The outstanding birding spot at Discovery Park is the West Point peninsula, jutting out into Puget Sound and bounded by sandy and rocky shorelines. Walk from the North Parking Lot along the North Beach Trail along the rip-rap wall. On the right you will find grebes, loons and ducks, including an occasional Harlequin or Oldsquaw. About 200 yards before you reach the Metro dock, a large rocky outcrop is exposed at low tide. Look for Whimbrel (usually in spring) and Wandering Tattler (fall). Both the north and south sandy beaches are good for many small shorebirds. West Point itself is a fine lookout for the 18 species of gulls and terns, and 5 species of alcids recorded so far, including Ancient Murrelets which are most likely in November. Careful observation of the large fall flocks of Bonaparte's Gulls may result in a sighting of a Little or Sabine's gull or a dashing Parasitic Jaeger. Thayer's, Heermann's and Franklin's gulls may be seen close offshore. During periods of stormy, strong southwest winds there is even a chance of seeing a Sooty or Short-tailed shearwater well offshore.

**Golden Gardens Park, Alki Beach Park** and **Lincoln Park** border on Puget Sound and are good in winter for many loons, sea ducks and alcids. Brant often feed along the shore at Golden Gardens during migration.

**Seward Park,** in SE Seattle, is on a peninsula extending into Lake Washington. It has coniferous and mixed woodland and open areas and is good for forest species. Dippers have been seen regularly on a small stream there. Bald Eagles have nested here in recent years. The open waters of the lake itself have some species like Western Grebe and gulls in winter, but never as many as there are in the protected coves. (DH, RL, MM, DP, ES, BT)

---

S: all year    E: 50'
H: FW WC BF RW WM ST PG
Maps: DLA 79:C-D 6-7

# Lake Washington East

C - 8

The urban-suburban area on the east shore of Lake Washington and around Lake Sammamish has parks on the lakes and in upland habitats. Several of interest are located within a short distance of the I-90 freeway. **Newport area:** On the E shore of Lake Washington, take the Newport Way exit from I-405, to W on Newport Way/118th Ave SE. Follow the main street until you reach SE 40th St. Turn left at the Public Boat Launch sign. This area is good for ducks, including Hooded Mergansers, during migration. Marsh Wrens, Barn Owls and Northern Shrikes have been seen here. Return to 118th Ave, go N until just before the road passes under I-90. On the left is a long pipe supplying Seattle with water. You can walk on the pipe, and may see Great Blue and Green herons, American Bittern, many species of ducks, Red-tailed Hawks, rails and muskrats. Hooded Mergansers, and red fox are also possible. Continuing down

118th Ave, the next stop is **Bellefields Park.**
The park is good during the spring and
summer for nesting birds, including
woodpeckers, vireos and warblers. In winter
and migrations there are many ducks and
marsh birds, Cooper's Hawks, kingfishers
and more. Wood Ducks often winter near
**Clyde Beach Park** on Meydenbauer Bay,
where there are large flocks of Mallards,
both wild and tame. **Lake Sammamish State
Park,** from I-90 exit 15, is at the S end of
Lake Sammamish. Hiking around the park

offers good birds at any season. Marymoor
Park is at the N end of the lake. S of the
main grounds are open fields (formerly
farms) and a dense growth of trees and
shrubs along the river to Lake Sammamish. It
may be wet, but a hike through this area
along the river almost to the lake is possible,
and many species typical of lowland habitats
seen in season. In summer, Purple Martins
nest in pilings out in the lake to the E of
Marymoor Park. (AM, RL)

---

S: Feb.-June  E: 100'
H: FW DF
Maps: DLA 63:B 6

# Blue Heron Marsh

C - 9

Beginning in early February, nesting Great
Blue Herons can readily be observed by
looking directly across the marsh to a
rookery with 25 nests on a steep hillside
with alders and a few firs. Nest building and
repairing, courtship, feeding young, flights
in, over and around nests provide
continuous action. Located at the
intersection of Peasley Canyon Rd and West

Valley Hwy in Auburn, it can be reached
from I-5, exit 143, at S 329th in Federal
Way. Follow 320th east (it soon becomes
Peasley Canyon Rd) to the end at West
Valley Hwy. Turn right into a small parking
area or use the large Park & Ride lot. Follow
a short path along the marsh to a rustic
bench at the viewpoint close to Peasley
Canyon Rd. (TB)

**KING, PIERCE COUNTIES, TACOMA**

---

S: Apr.-June  E: 50'
H: SW WC BF ST PG
Maps: DLA 63:A-C 5-6

# Des Moines to Tacoma's Lincoln St. Marsh

C - 10

A tour of area saltwater parks begins at the
**Des Moines Marina,** reached via I-5, exit
149, following SR 516 west to its end at
Marine View Dr, turning N to So. 223 then
left to the north marina's long fishing pier
and adjacent Beach Park where Des Moines
Creek empties into Puget Sound. Many gulls
line the pier's railings, Barrow's Goldeneyes,
scoters, grebes and wigeon provide close
looks. Continue S 1 mile to **Saltwater State
Park** for both upland and water birds. This is
a good place to find Black Scoter, Brant in

spring, and a variety of landbirds on the
forested bluffs. Continue S on Marine View
Dr (#509) to a flashing light at So. 272. Turn
right, go downhill to **Redondo Beach Dr** to
a boat launch and fishing pier. In season,
Rhinoceros Auklets and Marbled Murrelets
favor this area. Near Salty's restaurant take
Redondo Way So. uphill 1 mile to Dash Pt.
Rd (509). Follow the winding road about 5
miles, passing Lakota sewage treatment plant
to 44 Ave SW (dead end; usually unmarked);
it is the last right turn before 47 Ave SW.

Within 0.25 mile a **Dumas Bay Sanctuary** sign leads into a parking lot. From there walk through the woods to the beach and a large shallow bay, fed by 3 streams. Loons, rafts of wigeon, Brant in migration and shorebirds are among seasonal features. Both species of rails are summer residents in the freshwater marsh. A few steps down the road from the parking lot, you can glimpse a Great Blue Heron rookery with over 50 nests through the trees.

Returning to SR 509, continue S to **Dash Point State Park.** Trails and campgrounds are good for woodland birds like Hutton's Vireos and Townsend's Warblers and there are gulls and ducks along the shore.

After crossing into Pierce County turn right at Dash Pt sign and down into **Dash Point County Park** and fishing pier. This is often the most productive place around for Pigeon Guillemot, Marbled Murrelet, Ancient Murrelet (late Oct.-Nov.) and Rhinoceros Auklet. Continue S 2 miles to Brown's Pt, turn and go 1 mile to **Brown's Point County Park** at the lighthouse. Marbled Murrelets are seen in breeding plumage in June. Purple Martins, for which many boxes have been put up around the region, nested here in 1987.

Return to 509 and downhill to **Hylebos Waterway.** Pull off the road past the first marina (Crow's) to scan logbooms for thousands of gulls and dozens of herons, water for rafts of Western Grebes. Any of numerous pullouts can be productive; watch for pilings with boxes for Purple Martins. Ruddy Turnstones turn up each year with Black Turnstones on the logbooms, Least and Western sandpipers frequent the flats in migration and Dunlins are present in winter. Return to I-5 by turning left by the tideflats on the Port of Tacoma Rd. (If you are reversing this route, the Port of Tacoma exit from I-5 is #136.)

Or, alternatively, take the Port of Tacoma Rd as far as Lincoln Ave, turn right and continue to a gravel/dirt road before crossing the Puyallup River bridge; turn left to the newly created **Lincoln St. Wetland** or **Mitigated Marsh.** An opening into the river allows daily tidal action into the mudflats. Viewing from the levee road is excellent - no need to leave your car. Shorebirds use the mudflats (a Bar-tailed Godwit was recorded the first season!), Thayer's Gulls appear in nearly pure flocks during winter, road. Located in the vast wasteland of industrial Tacoma, the marsh has hosted more than 80 bird species in 2 years. Return to I-5 by crossing the Puyallup River bridge and turning left at the light onto Portland Ave. (If entering this route, the Portland Ave exit from I-5 is #135). (TB)

S: all year   E: 0-200'
H: SW RS SS WC BF ST
Maps: DLA 62:B-C 4

# Point Defiance, The Narrows

C - 11

Tacoma's Point Defiance Park has upland habitats, Pigeon Guillemots nesting in the north bluffs overlooking the sound, and other attractions. One of its birding features is a seasonal seabird event that ranks as one of the best in the state. From fall through spring huge numbers of Bonaparte's, Mew and other gulls, Common Murres and other diving birds feed in the Tacoma Narrows, from Point Defiance south to Fox Island, Hale Passage and to Carr Inlet. Many birds can be seen by scope from the beach or bluff overlooks during flooding or ebbing tides, and a boat trip would get right into the flocks of birds. This is a great place to search for Little Gulls and other rare species. (TW)

# Mount Rainier National Park

The summit of massive Mt. Rainier, the highest point in Washington, is visible from many miles away and this volcanic peak attracts visitors to its scenery, flowers and forests and many animals. Its mountain birds are within a short distance of the major population centers of western Washington.

Mt. Rainier's high elevations can be reached by any of three all- year entrances on the N, W and S sides. Additionaly, there are two summer-only entrances from the W and one from the E. All of these are shown on road maps, and visitors should check in advance to see if the summer-only entrances are open from October to May. Obtain maps of the park at any of the entrance gates. The park offers a wide variety of situations in which to look for birds of different habitats, all of which are easily reached by road. For birds of the wet lowland forest, a stop at any of the campgrounds or the visitor centers at Cougar Rock, Tahoma Creek, Longmire, Ohanepecosh, and Ipsut Creek should be productive. This is big conifer habitat (Douglas fir, western red cedar, western hemlock, grand fir). The ground varies from fairly open, often covered with logs, to very densely vegetated with shrubs of the rose and heather families.

The interior of these forests is often dark and wet, and birds may be scarce. Winter Wrens are the most obvious species of the ground level, and by looking up and especially by listening you may can find other common species - Blue and Ruffed grouse, Vaux' Swift, Hairy and other woodpeckers, Hammond's and Olive-sided flycatchers, Gray and Steller's jays, Chestnut-backed Chickadee, Red-breasted Nuthatch, Brown Creeper, Robin, Varied and Swainson's thrushes, Golden-crowned Kinglet, Solitary Vireo, Yellow-rumped, Townsend's and Wilson's warblers, Western Tanager, Evening Grosbeak, Purple Finch, Pine Siskin, Red Crossbill, and Dark-eyed Junco. Many of these will be singing from the canopy and not be visible except where the forest is lower or openings provide better visibility. Spotted Owls are resident in the park, and are sometimes seen or heard by lucky hikers or back-country campers. The species is often reported in late summer when young birds have left nesting territories and are wandering about. Some interesting species of flowers grow in these dense, dark forests. Salamanders are abundant, and obvious mammals include Townsend chipmunk, Douglas squirrel and the black-tailed form of the mule deer. Some of the species encountered in the lowlands can be found in the forests of mountain hemlock, alpine fir and Alaska yellow cedar above 4000', but many are replaced by higher elevation counterparts. These include Clark's Nutcracker, Common Raven, Mountain Chickadee, Hermit Thrush, Ruby-crowned Kinglet and, in more open areas, Mountain Bluebird. In dense thickets, Fox Sparrows (drier areas) and Lincoln's Sparrows (wetter areas) can be found. At still higher elevations (above 5500') the trees thin out and become stunted, and finally give way to alpine meadows which, in July and August, produce one of the finest flower shows to be seen anywhere. White-tailed Ptarmigan, American Pipits and Horned Larks nest in the meadows; Gray-crowned Rosy Finches nest in rocky areas. The ptarmigan are the most difficult of the high mountain species to find, and they should be searched for early in the morning or at other times before the trails become crowded with hikers. The two best places for easy observation of high mountain species are **Paradise** (5400') and **Sunrise** (6400'), both of which have visitor centers and hiking trails which lead higher up the mountain. Boreal Owls occur at Sunrise in the fall and may breed there. One of the better ptramigan locations in the park is **Burroughs Mtn,** reached from Sunrise; the birds occur on the trails above Paradise as well, but they are seen in both areas infrequently. Another accessible area nearby is the Chinook Pass summit (5400') on SR 410 on the E side of the park. Red-naped Sapsucker, Three-toed Woodpecker, Pine Grosbeak and many other interesting species are in that area. (EH, DP)

## PIERCE, THURSTON COUNTIES

---

The native prairies, mixed forest and oak woodlands typical of the south Puget Sound region vary from regions to the north, west and east in plant and animal species and offer a taste of similar habitats found in valleys south into Oregon.

# Fort Lewis prairies

S: April-June  E: 200'-500'
H: FW DC BF DG ST
Maps: DLA 46-47:A 3-5; 62:D 4

C - 13

Some excellent examples of the native prairies can be found on Fort Lewis and in adjacent areas. The best locations are located between Spanaway and Roy, in Pierce County, and northwest of Rainier, in Thurston County. You can explore the prairie ares off Hwy SR 507 or the Harts Lake Loop Rd (8th Ave), or visit the specific areas identified below.

Prairie birds common on Fort Lewis include Northern Bobwhite, Mourning Dove, Western Meadowlark, Vesper and Chipping sparrows, House Wren and Western Bluebird. In the early 1980s Fort Lewis began a bluebird nest box program. There are now over 100 nesting pairs of Western Bluebirds scattered about the Fort. These prairie areas are at their best in May. Common wildflowers include shooting star, camas, chocolate lily, blue-eyed grass and the endangered Aster curtus. Often, the butterflies can be as interesting as the birds.

NOTE: Many of the Fort Lewis training areas are open to the public when training activities are not occurring. However, you must have an access permit issued by the Fort Lewis Area Access Office. Enter the Fort through the Main Gate, at I-5 exit 120, and ask for a visitor's pass and directions at the M.P. station. You will need your driver's license and vehicle registration. Ask the MPs for directions to Range Control for this seasonal pass.

**Chamber's Lake area.** Go in from Roy, Pierce County. Roy is S of Tacoma on Hwy 7, then 507 or E of Olympia; take Marvin Rd exit 111 off I-5, SR 510 E to Yelm and 507 N to Roy. Where 507 makes a right-angle bend in Roy, go W on Water St for one block, turn right on Warren Rd, which zigs across railroad tracks and enters Fort Lewis at a public gate. Approximately one half mile N of the gate, make a sharp right at a yield sign onto a paved road which runs along the W side of the lake. This is a prairie area with scattered ponderosa pine and Douglas fir - habitat for Western Bluebirds, Vesper and Chipping sparrows and House Wrens. In winter the brush along the lake holds many passerines, and the lake itself has Lesser Scaup, Ring-necked Duck and an occasional Redhead along with other ducks. Bald Eagles are frequent here.

**Johnson Marsh,** located N of Chambers Lake, is best known for nesting Purple Martins, Wood Ducks and Hooded Mergansers. Look and listen for Yellow Warbler and yellowthroat. Bluebirds nest in boxes in the clearcuts W and E of the marsh. Go N from Chambers Lake, turning E on East Gate Rd. Or, turn W on East Gate Rd from SR 507, about half way between Roy and Hwy 7. The marsh is N of East Gate Rd, 2.5 miles W of SR 507.

**Weir Prairie,** near Rainier, Thurston Co., can be reached from Centralia by driving NE on SR 507, from Olympia by driving SE on the Rainier Hwy, or from Roy on SR 507. The prairie is NW of town, in two sections. To reach Upper Weir Prairie, turn NE on Military Rd one mile W of Rainier. The prairie lies N of the junction of Military and 123rd, which runs along its southern border. Just beyond Military Rd intersection, the Rainier Hwy bisects Lower Weir Prairie and well-maintained gravel roads lead off in several directions. This prairie has Northern Bobwhite, Western Meadowlark, Western Bluebird, Vesper and Savannah sparrows. The edges hold Ruffed Grouse, Hammond's and Pacific-slope flycatchers, Western Wood-Pewee, Black-headed Grosbeak, Orange-crowned and MacGillivray's warblers, Chipping and White-crowned sparrows.

**McKenna.** Another access to prairie habitats is near McKenna. SR 702 E of McKenna crosses extensive second-growth woodland, much of it fairly recently clear-cut. It is noteworthy for open-country birds otherwise rather uncommon and/or local in western Washington, particularly Bobwhites but also Western Kingbirds, Western Bluebirds and Lazuli Buntings. A walk down one of the many roads in the area on a spring morning will produce dozens of species of birds, with many of them singing from the prominent brush piles still remaining. It is good country for small mammals and therefore birds of prey, so scan the sky regularly. Harts Lake Loop Rd, turning S from SR 702 0.5 mile E of McKenna, loops through some interesting areas and returns to Hwy 702 approximately 5 miles E of McKenna. Crossing the highway and continuing N will lead to open prairies of Fort Lewis and, eventually, to SR 507 and Hwy 7 in Spanaway.

**Scatter Creek WRA.** Exit I-5 for Little Rock-Maytown, about 10 miles S of the junction of I-5 and the Shelton-Aberdeen freeway. Turn left on WA 121, cross the railroad tracks, go 0.3 mile, turn left on the Case Rd for about 5 miles. Turn right on 180th for 0.5 mile, turn right on Guava for 100 yds and then left into the parking lot. From here, walk SW through the grassy field. Lazuli Buntings may be found in early summer. Vesper, Chipping and Savannah sparrows and Western Meadowlarks are common. By following this trail between the barn and the creek you reach a brushy marsh. This stretch is usually good for warblers, vireos, flycatchers, thrushes, etc. White-breasted Nuthatches have been seen in the large oaks along the trail. Ruffed Grouse, Winter Wren and Chestnut-backed Chickadees are common on N side of the creek from the parking lot. (G&WH, DP, JS, BT)

## Bald Hill Lake

S: April-Oct  E: 500-1000'
H: FW WC BF RW
Maps: DLA 46-47:B 4-5

C - 14

This area of varied habitat between the Upper Deschutes and Nisqually Rivers has hilly terrain, several lakes, marshes, intensively-managed timberlands and scattered ranches. There is good access with many "exploring" roads. About 50 species are possible in a day in summer. Increasing recreational use makes weekends and holidays less attractive for birding. From I-5 take exit 111, follow SR 510 SE to Yelm, go SE on SR 507 for about 1 mile to Five Corners and turn right onto Bald Hill Rd. Continue SE for about 11 miles, and then about 1 mile past Clear Lake. At an intersection where the pavement ends turn left for 0.2 mile and stop beside a swamp. Marsh Wrens, yellowthroats, woodpeckers, Tree Swallows and Vaux's Swifts are some of the summer residents. Continue on this road, keeping left, and follow Weyerhaeuser signs to Bald Hill Lk. The lake is about 0.5 mile across and mostly covered with water lilies, with cattail patches along much of the

shore. A passable road goes part way along the W side, with a rough trail completing the circuit. Hiking time: about 3 hours. Lesser Scaup and other ducks are common, especially in spring. Wood Ducks nest in summer. Cliff Swallows nest on the cliffs on the NE side. Many common warblers are found along the trail, as well as busily foraging flocks of chickadees, nuthatches, wrens, creepers, kinglets and bushtits. Turkey Vultures are seen frequently and may nest here. Return to Bald Hill Rd, turn left for 2 miles to logging road 1161. Lazuli Buntings and Western Bluebirds invade recently opened areas (clear-cuts, burns). These two species, along with House Wren and White-crowned Sparrow, nest in open areas in the vicinity. There is a good opportunity for exploration where many roads traverse recently logged areas adjacent to dense second-growth forest, and abundant water which encourages a diversity of species. (JDa, GW)

**THURSTON COUNTY**

## Nisqually Delta

S: all year  E: 0
H: SW SS FW RW WM ST FL
Maps: DLA 62:D 2-3

C - 15

The Nisqually National Wildlife Refuge and state Wildlife Recreation Area make up the outstanding river delta-estuary birding spot left on southern Puget Sound. It is easily accessible from Seattle, Tacoma and Olympia via freeway. It is reached from I-5 exit 114 between Tacoma and Olympia. The NWR headquarters is on the N side of the freeway, reached via a road paralleling I-5. A check should be made at headquarters for access and trail conditions in the area. While varying seasonally, this delta has very large

numbers of waterfowl, wading birds, shore-birds, gulls, passerines and appropriately large numbers of birds of prey. The E side of the loop trail is wooded, the W side is open, and you may wish to choose one or the other of these trails rather than hiking the entire 5-mile trail. Red-breasted Sapsuckers and Great Horned Owls are regular in the woods. Birders who have checked the area regularly have compiled an impressive species list for the refuge, including rarities like the White-tailed Kite and

Red-shouldered Hawk. Access to the refuge is limited during the hunting season. Address is Nisqually National Wildlife Refuge, 2625 Parkmont Lane, Olympia WA 98502. Phone (206)753-9467. Check Winter gulls for rarities at the Thurston County dump, which is visible from the I-5 freeway about 3 miles E of Olympia and is reached by exit 111. Glaucous, Thayer's, hybrid Glaucous Winged X Western, and Glaucous-winged X Herring are among the challenging identification goodies possible. (DP, BT)

---

## Budd Inlet and Capitol Lake

S: all year   E: 0-300'
H: SW FW WC BF ST PG FL
Maps: DLA 62:C-D 1

C - 16

Located at the southern end of Puget Sound, Olympia is flanked on three sides by inlets and passages attractive to waterbirds especially during the winter and these varied areas, from mud flats to deep tidal channels have good potential for birders. **Capitol Lake.** Take I-5 exit at Plum St, follow Plum to Fifth St. Turn left on Fifth and continue on it to the N end of Capitol Lake. Although a good number of waterfowl species are present in winter, it is most interesting in November when as many as 1000 Barrow's Goldeneyes roost overnight. The birds start arriving about 3 p.m. and flocks continue to arrive until dark. This interesting species appears to prefer calmer waters than the Common Goldeneye and flocks of Barrows often feed well back under dark piers in protected waters and marinas. Across the road from Capitol Lake, **Budd Inlet** often yields many saltwater species such as scoters, alcids, gulls and Pelagic Cormorants. This long inlet is the Olympia harbor and is especially noteworthy for its large numbers of wintering Black Scoters, along with many other species. (BT)

## MASON, JEFFERSON COUNTIES

## Hood Canal, Great Bend

S: Sept-May   E: 0
H: SW SS WC WM ST FL
Maps: DLA 61:A-B 7-8; 62:A-B 1-2; 77:D 8; 78:A-D 1-4

C - 17

Much of this beautiful, sheltered arm of Puget Sound appears to have low numbers of wintering waterbirds. It is very deep and has limited areas of shallow edges for much of its length, but several estuaries offer rich habitats. The very deep, offshore waters of Hood Canal support only flocks of Western Grebes and Common Murres. Along Hwys SR 101 and 106 along the W and S shores of the Canal there are several small yet promising birding spots. **Tarboo Bay** (S of Dabob) and **Quilcene Bay** (at Quilcene), at the head of Dabob Bay, have estuaries and waterfowl habitat, as does **Thorndike Bay** SE of Dabob on Hood Canal proper. The **Dosewallips River mouth** (at Brinnon), the **Duckabush River estuary,** and the **Hamma Hamma estuary** (at Eldon) are also quite promising. One of the most important wintering areas for waterbirds in the inland waters of Washington is at the S end of the canal - the **Great Bend.** This area is from Potlatch SP south and east through Anna's Bay and the Skokomish delta and to Lynch

Cove at the end of the "hook" of the canal. The Yellow-billed Loon has been seen here and could be found in winter all along Hood Canal. The Great Bend of the canal, both in offshore areas and shallow nearshore waters has very large numbers of Western Grebes, diving ducks, dabblers, gulls and Marbled Murrelets. At the E end of the Canal, Lynch Cove flats (at Belfair SP) has more possibilities. Access routes into the Olympic mountains (as at Brinnon and Hoodsport) are worth birding. Mountain habitats are within a very few miles of salt water. (TW)

S: Nov-Apr    E: 0
H: SW SS FW WC ST PG FL
Maps: DLA 78-79:B 4-5

# Kingston, Port Gamble

C - 18

The northern part of the Kitsap Peninsula has fine prospects for waterbirds at almost any season of the year and the rugged, northernmost tip can be a landbird trip during migrations. Another area reasonably close to major population centers, it has only recently been covered by birders. Take the ferry from Edmonds to Kingston. Follow SR 104 to Port Gamble, go S on SR 3 and 305 to Poulsbo. Or, this route may be reversed by taking the Winslow ferry from Seattle and continuing on WA 305 to Poulsbo. Camping is possible at Kitsap Memorial State Park. The harbor and shore at **Kingston** can be studied by scope from the ferry dock. Park at the marina just S of the dock. Stop at the park in Port Gamble for passerines and to scan the water to the N. Permission may be obtained at the Pope and Talbot office to visit the **"Y" log dump,** 1.2 miles S of Port Gamble and unmarked. Park W of the highway near the gate to the watershed, cross the road and walk about a block down the road toward the water. This is the best place to scan the bay and is best on Sundays or after dumping hours. Black Scoters, Hooded Mergansers, Harlequins, Oldsquaws, Barrow's Goldeneyes and many other ducks, loons and grebes (including Eared), alcids, gulls, terns, Bald Eagles, cormorants, jaegers and Ospreys may be seen in season. Turn right 0.8 mile past Port Gamble, just before the sign "Hood Canal Bridge - 1/2 mile", to the public boat ramp where there is parking and birds. Continue S on the main highway to **Kitsap Memorial State Park,** where there is a beach, forested areas, thickets and a stream. Continue on S to Poulsbo and the waterfront public parking area. Wintering Eared Grebes can often be seen from the docks. This route is especially good in winter, but there are many birds in other seasons. (B&PE)

# Foulweather Bluff area

Coverage of the area can be done in a loop. Turn N onto Hansville Rd from SR 104 for a little more than 4 miles and turn E onto Eglon Rd. This road passes through farmland, turns S and eventually ends at **Eglon Public Boat Launch.** Grebes and seaducks can be seen off the shingle beach in fall and winter.

Return to Hansville Rd and turn N for 3 miles, descend to the shore and the town of Hansville. Watch for the first intersection with a large sign directing you to the Point No Point Marina to the right. Follow this road but instead go straight ahead on the road signed "Dead End" to the parking lot of the **Point No Point Coast Guard Station.** Park here (don't block access). Tidal convergences attract many birds, including rarities like Brown Pelican, Magnificent Frigatebird, Short-tailed Shearwater and Black-legged Kittiwake. Landbirds may be found around the point to the E, part of an undeveloped County Park. Retrace and cross Hansville Rd onto Buck Lake Rd to **Buck Lake County Park,** the only sizable lake on this route. The dirt road fishing access at the north end of the lake has promise for waterfowl, raptors and landbirds.

Back to Hansville Rd: turn left and within a block the main road turns W and after about 2.4 miles look for red and white posts on the left side of the road and an alder-screened opening to the left. Park on the shoulder (if you've reached Skunk Bay Rd you've gone about 2 blocks too far). Look for an obvious foot trail on the S side of the road with a well-hidden sign welcoming you to the **Nature Conservancy**

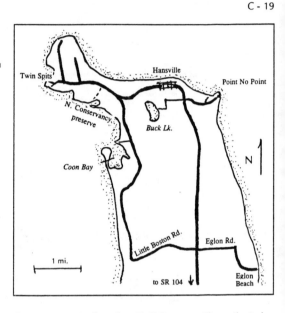

**Foulweather Bluff Preserve.** The trail winds through thick second-growth next to a tidal marsh and to the beach at about 0.2 mile. The marsh is good for ducks and shorebirds and the woods for passerines. Gulls roost on the sand/cobble beach, and grebes, seaducks and alcids are visible on Hood Canal.

The main road continues farther W to Twin Spits Resort (stay to the left at any major intersection) and deadends at a tiny public access parking lot next to the resort. You can walk around a muddy little bay to the E and to one of the **twin spits** where many gulls, including Heermann's, may be seen. By continuing down the main road, past the Sanctuary, you can turn S (right) onto Hood Canal Dr. This becomes Little Boston Rd and eventually reaches Hansville Rd. (JC, TS, RT)

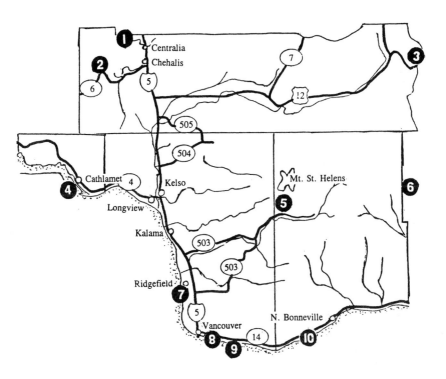

Lewis County
1 - Lincoln Creek
2 - Rainbow Falls State Park

Lewis-Yakima counties
3 - White Pass Highway

Wahkiakum County
4 - Puget Island

Cowlitz-Skamania counties
5 - Mount St. Helens area

Skamania-Yakima counties
6 - Mount Adams area

Clark County
7 - Ridgefield area
8 - Vancouver area
9 - Steigerwald Lake

Clark-Skamania counties
10 - Columbia Gorge

## Lincoln Creek Valley

D - 1

S: May-Sept E: 200-300'
H: FW WC BF ST
Maps: DLA 45:C-D 6-8

One of the best places in western Washington to look for Wild Turkeys is reportedly the Lincoln Creek drainange in northwestern Lewis County, W of Centralia. The Department of Wildlife has been releasing birds from Pennsylvania for several years in this area and the population appears to be increasing, Take Exit 81 from I-5, go W on Stephens Rd to Galvin and onto Lincoln Creek Rd which goes W several miles. No stake outs, but dedicated looking and listening may turn up turkeys as well as other interesting species. Reports of sightings of turkeys in SW Washington would be appreciated by the staff at the WDW Game Farm in Centralia at (206)736-4615. (JS)

## Rainbow Falls State Park

D - 2

S: May-Sept E: 300'
H: FW WC ST PG
Maps: Lewis; DLA 45:C-D 7

An easy-to-reach spot for Hermit Warblers is at Rainbow Falls State Park where, next to the playfield is a good stand of conifers. Several birds have been seen at once, responding aggressively to calls and coming from treetops to ground level. Screech-Owls have been seen in the past nesting in large snags at the same location in the park. Other Hermit Warblers were noted in suitable habitat along the highway. Take Exit 77 from I-5 at Chehalis to Hwy 6, follow signs for about 20 miles to the state park. (PH)

## White Pass Highway

D - 3

S: May-Sept E: 500-4500'
H: FW WC DC BF RW WM ST
Maps: DLA 48-49:C-D 3-8; 50:C 1-2

One of the better high mountain passes for birds crosses the Cascades over the White Pass Highway, US 12, southeast of Mt. Rainier. Several sought-after species have been found consistently in the area of the summit and downhill to the east in May-July. Hermit Warblers are reached by logging roads going S from US 12 from **Randle** and near **Packwood.** Just a short distance from the highway, where tall trees begin, you may hear the species' song - very similar to Townsend's but ending with CHUP CHUP. Lincoln's Sparrow has been seen in scrub willows right next to the road at the **White Pass summit.** A small colony of Williamson's Sapsuckers has been found just west of the summit, across from the ski lodge, in recent years from early May through late July. Rock

Wrens have been recorded in talus slides. Three-toed Woodpeckers are found widely, sparsely, in the forests, particularly E of the summit.

About 0.5 mile E of the summit on the N side of the highway look for the turnoff to **Leech Lake**. Park at the lake and check the area. Many species, including Ospreys, are possible. Three-toed Woodpeckers have been seen right next to the lake at the parking lot. Further downhill to the E along the mountain pass Red-naped Sapsucker, Clark's Nutcracker, Pine Grosbeak and more may be seen. Near the W end of **Rimrock Lake** there is a highway rest area/boat launch next to the lake. Calliope Hummingbirds are seen here in June, displaying and feeding at flowering shrubs, on the hillside below the entrance to the rest area. White-headed Woodpeckers have been seen at the E end of Rimrock Lake. Other stops, side hikes or drives up side roads will turn up many other birds. (G&WH, BT, TW)

## WAHKIAKUM COUNTY

S: all year   E: 0
H: SS FW RW WM ST FL
Maps: DLA 31:C 5-6

# Puget Island

D - 4

Puget Island is an interesting spot for birds and should be good any time of the year, but especially good during winter and migrations. It is reached via SR 409 and bridge from Cathlamet. The island is extensively farmed, but has many areas of brush and deciduous trees, ditches and dikes with passarines, raptors, waterfowl and wading birds. Nearby islands are NWR refuges set up to protect Columbian white-tailed deer and have brush and wooded areas. The Japanese Green Pheasant (Phasianus versicolor) was introduced here. (FC, TW)

## COWLITZ, SKAMANIA COUNTIES

S: June-Aug   E: 500-3000'
H: FW WC DC BF RW WM ST
Maps: DLA 33:C 5-7

# Mount St. Helens

D - 5

The area around Mt. St. Helens is now in a state of recovery from the dramatic volcanic activity in 1980. Extensive areas once covered with big timber and flattened by the blast are gradually recovering. Closed areas around the mountain are being opened again to visitors, and access to all Mt. St. Helens areas should be checked locally. A Hermit Warbler area is reached by following SR 503 from I-5 exit 21 at Woodland, E to Yale and Cougar, along the N shore of Swift Creek reservoir. Past the ranger station, take the left fork toward Cedar Flats and Muddy River (about 25 miles E of Cougar). Pass Muddy River and Clear Water campground; you may follow the road along Smith Creek to the end or until stopped by snow. The area is most rewarding during June or July at higher elevations. The road may be difficult or impassable in early spring or late fall.

From Woodland the highway follows the Lewis River, climbing slowly through lowland farm country into the coniferous forest beyond Cougar the birdlife begins to change fairly rapidly. Five miles E of Cougar, watch and listen for Hermit Warblers; they become numerous within an area of a few miles. In another 5-10 miles you are high enough for Hammond's Flycatchers, Gray Jays and Varied Thrushes. Look for Vaux's Swifts and Dippers (in Muddy River and Swift Creek). About 2 miles past Clearwater campground is an interesting mountain marsh with nesting Spotted Sandpipers. (FC, JD, R&JR)

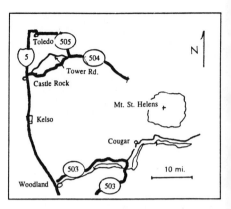

The area around Mount Adams is among the mountain areas in Washington that are least explored by birders, probably due to its remoteness, but it has interesting birds and scenery and, with preparation and care, the area can be covered.

# Mount Adams area

S: July-Sept  E: 1000-3000'
H: FW WC DC BF RW WM ST
Maps: DLA 34-35:A-D 1-6 48:D 1

D - 6

Hermit Warblers have been seen during the nesting season along FS Rd 123 (open in mid-summer) SE of Randle on US 12, at Adams Fork Campground, Ollalie Lake, and also at Takhlakh Lake. Based on recent observations, principal Hermit Warbler range is W of the Cascade crest and S of US 12, with Townsend's Warbler predominating E of the crest and N of the highway.

**Indian Heaven area** - A map of the Gifford Pinchot NF is required. From St. Helens RS at the E end of Swift Reservoir drive E on N90, then S on N174, then NE on N73 to the Surprise Lakes area. From Trout Lake, go

NW on N88, NW on 819, then S on 123 to the Surprise Lakes. Surprise Lakes is the hub of the area and offers wonderful camping when the Indians are not picking huckleberries in August and September. The terrain here includes large huckleberry meadows (maintained by burning), numerous small lakes, and extensive forests typical of the mountain hemlock and silver fir zones. Birds of the meadows and bogs include Hermit Thrush, Mountain Bluebird and Fox and Lincoln's sparrows. Forest birds include Black-backed Woodpecker, Gray and Steller's jays, Mountain and Chestnut-backed chickadees, Townsend's and Hermit warblers and Varied Thrush. Mosquitos can be very bad. Starting in late July, large flocks of sparrows, warblers and other small passerines can be found around the meadows; Nashville Warblers are common. Based on habitat availability, Great Gray Owl should be a possibility in this area. Many opportunities exist for walking. The Pacific Crest trail leads S from Surprise Lakes through some of the most beautiful parts of Indian Heaven. The trail can also be reached from the Thomas Lakes area. Go SW on N73 from Surprise Lakes, then 3 miles S on N605 to Thomas Lakes trailhead which leads E for 2.5 miles to the crest trail in the heart of Indian Heaven. Other good trails take off from N73D (not shown on the FS map) two miles W of Surprise Lakes on N73. This high point on the plateau has good views of the surrounding country.

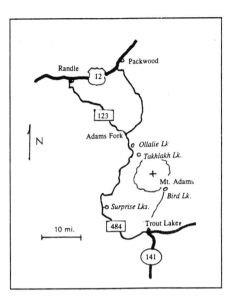

**Bird Creek Meadows** and **Bird Lake** - On the Yakima Indian Nation lands, near timberline on the SE slopes of Mt. Adams, there are beautiful displays of wildflowers in the subalpine and alpine meadows. Go N from Trout Lake on N80, right on N17 for 2.4 miles, then NE on N700 for 4.8 miles, then N on N80 (again!). It is 7.2 miles to Mirror Lake and another 3 to Bird Creek Meadows over a moderately bumpy dirt road (a large trailer might not make it). There is a fee for camping here. Several trails leading to the mountain meadows from here join the round-the-mountain trail, portions of which are particularly worth hiking. Birds include Steller's and Gray jays, Clark's Nutcracker, Mountain Chickadee, Hermit Thrush, Townsend's Solitaire, Cassin's Finch and flocks of warblers and sparrows in late summer with many other scattered up-mountain migrants (A House Wren was seen at 6700'!) (EH, BT)

Some of the best birding in the state is in the Columbia River lowlands around Vancouver, with many sloughs, lakes, marshes, brush and farmlands supporting large numbers during all seasons, with winter numbers especially impressive.

S: all year   E: 20-50'
H: SS FW BF RW DG WM ST
Maps: DLA 22:B 2

# Ridgefield

D -7

This is an important migratory bird area along the Columbia River dikes, with open oak woodlands and ponds where many birds are possible. In addition such species as Wood Ducks, seasonal waterfowl and hawks, Scrub Jays are found here. This latter species is known to range the lowland Garry oak habitat to Longview, at least, and reports of Scrub Jays elsewhere would be welcomed. One entrance to the Ridgefield NWR is via road about 0.5 mile north of Ridgefield on Main St. The refuge is along the river, below the town. Park above the railroad tracks and walk down hill and to the N. Solitary Sandpipers are regular fall migrants, stopping at secluded ponds on the refuge. Interesting passerine migrants are likely in the oak habitats, too. Just S of Ridgefield on S 9th St a sign marks the southern entrance to the refuge. You can follow the narrow, one-lane road down the hill and across the railroad tracks. This road allows in-car birding until it ends at a large dike at the W side of the refuge. Between early October-March, larger numbers of Sandhill Cranes can usually be seen here than anywhere else in Washington. If you have not seen them by the time you reach the dike, scan the fields on the refuge from the top of the dike, and also check the channel and Bachelor Island, W of the refuge. Bald Eagles may be seen in winter, along with perhaps 1000-2000 Tundra Swans and many thousands of Canada Geese. The world's entire

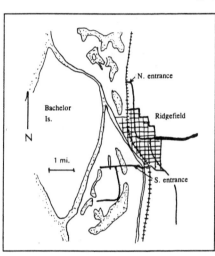

population of the Dusky subspecies of the Canada Goose winters in this section of the Columbia River valley and adjacent Willamette River valleys. White-fronted and Snow geese can be seen in smaller numbers during migration. Large numbers of dabbling ducks including Mallards, Northern Pintails and wigeon, winter here also. White-throated Sparrows and Harris' Sparrows, Say's Phoebe and Stilt Sandpipers have also occurred. See D-8 (Vancouver, below). (G&WH, EH, JS, TW, GW)

S: all year  E: 50'
H: FW BF WM ST FL
Maps: DLA 22:C-D 2-4

Vancouver Lake is west of the city, with a number of nearby small lakes, potholes, and sloughs between the farm fields and rows of trees which all provide good habitat. Large numbers of dabbling ducks and Canada Geese winter here, and Sandhill Cranes may be seen in the fields. Many raptors and passerines are possible. Yellow-headed Blackbirds have been reported nesting here in recent years. The area is reached from Vancouver via W Fourth Plain Blvd and then Lower River Rd past the aluminum plant and other major industrial activities. Signs mark the parking lot. Following the road W and N from Vancouver Lake provides access to more lakes, brush, fields and Columbia River shoreline. During fish runs, thousands of gulls feed along the river; the largest concentrations of Herring Gulls known for Washington are seen here in early spring. A Great Blue Heron rookery with several hundred nests is northwest of the lake. Ridgefield NWR is to the north of this area and birds cross the river between these Washington areas and the Sauvie Island in Oregon. There is great potential for careful, thorough birding here. If you plan to be birding here during the hunting season, check to see on what days hunting is permitted and avoid those days. Fruit Valley Rd, which goes N from Fourth Plain Blvd just W of Vancouver, goes to Ridgefield (D-4). About 1.5 miles N from Fourth Plain Blvd on Fruit Valley Rd is a railroad track crossing and an old burnt railroad bridge. Scrub Jay, Anna's Hummingbird and many other species may be encountered by walking E along these tracks up Burnt Bridge Canyon for several hundred yards. Lesser Goldfinches have been seen about 3 miles E of Pearson Airport in S Vancouver. The distribution of this species in the state is poorly known and sightings should be reported to the Washington Records Committee and American Birds regional editor. (EH, TW, GW)

S: all year    E: 50'
H: FW RW WM
Map: DLA 23:D 6-8

The Steigerwald Lake NWR area of open fields and marshes located near milepost 18 of SR 14 at the western end of the Columbia River Gorge attracts a wide variety of waterfowl and migrants. Wintering raptors include Bald Eagles, Northern Harriers, Red-tailed and Rough-legged hawks. Tundra Swans, Canada Geese, dabbling and diving ducks are present but difficult to see from the highway. The best viewing spot for these birds is the Washougal sewage lagoons at milepost 18.5 on SR 14. Every winter Redheads, Canvasbacks and both species of goldeneyes can be found here. The dike between the refuge and the Columbia River provides a three-mile walking trail with views of birds on both the river and the refuge. Just offshore is Reed Island, an undeveloped state park with a heron rookery. Breeding species here are American Bittern, Green-backed Heron, Wood Duck, Northern Harrier, Virginia Rail, Sora, Purple Martin and Yellow-headed Blackbird. Due to the near-sea level passage through the Cascades, birds that are not normally found on the west side have been located here.

Among these have been White-faced Ibis, Prairie Falcon, Wilson's Phalarope, Acorn Woodpecker, Say's Phoebe and Western Kingbird. The refuge is in the process of being restored with the wetlands being re-established, the fish runs in Gibbons Creek restored, and a visitors' center and public access is in the planning stage. (WC)

S: October - May     E: 100'
H: FW
Map: DLA 24-25:C 1-5

# Columbia Gorge

D - 10

A number of areas reached via SR 14 along the Columbia River offer access to wintering waterfowl flocks and other species at other seasons. (See also Klickitat County area F - 16.)

**Rock Creek Lake,** at milepost 44, is an impoundment at the western edge of the city of Stevenson and provides a sheltered area for waterfowl. Wigeon, goldeneyes, mergansers, Redheads and Canvasbacks are joined by loons and grebes. A male Smew was found here and seen at other locations nearby during one recent winter. The islands in the lake are used for nesting by Canada Geese and the large snag on one of the islands should be checked for Bald Eagles in the winter and Ospreys during the summer. While there is access all around this small body of water the best viewing is from SR 14 and the two small peninsulas that extend ino the lake from the highway. Be sure to check the Columbia River from the railroad tracks; diving ducks congregate around the island there.

**Home Valley Park** is between SR 14 mileposts 51 and 52. The small county park at the confluence of the Wind River and the Columbia is used extensively by sailboarders and ballplayers during warm weather. In spring migration the willows around the small pond W of the park are good for passerines. In May and June, Harlequin Ducks can occasionally be found at the mouth of the Wind River - they nest along the upper river and its tributaries.
The large bay E of the park holds diving ducks in the fall and winter. These are best observed from the highway shoulder.

**Dog Mountain Trailhead,** at milepost 53.8, offers a good concentration of diving ducks inthe bay. Park in the trailhead parking lot and cross the highway to scan the rafts of scaup and Ring-necked Ducks for Greater Scaup, Redheads and Canvasbacks. In the spring the trail up Dog Mountain (to 3000') goes through one of the most spectacular wildflower displays in the Gorge. Watch, however, for rattlesnakes.

**Drano Lake** is an impoundment at the mouth of the Little White Salmon River, milepost 57, offering a wind-sheltered haven for large rafts of ducks. Wigeon, Gadwalls, Buffleheads, Ring-necked Ducks and Scaup are present and Redhead and Canvasback should be looked for. The road along the western shore that leads to the fish hatchery has numerous pulloffs from which you scan the lake. The upper arm near the hatchery attracts Common and Hooded mergansers as well as both goldeneyes.

On SR 14 just E of the bridge, park near the boat launch and climb to the top of the railroad tracks to check for flocks of diving ducks in the Columbia River. (WC)

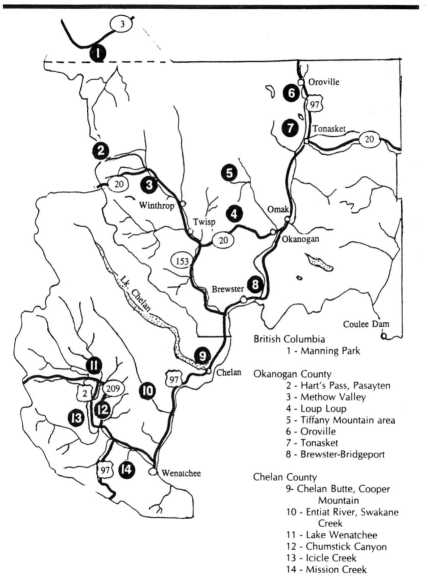

British Columbia
    1 - Manning Park

Okanogan County
    2 - Hart's Pass, Pasayten
    3 - Methow Valley
    4 - Loup Loup
    5 - Tiffany Mountain area
    6 - Oroville
    7 - Tonasket
    8 - Brewster-Bridgeport

Chelan County
    9- Chelan Butte, Cooper
        Mountain
    10 - Entiat River, Swakane
        Creek
    11 - Lake Wenatchee
    12 - Chumstick Canyon
    13 - Icicle Creek
    14 - Mission Creek

103

Birds of the high mountains are found in several accessible locations in northern Washington and just across the border in British Columbia. Highways and roads attain several thousand feet elevation and trails take off from these to lead to points above treeline to meadows and snowfields.

S: May-Oct    E: 3000-6000'
H: FW WC DC RW WM ST
Map: British Columbia, park

# Manning Park

E - 1

At Manning Park, Spruce Grouse, Three-toed woodpecker, Boreal Chickadee, Pine Grosbeak, Mountain Bluebird, Clark's Nutcracker are among the highlights of visits in summer, which is when most birding is done at this altitude. Go E from Hope, B.C., on Highway 3 ("Hope-Princeton Highway"). The park headquarters and interpretive center are about 6 to 7 miles E of Allison Pass. Obtain a map and birding information there.

At a major intersection at Manning Park Lodge, about 1 mile W of headquarters, one road goes 1.5 miles W to **Lightning Lake,** where the Three-toed Woodpecker is resident in the spruce stands. Look for them at Spruce Bay Beach parking lot trailhead, along with Boreal Chickadees. Spruce Grouse have been found in the parking lot. The woodpeckers have also been found in the area of the Lookout, reached by the road going uphill right across the highway from the lodge, and near the Beaver Pond, a nature area about a mile E of the lodge on Highway 3. The **Beaver Pond** often has a

good variety of species. The Black-backed Woodpecker has been reported along Cambie Creek Trail, about 4 to 5 miles W (uphill) from the lodge. It is uncommon at best and certainly difficult to find.

The **Windy Joe Mountain** trail is a good trail for birding. Spruce Grouse and Boreal Chickadees have been seen, the latter also at Lightning Lake, and many other places. Park naturalists say that Mountain, Boreal, Chestnut-backed and Black-capped is the order of chickadee abundance at Manning. Hawk Owls were found nesting recently near Buckhorn Campground in alpine meadows several miles uphill from the Lookout.

Manning Park has several fine campgrounds and the lodge. A large forest fire "burn" W of Allison Pass shows the devastation caused by a forest fire and the long time required for recovery from such a catastrophe. The site of tremendous earth-slide between Manning Park and Hope is another worthwhile stop. (TW, GW)

## Hart's Pass, Pasayten

S: June-Sept  E: 4000-7000'
H: WC DC RW WM
Maps: DLA 112: B-C 2-4

E - 2

This rugged wilderness area is explored by few birders as yet but has interest and attraction to those looking for birds of the northern mountains which are infrequently if ever seen further south. This vast area lies E of the Ross Lake National Recreation Area, N of Hart's Pass, and includes the extreme NW corner of Okanogan County. While Ross Lake access is possible on the W side, primary access and interest lies in the central area reached through Mazama, 75 miles E of Marblemount on the Hwy 20.

**Hart's Pass.** From Mazama on SR 20, NW of Twisp, cross over the N bank of the Methow River and follow the road for about 20 miles to Hart's Pass. The road becomes a steep dirt road that is cut into the side of the mountain. In the last 5 miles it is wise for the driver to keep his or her eyes on the road and let someone else do the bird-watching. Two campgrounds are in the area, one right at Hart's Pass. One can in go four directions by car and in any direction by foot from the pass. The road to the right at the pass leads to Slate Mt.lookout and is an especially interesting hike or drive. The Cascade Crest Trail runs through Hart's Pass. Some of the birds possible include: Three-toed Woodpecker, Hermit Thrush, Fox Sparrow, Mountain Bluebird, Cassin's Finch, the Alaska subspecies of the White-crowned Sparrow and two swifts. Scenery and wildflowers are rewarding, too.

Mid-June is a very good time, since many birds are singing then. Hiking 12-16 miles into the Pasayten Wilderness Area may produce species like White-tailed Ptarmigan,

Boreal Owl, Black-backed Woodpecker, (Three-toed is much more common), Boreal Chickadee, Bohemian Waxwing, White-winged Crossbill. This trail is usually open only from mid-August through early October.

**Pasayten.** About three miles up this road, a locked gate signifies the start of birding on foot. The area up this trail, West Fork Pasayten River Trail, has been one of the state's most dependable for White-tailed Ptarmigan and Boreal Chickadee in recent years. Just past the gate look for the road to Slate Mtn Lookout - the ptarmigan have been seen here, and in fact in the parking lot itself and on the ridge to the E. The West Fork trail, about 500' from the parking lot, starts very steeply and you may well encounter snowfields. The trail then descends into the valley where Three-toed Woodpeckers, Boreal Chickadees and Spruce Grouse have been seen. Bohemian Waxwings, White-winged Crossbills and other more common "mountain" species occur here, too, and Spotted Owls should be watched for. The hike from the parking lot to Holden Creek (about as far as you may have to go for the special birds of the area) is about 8 miles, so overnight camping may be advisable. For backpacking birders this area holds great potential. As in most mountain and back-country areas, topographic maps are desirable. Check in at the ranger station, just N of the campground, for trail conditions and information on where to park your car, and back-country permits if they are required. (JD, G&WH, EH)

From the northern Cascades, the Methow River descends alongside SR 20 through pine forests, orchards, dry grassy areas and desert plants to the Columbia River at Pateros and offers scenery and many interesting birds. Birding between Pateros and Winthrop is productive, especially in the early morning in spring (and from roads on the opposite side of the Methow River from SR 153 and 20). About 65 species of breeding birds can be noted in mid-June, including those from a wide variety of habitats - ponderosa pine forest, Douglas fir forest (wetter and shadier), aspen swamp, cottonwoods, thickets, patches of sagebrush and farmlands. Many of the characteristic birds of open farmland - crows, magpies, swallows, kingbirds, Killdeers, meadowlarks and blackbirds - are abundant. Several species of "eastern affinity" - Eastern Kingbird, Veery, Gray Catbird, Red-eyed Vireo - are common in the deciduous forests, American Redstarts are found in cottonwoods, and typical western species - Western Wood-Pewee, Yellow-rumped Warbler, Cassin's Finch - can be found in the pines. Lewis' Woodpecker can be seen flycatching from the pines on the cliffs high over the valley or feeding on fence posts next to the road. With similar silhouette, Clark's Nutcracker inhabits the same rocky cliffs, a very different habitat from its usual timberline haunts in the high Cascades. Ruffed, Blue and Spruce grouse and Turkeys are reported resident in the **Methow WRA** which is in the high country E of Winthrop and Twisp. Access is via a road at the N end of Pearrygin Lake, two roads from the road along the E side of the Methow River and one about 2 miles up WA 20, E of the junction with WA 153. One mile up the S side of the river from Pateros, then 2 miles up hill is **Alta Lake State Park.** This is a delightful camping and fishing spot, but very crowded at times. The pine forest and other habitats yield a good representative bird list and the trail up from the park campground yields more. Species like Chukar, Rock Dove (nesting), Poorwill, White-throated Swift, Calliope Hummingbird, Western Wood-Pewee, Olive-sided Flycatcher, Clark's Nutcracker, Mountain Chickadee, Red-breasted Nuthatch, Gray Catbird (found in riparian growth near the end of the lake), Western Bluebird, Nashville Warbler, Western Tanager, Black-headed Grosbeak, Cassin's Finch and many others are found in the park in summer. (DP, TW)

The mountainous area between the Methow and Okanogan rivers has dry pine forests, wet fir stands, aspen groves and meadows which support bird populations of many species. Two such areas are Loup Loup and Tiffany Mountain.

# Loup Loup

S: May-July  E: 2300-5500'
H: DC BF RW WM ST
Maps: DLA 100:A 1

E - 4

Turn off SR 20 at the "Starvation Mountain Rd", about 11 miles E of Twisp. Loup Loup campground, in the Okanogan NF, is about 0.7 mile up this graded FS road which leads through varied mountain forest habitats to Conconully where there is a state park and fishing lake. Birding at Loup Loup especially good in May and June. Nights can be cold, but the camping area is usually uncrowded at this time. Interesting pine forest species including Williamson's Sapsucker, Great Horned and Barred owls, N. Pygmy-Owls, Hammond's and Olive-sided flycatchers, Western Wood-Pewee, Ruby-crowned Kinglet, Mountain Chickadee, Western Tanager, Townsend's and Yellow-rumped warblers, Cassin's Finch and Red Crossbill nest in and around the campground.

A small wet meadow adds many other species. Snowshoe hares, flying squirrels and black bears are among the mammals observed here. The road uphill climbs to other habitats and stops and side hikes may produce many other species like Goshawk, Calliope Hummingbird, Red-naped Sapsucker, Clark's Nutcracker, Pygmy Nuthatch, Townsend's Solitaire and bluebirds. From Conconully, roads go to US 97, or **Blue Lake** and the **Sinlahekin WRA** which includes a beautiful valley that is range for introduced Turkeys, bighorn sheep and many other animals. And you can go to Tiffany Mountain (E-5). You can also continue N to Loomis, Chopaka or Nighthawk, then to Canada or back to Oroville. (TW)

# Tiffany Mountain area

S: June-October  E: 4500-8400'
H: WC DC WM
Maps: DLA 114:D 1-2

E - 5

The crest of the Okanogan Highlands W of the Okanogan River can be productive for boreal species. A map of the Okanogan NF, obtainable at Forest Service headquarters in Okanogan, is useful to find one's way amongst the maze of logging roads. One approach is via **Conconully Lake** 15 miles NW of Okanogan. Forest birds typical of the Ponderosa pine belt are fairly common here, including N. Pygmy Owl, White-headed Woodpecker, all three nuthatches, Cassin's

Finch and Evening Grosbeak. Red-necked Grebes have nested recently on the lake and other waterfowl and shorebirds are common in season. From the park in Conconully, take Forest Rd 37 W to the crest at 6500' at Old Baldy Pass, then W down into spruce and fir forests and bearing N on Forest Service Rd 39 to **Roger Lake**. Rd 37 continues into Winthrop from here. Although logging will change the birding possibilities, the Roger Lake area has been set aside as a Natural

Area, as has Tiffany Mtn proper. There, Spruce Grouse, Three-toed Woodpeckers and Boreal Chickadees are regular. Boreal Owls may be resident here in very small numbers and along Rd 39 N to the Long Swamp area.

Just N of Roger Lake, a trail climbs Freezeout Ridge to **Tiffany Mtn,** where extensive "continental" or Rocky Mountain-type alpine grasslands occur. Blue Grouse are fairly common on this ridge to timberline as on many of the south-facing treeless "balds" in the region, and Clark's Nutcrackers are conspicuous amongst the many whitebark pines. White-tailed Ptarmigan are scarce here above treeline, but occasionally noted. The fall raptor migration can often be exciting from these slopes and in October a magnificent display of color from the alpine larch is worth the hike alone. At Tiffany Spring Campground another trail climbs past beautiful Tiffany Lake to Middle Tiffany Mountain. Possibilities there may be as for Tiffany Mountain but more raptors have been noted. North from the Tiffany Mtn area, Rd 39

traverses the **"Meadows" area,** threatened by logging, and is prime habitat for some of the few remaining lynx in Washington. The entire area is good for Northern Goshawk, Spruce Grouse and Boreal Chickadees. White- winged Crossbills are irregularly common. Irruptions from Canada occur at unpredictable intervals. Invasion years see an influx beginning in July and lasting through the following winter. Scattered records in non-invasion years hint there may be a very small resident population.

At the north end of the roaded complex, **Long Swamp** boasts many Ruby-crowned Kinglets and Lincoln's Sparrows and some nesting waterfowl. The Toats Coulee Rd from Long Swamp is another approach to the area.

Another approach is north from **Salmon Meadows** which is reached by continuing N out of Conconully. The area around Salmon Meadows Campground contains mixed-conifer habitats and openings which harbor many of the breeding birds of this zone, including Pileated Woodpecker. (AS)

---

S: May-July    E: 1000'
H: DG FL
Maps: DLA 115:B 5

# Oroville

E - 6

Along the W side of the Okanogan River, about 7.2-7.5 miles S of Oroville, there are several extensive hayfields where Bobolinks are present during the nesting season. These colonies have been known for several years, and birds were present in 1981. Other species, including Grasshopper Sparrows,

occur along this road. In winter there are flocks of Bohemian Waxwings in the orchards, flocks of Common Redpolls are present in some years, and Sharp-tailed Grouse may be found feeding on buds in leafless shrubs along watercourses through open country. (EH, DP, TW).

Between the Okanogan River and timberline are irrigated orchard, farmland and riparian growth, desert shrub and grassland which present a corresponding variety of birds and other animals, including many characteristic of the high plateaus now being lost to change. Two examples follow.

# Tonasket

S: April-July   E: 1000-1600'
H: FW DG WM SD
Maps: DLA 114-115:C 4

E - 7

One of many beautiful grassland habitats found in the Okanogan Valley slopes is W of Tonasket. Cross the Okanogan River at Tonasket to the W side, go S for about 0.6 mile and turn right, up hill. At about 2.5 miles, bear straight ahead (not left to Aeneas Lake) and continue about 1.5 miles farther to a junction and take the **"Horse Springs Coulee Rd"** on the right for about 3 miles and pass an old concrete foundation, and turn right at an old car onto the less-developed road. These quiet, open, cattle country grasslands feature beautiful scenery and wild flowers in the spring. The road going straight ahead (W) at the "old-car junction" leads to Spectacle Lake, one of many popular fishing spots in the area. The cattle road you're on wanders through the grasslands to small lakes and marshy areas. Grasshopper Sparrows, Horned Larks and Long-billed Curlews are found here, along with many other birds. **Aeneas Lake,** just S of the first turnoff (above), is a reservoir and heavily used fishing spot which has interesting waterbirds on occasion. (TW)

# Brewster-Bridgeport

S: April-June   E: 1000-2000'
H: FW DC RW DG SD ST FL
Maps: DLA 100:C-D 2-3

E - 8

The grassland and sagebrush areas around Brewster offer a good variety of nesting birds. Bank Swallows nest in road cuts and washes, often in very large colonies. Mourning Doves, kingbirds and orioles abound. Black-chinned Hummingbirds have been found in the country N of Brewster. **Note:** the site in this area, **Brewster Flats,** mentioned in previous editions as the space satellite communications site may not be open to birders. Searching other areas of sagebrush flats may turn up Horned Larks, Sage Thrashers, and Lark, Brewer's and Grasshopper sparrows in the spring. About 3 miles E of Brewster is the junction of the Okanogan and Columbia rivers. On the flats there are many birds, including Burrowing Owls, magpies, kingbirds and swallows. Many species of waterfowl, some grebes, gulls and Forster's Terns may be found along the river in the area of **Old Fort Okanogan.** The Fort Okanogan Memorial Cemetery is on the E side of the Okanogan River on US 97, 1.5 miles N of the bridge at Monse. Opposite the cemetery, the dirt **Soap Lake Rd** climbs the hill on the Colville Indian Reservation and leads through good birding habitats. The bunchgrass at the top of the hill, 1 mile from 97, is Grasshopper Sparrow habitat. About a mile further, look for

Long-billed Curlews. Sharp-tailed Grouse, hawks, Golden Eagles, Burrowing Owls and various sagebrush-grassland passerines are likely. The road eventually leads to Little Soap Lake (nesting ducks) and Soap Lake (alkaline and not too birdy, but sometimes Wilson's Phalaropes). The road up the hill from the E end of the Monse bridge leads to ponds and lakes on the plateau where nesting teal of 3 species and other puddle ducks, grebes, Wilson's Phalaropes and other birds may be seen. Nine miles up the

Columbia River just E of Chief Joseph Dam, is **Bridgeport State Park.** A walk up the hill from the campground should produce Rock Wrens, Western Kingbirds, Northern Orioles, Sage Thrashers, Lark Sparrows and other birds. During winter, flocks of Bohemian Waxwings are encountered in this general area, and Common Redpolls also may occur in some years. The open water at the confluence of the Okanogan and Columbia rivers attracts large concentrations of waterfowl and Bald Eagles. (HS, TW, GW)

S: April-July   E: 1200-3900'
H: DC DG ST
Maps: DLA 83:A-B 8; 84:B 1

# Chelan Butte, Cooper Mountain

E - 9

Immediately after passing the SW city limits of Chelan on SR 97, watch for a sign on the right, indicating the road to **Chelan Butte Lookout.** The road is paved for only a short distance and then changes to dirt; dusty in spring and summer, slick and often impassable after a rain, closed by snow in winter. The road is steep and rough in places, but the deciduous thickets, ponderosa pines and grassy hillsides with some sage all attract interesting birds. Park where there is room and walk all over the hillsides, particularly near the summit, but in rocky areas watch out for rattlesnakes. Views of Lake Chelan, the Columbia River, and the surrounding regions are impressive. In spring and summer look for Swainson's Hawk, Golden Eagle, California Quail, White-throated Swift, Lewis' Woodpecker, White-headed Woodpecker, both Eastern and Western kingbirds, Say's Phoebe, Clark's Nutcracker, all three nuthatches, Gray Catbird and many others. Fall and winter seasons add other possibilities, including accipiters, Pygmy-Owl and Pine Grosbeak.

For an alternative spot, one can continue through the town of Chelan to the N shore of the lake (Highway 150). A mile or so after leaving Chelan watch for a sign on the right for **Cooper Mountain.** By following this road, which is an easier grade than the butte road, particularly the paved, lower reaches, you can see many of the birds also found on Chelan Butte. Beyond the local ski area, the road follows a small stream within a wooded gully where N. Pygmy-Owls, catbirds and many other birds have been found. After leaving the stream, the road climbs toward the summit of Cooper Mtn. Three-toed Woodpeckers have been found here in the burned-over area. The adventuresome can follow the road over the ridge and into the Methow River valley.

In addition to good local birding areas noted below, boat service from Chelan allows access to forest and recreation areas at the head of the lake and to trails crossing the northern Cascade mountains. (BW, TW)

S: May-June E: 700-1000'
H: FW DC BF RW DG WM ST FL
Maps: DLA 83:B-D 5-7

About 16 miles N of Wenatchee on US 97, turn W and go up the **Entiat River Valley.** For about 20 miles along the river there is open farmland, orchards, higher open mountains, forested hills, some wet meadows and boggy areas. Further along, there are forested and rocky areas and numerous logging roads into the small side canyons. Several forest camps are located along the river. The mountainsides have had several extensive forest fires in recent years, and woodpecker activity on the mountain slopes should be widespread. The road goes up the valley for miles, but detours and closures due to logging and fire control are possible. Many species are seen in the area, including Golden Eagle, Dipper, Yellow-breasted Chat, Hermit Thrush, Veery, Mountain Bluebird, Gray Jay, Clark's

# Entiat River, Swakane Creek

E - 10

Nutcracker, three-toed woodpeckers, White-headed Woodpecker, sapsuckers, Calliope Hummingbird and Chukar. The Entiat WRA lies to the N of the river and, with the adjoining Chelan Butte WRA, includes almost the entire uplands area W of the Columbia River from Entiat to Lake Chelan, to the ridge divide above the river drainage.

About 6 miles N of the junction of US 2 and 97 N of Wenatchee there is a road going W up **Swakane Creek.** Within 1-2 miles the road enters the Swakane WRA, another area important for hunting in the fall but also featuring many of the birds of the Entiat area and other "east slope" sites. Wildflowers in these areas support many butterflies. (WD, TW)

---

S: May-July E: 2000-4000'
H: FW WC DC RW ST
Maps: DLA 82:B 2-3

Birding areas along the east slope of the Cascades can be reached via several roads off US 2, the Stevens Pass highway. Spring and early summer sunshine and the birds attract visitors from west of the mountains. Leave Hwy US 2 at Coles Corner, 16 miles W of Leavenworth, drive approximately 5 miles to Lake Wenatchee. Two rivers feed this resort lake - the Little Wenatchee and the White. You can drive up either river for about 10 miles and there are forest service camping areas on both. There is camping also at Lake Wenatchee SP. The area is mostly forested, with some clearings in the valleys. Birds here include Golden Eagle, Common Merganser, Osprey, Ruffed

# Lake Wenatchee area

E - 11

Grouse, Chukar, Black Swift, Vaux's Swift, Calliope Hummingbird, White-headed Woodpecker, Red-naped Sapsucker. Hammond's, Willow and Pacific Slope flycatchers, Western Wood-Pewee, Olive-sided Flycatcher, Gray and Steller's jays, Black-billed Magpie, Common Raven, Clark's Nutcracker, Black- capped, Mountain and Chestnut-backed chickadees, Red-breasted and White-breasted nuthatches, Dipper, Veery, Western and Mountain bluebirds, Townsend's Solitaire, Nashville, Townsend's and MacGillivray's warblers, Yellow-breasted Chat, Western Tanager, Purple and Cassin's finches, Lazuli Bunting and Red Crossbill are here, too. (WD)

S: April-June  E: 1200-1800'
H: FW DC BF RW ST
Maps: DLA 82:B-D 2-3

# Chumstick Canyon

E - 12

This route is along SR 209 for about 16 miles between Plain and Leavenworth and offers a birding alternative to the heavy traffic of US 2, over a stretch more or less paralleling that busy highway (See C-4, Tumwater NF campground). By taking some additional time you can enjoy the scenic Chumstick River canyon, stop at likely birding spots, and connect again with US

2 at either Leavenworth or near Lake Wenatchee at Coles Corner. Spring through summer is best. Species possible include Calliope Hummingbird, House Wren, Mountain and Western bluebirds, a good number of wood warblers including Nashville and Yellow-breasted Chat, and Gray Catbird, Veery, Cassin's Finch and Lazuli Bunting. (FR)

---

S: May-July  E: 2000-2800'
H: FW DC BF RW ST
Maps: DLA 82:D 1-3

# Icicle Creek

E - 13

This area is good for a wide variety of east-slope species (see E-12, above, but don't expect Chukar) within a concentrated area. Leave US 2 W of Leavenworth, at the mouth of Tumwater Canyon. The well-marked road crosses the Wenatchee River, goes past the

Fish Hatchery and Camp Field roads, and continues up the Icicle River. Blacktop ends after about 10 miles, but birding continues good. Harlequins have been seen here in May. Minimum facilities are available at several FS campgrounds along the river. (BJ)

---

S: May-July  E: 1500-3400'
H: FW DC BF RW ST FL
Maps: DLA 66-67:A-B 4-5

# Mission Creek

E - 14

Leave US 2 at either bridge entering Cashmere, follow either Cottage Ave or Division St until they meet at a blinking light, follow Division St over railroad tracks about 0.5 mile and turn left onto Mission Creek Rd, which runs approximately 25 miles along Mission Creek, through orchards

and meadows bordered by open and forested mountains into a long valley gradually rising to the top and then down into #2 canyon into Wenatchee. Bird species are similar to the east-slope areas described above. (WD)

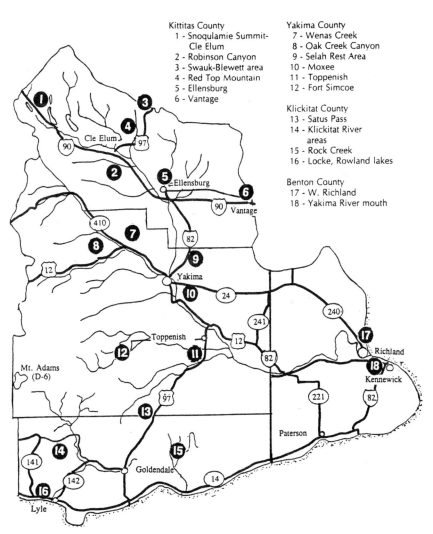

Kittitas County
1 - Snoqulamie Summit-
    Cle Elum
2 - Robinson Canyon
3 - Swauk-Blewett area
4 - Red Top Mountain
5 - Ellensburg
6 - Vantage

Yakima County
7 - Wenas Creek
8 - Oak Creek Canyon
9 - Selah Rest Area
10 - Moxee
11 - Toppenish
12 - Fort Simcoe

Klickitat County
13 - Satus Pass
14 - Klickitat River
     areas
15 - Rock Creek
16 - Locke, Rowland lakes

Benton County
17 - W. Richland
18 - Yakima River mouth

S: May-Oct    E: 2000-3000'
H: FW WC DC RW WM
Maps: DLA 65:A-C 5-8; 66:C-D 1-2

# Snoqualmie Pass - Cle Elum

F - 1

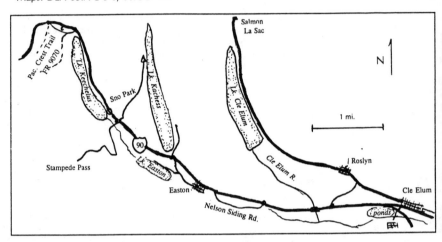

Snoqualmie Pass, the most travelled and accessible mountain pass in the Cascades, has good birding spots east of the summit and along the Yakima River paralleling I-90. **Snoqualmie summit,** just over 3000' elevation, is not high enough for subalpine habitats, but the combination of forests, fake "meadows" of ski slopes and some clearcuts has produced varied habitats. The summit area can be reached from any of three I-90 exits. The westernmost is W Summit Dr (exit 52). By turning N (under I-90 if coming from the W) you will come to a turnoff within 200' to a Pacific Crest Trail parking lot. The trail heads N up Commonwealth Creek Basin, mostly through old silver-fir forest, with Hermit Thrushes, kinglets and other forest birds. To the S, the trail crosses ski areas with birds like MacGillivray's Warblers and Lincoln's Sparrows. The road rejoins I-90 at Hyak (exit 54). Turn in to the Hyak ski resort parking lot and cross it an angle to the SE. In 0.25 mile it turns right and passes the Hyak sewage ponds, which can harbor

ducks and occasional shorebirds. Past the sewage plant you link up with FS Rd 9070, which can be followed for 4 miles to the Twin Lks Trail trailhead. The trail ascends for about 1 mile through an old clearcut excellent for hummingbirds and warblers, then old forest to a subalpine lake complete with Dipper.

I-90's descent to the E passes Hyak and along **Lake Keechelus.** The rest stop/snow park just past the lower end of the lake is good for birds like Gray Jay, Mountain Chickadee, Fox Sparrow and Red Crossbills. Williamson's Sapsuckers have been seen here. Next stop is exit 62, for Lake Kachess/Stampede Pass. A road to the N goes along **Lake Kachess** to a FS campground, good for Gray Jays and Osprey, and other typical montane birds.

Exit 70 leads to a state park on the N shore of **Lake Easton,** which may have loons and/or mergansers. The old road SE past the

114

park entrance leads to an old bridge over the Yakima which is a good place to look for Dippers. The road rejoins I-90 in Easton. Look for Mountain Bluebirds along the tracks at the SE end of town and along Nelson Siding Rd, which parallels I-90 to the S just beyond Easton. Lake Kachess dam, N from the exit 70, can feature Ospreys.

After entering Ponderosa pines you reach the Roslyn exit (80), and Mountain Chickadee, Nashville Warbler, Cassin's Finch and Chipping Sparrow are along the road. By continuing through Roslyn you can bird the shoreline of the easternmost reservoir, **Lake Cle Elum.** From exit 80 you reach Roslyn and Salmon La Sac via the Bullfrog Rd. Go N over the freeway about 0.4 mile to the **Cle Elum River.** About 100 yds E of the bridge there is a short, paved dead-end road back to the river. Red-eyed, Solitary and Warbling vireos and Veeries are regular here in summer. An American Redstart stayed here one season and a small colony of Bushtits has been discovered at the edges of the marsh under the powerline just N of the road. The pine flats nearby are riddled with ORV trails and are good for Purple Finch (with Cassin's Finch an occasional visitor), Chipping Sparrow and Western Tanager. Continue on Bullfrog Rd 2.5 miles to its intersection with Hwy 903. Go left (N) here for excellent campsites at Salmon La Sac and Cooper Lake and access to the high country hiking trails of the Alpine Lakes Wilderness.

Go right 2 miles into Cle Elum. Go W a few blocks on First St and just past the railroad tracks on the W edge of town make a sharp turn S into South Cle Elum. Go under the

freeway and immediately turn right (W) onto a dirt road beside the **railroad ponds,** formed as borrow pits for constructing the railroad grade across the floodplain of the Yakima River. The ponds are at the very western edge of Cle Elum and can also be reached by exiting I-90 at exit 84 for Cle Elum. The steep-sided ponds have a good fringe of reeds and sizeable cottonwoods. Ospreys, Wood Ducks, Hooded Mergansers, Eastern Kingbirds, Tree Swallows, catbirds and Nashville Warblers nest here.

In Cle Elum stop at the excellent Cle Elum Bakery on First St and Peoh Ave. Continuing E from Cle Elum the main roads reaches SR 970 to Swauk Pass and Wenatchee from exit 85. About 3 miles E of town scenic Hwy 10 turns off to the right (SE) and follows a winding canyon along the Yakima River. One mile E along Hwy 10 is the **Teanaway River** bridge. A popular rafting put-in spot, it hosts Dippers under the bridge, Veery, Western Tanager, catbird and Nashville warblers and Red-eyed Vireos. Cinnamon Teal and Wood Ducks are regular on the small pond just W of the bridge. Just W of the junction of Hwys 10 and 970, W Masterson Rd goes N 0.7 miles past the fire station to a very productive pond at the junction with Airport Rd. Continue E on Masterson Rd about 4 miles to its bridge over the Teanaway River. "Baltimore" Oriole and many common riparian species have been seen here. Teanaway Rd and the North Fork Teanaway Rd are excellent also, with several good campgrounds, access to excellent hiking trails, and a passable back road up Dickey Creek to Red Top Mtn. (PM, RT)

## Robinson Canyon

S: May-July   E: 2000-4000'
H: FW DC RW WM ST
Maps: DLA 66:D 2-3

F - 2

Leave I-90 via exit 101 at Thorp and go S straight ahead (not taking the road to Ellensburg) for 1.7 miles. Turn right 0.5 mile, left 1 mile, and then right up Robinson

Gulch for about 4 miles. Northern Pygmy-Owls, Flammulated and Saw-whet owls are regular here, and Common Poorwills forage from the road at night.

Robinson Canyon has the same species as the Wenas Creek area. Gray Flycatchers and other birds typical of the ponderosa pine forest and adjacent habitats are here. Birds of higher elevation forests are found NW of Thorp. From the Elk Heights exit, go up the road paralleling I-90 on the SW side - this is the Taneum Creek area, served by Forest Service campsites and trails. Much of this area, S to the Wenas region, lies within the Oak Creek and L.T. Murray WRAs - 200,000 acres. Many back-country drives and hikes are possible here. (DP, TW)

---

S: May-Sept   E: 3500-4100'
H: DC WM ST
Maps: DLA 66:A-C 2-4

## Swauk Pass - Blewett Pass area

F - 3

Forested slopes and meadows up to and around the old Blewett Pass feature a good variety of owls, as well as for birds like Three-toed Woodpecker, Williamson's Sapsucker, Nashville Warbler. Hwy US 97 crosses **Swauk Pass.** About 5.7 miles S of the junction of US 97 and US 2 turn E off 97 onto the Camas Creek Rd (FR 7200) for 1.5 miles to a relatively small burn on the N side of the road. Park at a small pulloff to the left. Black-backed Woodpeckers have nested near this pulloff since the burn occurred. Listen for their quiet tapping. Red-naped Sapsuckers, White-headed and Hairy woodpeckers are here also, as are N. Pygmy Owls, Dusky Flycatchers, Cassin's Finch, Red Crossbills, and many other common east-slope species. About 0.5 mile further up the road to the E is an extensive Camas meadow. Black bear are seen regularly in the area and cougar have been occasional.

You can park and walk roads at the summit or, after checking conditions with the US Forest Service, drive FS roads from here. There are roads (e.g. FR 9716) leading from Swauk Pass to the E and S which to Naneum Meadow (location of a recent Boreal Owl sighting in October) and Haney Meadow a few miles to the N (Three-toed Woodpeckers nest here) and Lion Rock, a few miles S (a hawk-watch overlook on the W rim of Table Mtn). Interesting and easy access south to Ellensburg can be made via Reecer Canyon and Reecer Crk Rd.

The old highway (FR 7320), reached from US 97 about 1 mile SW of Swauk campground or about 7-8 miles N of the Swauk summit, crosses **Blewett Pass.** The area along the road just S of the summit has been quite good for owls in recent years, with Great Horned, Spotted, Saw-whet, Flammulated and and Pygmy-owls all having been found here. A trail connects the Swauk and Blewett pass roads. There has been horrific clearcutting along parts of the Blewett Pass road recently.

There are several NF campgrounds in the area, and near the Swauk campground, for example, there are Veeries, Swainson's and Hermit thrushes in summer. Nashville, Townsend's and MacGillivray's warblers are common. Very large flocks of Evening Grosbeaks and Pine Siskins are often noted in this area.

Just W of the intersection of Hwys 97 and 970 is the extensive Swauk Prairie with many Western and Mountain bluebirds and other grassland species. The entrance to the Hidden Valley Ranch is S off Hwy 970. The ranch hosts Ruffed Grouse, Townsend's Solitaire, Dippers, both bluebirds, three species of Empidonax flycatchers, numerous Rufous and Calliope hummingbirds at several feeders by the lodge windows, and many other forest, grassland and riparian species accessible by trail and horseback. (BJ, PM, AR, TW)

S: June-August  E: 2800-5400'
H: DC WM ST
Map: DLA 66 B 2-3

# Red Top Mountain

Go E from Cle Elm on SR 970 toward
Wenatchee, or W from Ellensburg on SR 97
toward Wenatchee. The two roads intersect
at Swauk Creek. About 6 miles N of this
intersection on SR 97, just past the Mineral
Springs campground and resort, turn W on
an obscurely-marked by well-travelled FS
road along Blue Creek to Red Top Mtn.
Lookout. In about 2 miles turn left (S) at the
only major intersection as the road winds
upward on the E side of a long N-S ridge.

From the parking lot at the end of the road
take the trail about 0.5 mile uphill to the
lookout tower. There is an extensive agate
bed for rockhounds at 0.5 mile further N
along the ridge. Hawk-watching in Sept.-
Oct. here (and at Hart's Pass and Slate Peak,
see E - 2) is as good as can be had in
Washington. Most raptors seen are Cooper's
and Sharp-shins, but Goshawks, both eagles,
Red-tails, Ospreys, Merlins, Turkey Vultures
and Ravens are noted. (PM)

---

S: all year  E: 2000'
H: SD FL
Maps: DLA 50-51:A 3-8; 66:D 4

# Ellensburg

An island in the midst of irrigated farmland,
Ellensburg has many enticing birding areas.
Right at exit 109 from I-90 there is a large
pond behind the Bar 14 restaurant, usually
with several hundred Canada Geese, ducks
of several species, an occasional swan in
winter, and Sandhill Cranes in spring and
fall. S of this exit Main St becomes Canyon
Rd and winds through the Yakima River
Canyon with numerous Bald Eagles present
in winter and several nesting pairs of Golden
Eagles and many other raptors year-round.
The I-82 freeway S over Manastash Ridge
passes several Dept. of Wildlife ponds about
2 miles S of town. Drive-up access (do not
stop on the freeway shoulder) is from No. 6
Rd along the E edge of the ponds reached
from the Thrall exit from I-82. These ponds
are a popular migration stopover with
regular occurrences of scoters and
Oldsquaws en route to the ocean. One can
walk the east bank for birds of scrub and
marsh. Back in Eilensburg, go N 0.5 mile
from exit 109 and turn W at McDonalds
onto Damman Rd. A few yards before the

bridge over the Yakima River turn N into
Riverside Park. A mile of flat, well-kept trail
parallels the river through a thick stand of
cottonwoods. House Wrens, Downy
Woodpeckers and Robins are numerous,
with Dipper and Spotted Sandpiper in the
river, Osprey overhead (Dept. of Wildlife
nest platforms are nearby), and Warbling
Vireo, Yellow Warbler and the regular
species of riparian woodland are present in
season.

From December through February a flock of
about 200 Bohemian Waxwings can be
found E of downtown generally between 1st
and 8th avenues.

North of town in the Ellensburg airport with
resident populations of Gray Partridges and
Short-eared Owls. Take Main St north
through town and go right at a stoplight onto
8th Ave. Past the Central Wash. Univ.
campus, 8th bears left and becomes 10th
Ave. Turn N onto Brick Rd (the turn is
poorly marked, but is between the DQ and

the radio station). After Brick Rd bends sharply to the W, turn N immediately onto Look Rd. Park at the intersection of Look Rd and Brick Mill Rd and cross the green gate onto the unused E end of the airport. The area is presently leased for horse grazing, so do no spook the horses. Walk along the ditches and fencerows back toward the airport and Gray Partridges will flush. Or visit at dawn and hear them calling. Short-eared Owls forage the in area at dusk.

To go W from town take 8th Ave which becomes the Dry Creek Rd and scenic Hwy SR 10 to Cle Elum; to E, 8th Ave becomes the Old Vantage Hwy to the Columbia River. E of town in the spring and summer Long-billed Curlews nest in the irrigated fields, in winter Rough-legged and Red-tailed Hawks are numerous. As the road enters the sagebrush country watch for Prairie Falcons

and stop at places and listen for the long, continuous song of Sage Thrashers and watch for their incredible display flight. There are Mountain Bluebirds, Loggerhead Shrikes, Sage, Vesper, and Brewer's sparrows and meadowlarks present also. Sage Grouse have been seen occasionally. Winds often blow fiercely through this country and can make birding by sight or sound difficult. The Colockum and Quilomene WRAs are N of the road, and worth exploring on their own, and they include diverse habitats, good species like Sage Grouse and Turkey and a great variety of other species. There are also pronghorns, elk, deer, bighorn sheep and many small mammals, and spectacular desert wildflowers in May. The northern part of the WRA can be reached from Kittitas, going N on Rd 81, E on Erickson, or from Malaga on the Columbia River. (PM, DP, AS, TW)

---

S: April-July    E: 500-1000'
H: SD FL
Map: DLA 51:A 8; 52:A 1

# Vantage

F - 6

At Vantage, you can visit the Gingko State Park interpretive center hundreds of feet above the Columbia River. White-throated Swifts may be seen below the cliff. Winds can be terrific here - at Vantage drive-ins your food to be eaten while parked is delivered to you securely wrapped up "to go." On I-90, the fast-traffic alternative freeway to the S of the Old Vantage Hwy (see F-5, above), Sage Thrashers can be heard and observed in season at the westbound rest stop W of Vantage.

South from Vantage, as the road travels between the Columbia River and the base of the rimrock, is an excellent place for Chukars. Often they are seen motionless on a rock beside the road, or clucking to the rest of the covey as they walk through the rocks and sagebrush. About 3 miles S of Vantage is **Wanapum State Park** with a large

Bank Swallow colony near the boat launch. Extensive tree plantings beside the river here have been discovered to be a "vagrant trap" or rest stop for migrants of many species. Further S at a small bridge over an inlet to the W, Getty's Cove, the trees and brush have the same attraction for migrants. From Wanapum SP south over the next 5-6 miles or road there have been scattered pairs of Black-throated Sparrows found every June-July for several years. The light, tinkling song of the Black-throated Sparrow can easily be lost among the ubiquitous Rock Wrens or in the howling wind. Generally the wind is lightest or absent at dawn and increases in intensity as the sun reflected from the bare rock heats the overlying air. Prairie Falcons and Canyon Wrens (and Rock Doves) nest on the cliffs near the railroad bridge, and numerous gulls are often found on the flats below Wanapum Dam. (PM, DP, AS, TW)

Within easy driving distance of the major cities on Puget Sound and one of the first east-slope birding spots to be "discovered" by west-side birders, the Wenas Creek area justifiably remains one of the most popular, varied and productive locations for many species in the state.

S: May-Aug  E: 1500-2500'
H: WC DC RW SD ST
Maps: DLA 50:A-B 1-3

# Wenas Creek

F - 7

Wenas Creek can be reached from either Ellensburg or Yakima (Selah or Naches). From US 97 in Ellensburg go to the end of Main St, just N of I-90. Turn west from Main onto Damman Rd, which bends S and becomes Umtanum Rd. Follow this road over the hills for about 19 miles to where pavement begins. About 0.2 mile farther, turn off on a dirt road to the right (upper the road) that leads off to the NW. At about 2 miles from the end of the pavement take left hand fork ("Dry Creek") to reach the campground and bird sanctuary along the stream. To get to Wenas from White Pass (US 12), drive 1.5 miles from the city limits (stop light) at the W side of Naches to the Allen Rd, turn left. After the first stop sign you are on the Wenas-Naches Rd which climbs over the hills. At the Y in the road, turn left and at the next stop sign, left again onto the Longmire Rd. At 17.5 miles from US 12 you should see a large old stump on the left with a Triple B Ranch sign. Take the upper dirt road. From the S, take the road that goes N through the middle of Selah, continuing to the first stop sign where you take the right fork - the Longmire Rd.

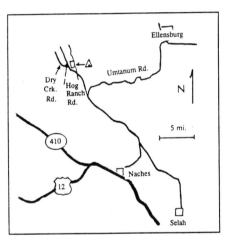

Dense stands of quaking aspen, cottonwoods, and shrubs grow along Wenas Creek, and ponderosa pine and sagebrush cover the slopes. Farther up the valley, beyond the end of the drivable road, more and more grand fir and Douglas fir appear, eventually producing conditions suitable for birds of the wet coniferous forest. A great variety of birds can be found near the

Wenas campground, varying with the effects of the on-going logging in the area. The birds inhabiting the dry hillsides are quite different from those of the moist stream bottom. The area has been good in the past for hole-nesters - woodpeckers (the White-headed being the most sought), both species of bluebirds, Mountain Chickadees in the pines, Black-capped Chickadees in the riparian growth, and all 3 species of nuthatches. Sapsuckers are seen often here, with some individuals intermediate between Red-naped and Red-breasted. All four of the common Washington empidonax can be heard and seen in the appropriate habitats along the stream, Gray Flycatchers nest in open ponderosa pine habitat about 0.7 mile up the "Hog Ranch Rd" W from the campground, and Least Flycatchers have been seen recently in aspen groves. Western Wood-Pewees, Veeries, Cassin's Finches and Chipping Sparrows are especially common. Northern Orioles, Western Tanagers, Black-headed Grosbeaks and Lazuli Buntings are common and furnish bright flashes of color among the tall cottonwoods. American Redstarts have been recorded here. Poorwills are present on the dry slopes and may be seen on the dusty roads at night. Vesper and Brewer's sparrows nest on slopes to the W of the campground. Great Horned and Flammulated owls and Screech-Owls have chipmunks and golden-mantled ground squirrels. During the spring, particularly after a wet winter, the desert and pinelands present a beautiful display of wildflowers.

The drive to Wenas from the N is very interesting, as the road gradually proceeds from sagebrush desert into pines and aspens, with much intermingling of plant associations and birds as well. The intermittent streams along the road allow a dense growth of serviceberries, roses, willows and cottonwoods to flourish, and in spring through summer these areas may have Downy Woodpecker, Eastern Kingbird, Gray Catbird, Warbling Vireo, Yellow Warbler, Yellow-breasted Chat, Northern Oriole, American Goldfinch and other riparian species. Birdlife is less abundant in the open desert, but Rock Wrens, Sage Thrashers, Loggerhead Shrikes and Vesper and Brewer's sparrows can be seen. Hawks are not common except in migration when dozens of Kestrels, for example, have been seen along the high country roads. Red-tails, Swainson's Hawks, Prairie Falcons and accipiters have also been recorded. Blue Grouse and Chukars bring their chicks out onto the road in late summer, and flocks of bluebirds and sparrows furnish much bird activity after the nesting season. Wenas Lake, along the road to the S, can be good for shorebirds in fall, though access is restricted. (G&WH, EH, PM, DP, TW)

---

S: April-July  E: 2000-3500'
H: DC BF RW DG ST
Maps: DLA 50:C 1-2

## Oak Creek Canyon

Entrance to this Wildlife Dept. WRA is about 2 miles W of the junction of US 12 and SR 410, W of Naches. Watch for the WRA sign where the road goes off the N side of US 12. This road can be closed during the winter. It follows Oak Creek along the riparian/oak woodland bottom of the canyon for 5 miles, slowly gaining elevation, and aspens replace cottonwoods in a few miles. The canyon walls are grassy bluffs with rock outcroppings. After 5 miles, the road goes into Snoqualmie NF and a maze of forest roads lead to higher elevations. Exploring these can be profitable, if one has a map of the Tieton Ranger District of Snoqualmie NF. Some birds of the lower canyon areas include Poorwill, Lewis' Woodpecker, Western Wood-Pewee, Rock Wren, Veery, Red-eyed Vireo, Nashville Warbler, Yellow-breasted Chat, Northern Oriole, Western Tanager, Black-headed Grosbeak and Lazuli Bunting. Least Flycatchers have been seen during two different years in the aspens 4-5 miles up from the highway. Occasionally, Canyon Wrens and Golden Eagles are seen here. Western gray squirrels are abundant here, one of the places in the state where they can be readily seen. Strikingly plumaged White-throated Swifts nest on a rocky outcropping along US 12 about 1 mile W of the Oak Creek Canyon road. (BT)

S: March-July  E: 1500'
H: DG
Maps: Yakima; DLA 51:C 5

Much of the land in the Yakima area has been converted to agriculture. Among the farmlands there are areas where original desert habitats remain. Native and introduced species thrive in both these habitat types. The southbound Highway Rest Area on I-92 between Ellensburg and Yakima has a sweeping overview of the Selah Creek canyon and a number of sought-after species are regular in the area, including Ferruginous Hawks. Prairie Falcons, Canyon Wrens and White-throated Swifts nest on the canyon cliffs. The northbound rest area is also worth a stop.

To the N and E is the U.S. Army's Yakima Firing Range. There is no public access to this area; however, in March each year several Audubon Society chapters have escorted field trips into Sage Grouse leks on the firing range. By the end of March, these trips also may encounter Burrowing Owl, Sage Thrasher and Sage Sparrow. (GW)

S: all year  E: 1500'
H: DC FL
Maps: DLA 51:D 7-8

The Moxee City Agricultural Experimental Station is worth a stop by birders passing through the area. It features ten long rows of coniferous trees planted as windbreaks sheltering field crops, and appears as a wooded "island" in the midst of the wide-open country southeast of Yakima. Long-eared Owls have nested here. Short-eared, Great Horned, Barn, and other owls roost in the trees in winter. This "oasis" also attracts migrant passerines in season. Take Highway 24 east from Yakima (Exit 34 from I-82). About 12 miles E of Moxee City, look for the rows of trees on the S side of the highway. Pull off and park near the caretaker's house between the road and the rows of trees, and obtain permission to enter. (PM, DP)

S: all year  E: 900'
H: FW WM SD FL
Maps: DLA 37:B 5-6

The Toppenish NWR and Toppenish Creek bottomlands are a rich birding area. While of prime interest during the summer because of nesting birds like Bobolinks, it also features a wide variety of waterfowl, waders, raptors and passerines during all seasons. The refuge is about 3 miles S of Toppenish on US 97. Turn in to the refuge just past a bridge over the creek and before the highway starts the long climb uphill to Satus Pass. If the gate to headquarters is open, information may be obtained there. There are many birding spots in the area. Bobolinks are resident in summer along the creek along the Pumphouse Rd, which is the road entering the refuge from 97. You can exit to the E via Marion Drain Rd where there are nesting Burrowing Owls. Huge numbers of ducks in migration, large numbers of wintering sparrows and blackbirds, numerous migrating warblers and many hawks are some of the attractions. NOTE: Access has been prohibited on some weekends. (G&WH, EH, DP, EP, TW)

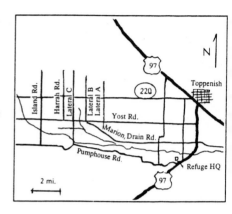

## Fort Simcoe

S: April-Aug   E: 1100'
H: RW BF SD PG
Maps: DLA 36:B 2-3

F - 12

Hwy SR 220 N from Toppenish ends at Fort Simcoe, in the Yakima Indian Nation. One of the area's top bird attractions are large numbers of Lewis' Woodpeckers (birders' descriptions range from "at least 100 in the immediate vicinity" to "an almost unbelievable concentration") are resident in the impressive stand of oaks here. Ash-throated Flycatchers, Yellow-breasted

Chats are among other songbirds seen and sagebrush areas along the road into Fort Simcoe have Loggerhead Shrikes, Brewer's Sparrows and other birds. There is good creek habitat on Yost Rd between Shaker Church and Pom Pom Rds. We suggest you stay on SR 220 unless you know the country well - many back roads come to dead ends. (G&WH, EH, EP)

## KLICKITAT COUNTY

## Satus Pass

S: May-Aug   E: 2000-4500'
H: FW DC BF RW WM SD ST
Maps: DLA 26:A 3

F - 13

At the Satus Pass summit on US 97, a road goes W and uphill to a ski area. A good variety of of birds occurs in summer along this road, both below and above the ski area. Fox Sparrows are common in open shrubby areas. At an old barn about 4.2

miles uphill from Hwy 97, Three-toed Woodpeckers are found, and a Black-backed Woodpeckers was here years ago. Turkeys reportedly visit the spring, and at 6.5 miles near a spring Flammulated Owls have been seen and heard. The combination of habitats

- from oaks to mountain conifers - includes other birds. At Brooks Memorial SP, a few miles SW of the summit, there's a good campground and birds like Nashville and

MacGillivray's warblers, House Wrens and other species. Gray Flycatchers have been found in the area along the power line. (EH, NL, TW)

---

S: May-Aug   E: 200-4400'
H: FW DC BF RW DG WM ST FL
Maps: DLA 24-25:A-C 4-8; 26:B 1-2

# Klickitat River areas

F - 14

A good birding area is about 16 miles W of Goldendale on SR 142, the Goldendale-Glenwood Rd. A state WRA is between the Klickitat River to the E and the Yakima Indian Nation to the N. There are steep, rugged canyons, with Garry oak groves, and park-like grassland benches interspersed with ponderosa pine, Douglas fir and quaking aspen thickets. Birds include Turkey, Blue Grouse, Ruffed Grouse, California Quail and Chukar. Other birds common to the area include Lewis' Woodpecker, Dipper, Lark Sparrow and Golden Eagle, and mule deer, bighorn sheep, bobcat, coyote and raccoon are among the mammals in the area. Southern alligator

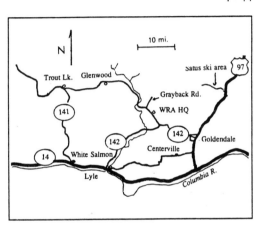

lizards are common in the summer, along with western skinks, western rattlesnakes and gopher snakes. About 1 mile NW past WRA headquarters, past a house on the right, turn up a dirt road (**Grayback Rd,** if there is a sign; a WRA sign is opposite the entrance to this road). From here to about 1 mile up the road, watch for striking pearl-gray Gray Flycatchers, and listen for their very regular, two-part song, the second part higher than the first part (as CHOOP CHEEP or SS-PUT SS-PEET, and there may be a lesser third note). Look for Mountain and Western bluebirds, all 3 nuthatches and many other species in May-June as well as outstanding views of Mt. Adams and Mt. Hood in Oregon, and many beautiful wildflowers. Hermit Warblers are seen in summer at **Trout Lake campground** W of the town of Trout Lake. Black-backed

Woodpeckers have also nested at Trout Lake. Going up Rd N 84 to Babyshoe Pass and Olallie Lake (the road may be open only after July 1 or later) leads N through Skamania County and eventually to Randle, on US 12.

Going S and W towards the **Klickitat River** on SR 142, you pass through open fields with Vesper Sparrows and Mountain and Western bluebirds, then drop down steeply to the Klickitat River canyon far below. The view as you descend, Lazuli Buntings singing all around on the slopes, is one of the most beautiful in Washington - and one of the least typical, since the dry terrain of and the chaparral and oak savannah is much more reminiscent of northern California. The wildlife seen here accords with this: California ground squirrel, western fence lizard, and gopher snake. When you arrive at the bottom of the hill and swing around to the left to follow the river, pull off and look back toward the steep hills and cliffs from which you have just descended and listen for the cascading song of a Canyon Wren. The dense deciduous vegetation along the river abounds with chats and other species.

Lesser Goldfinches have been seen in summer at a small campground about 0.8 mile up the Klickitat River from **Lyle.** Canyon Wrens are also found here. Mountain Quail and Turkeys are reported here and along the road from Lyle east to Centerville. In and around Lyle,

Ash-throated Flycatchers are easily found, and Acorn Woodpeckers have moved in in recent years. Just E of Lyle on WA 14, at the E end of a tunnel, there is a rest area on the N side of the road. Ash-throated Flycatchers may be seen or heard here - listen for the loud PRIT PRIT call notes and watch for the flash of a rufous tail. Other pulloffs along this road should produce more flycatchers, Lewis' Woodpecker, and, if you keep an eye on the tops of the cliffs, Prairie Falcons and recently reintroduced Peregrines.
WARNING: the attractive ground cover here, with its shiny green leaves dying off to a bright red, is poison oak, the particularly virulent Pacific Coast relative of poison ivy. (EH, NL, TW)

---

S: May-August E: 1000'
H: FW DC BF RW DG ST
Maps: DLA 26-27:B 4-5

# Rock Creek

F - 15

An area of ornithological and botanical interest to the E of Goldendale is reached via the Goldendale-Bickleton Rd. About 12 miles E of Goldendale where the bridge crosses Rock Creek, take Rock Creek Rd S for about 2.7 miles and park.

At this point Rock Creek sustains a riparian zone about 300-600 feet wide, with dry slopes rising abruptly on either side. The creek passes through a series of active beaver dams. The canyon slopes are dry and grassy, broken up by areas of sage, ponderosa pine-Garry oak woodland and a few junipers. Along the creek the oak is joined by white alder, willow and cottonwoods. There are extensive thickets of sumac and other common dry-region shrubs. Interesting features are the many introduced species of plants: Ailanthus, apple, pear and black walnut are common. Hawthorn is very extensive and burdened with fruit, which the birds may be busy consuming. Blueberry,

elder, Himalayan blackberry, hazelnut and other food is often plentiful. A wide variety of birds is present. California Quail, Chukar, Lewis' Woodpecker (abundant), Ash-throated Flycatcher (common), Canyon Wren and Gray Catbird are only a few highlights of an extensive list of species noted in the area.

By proceeding on to Bickleton on the Goldendale-Bickleton Rd, you pass through some very interesting oak/ponderosa pine/juniper habitat that is unique to the state. Along all the rural roads in and around Bickleton there is an extensive trail of bluebird boxes. From mid-March on you should encounter many Western and Mountain bluebirds. Western Bluebirds are more common in the scattered oak habitat W of town; Mountain Bluebirds are more common in the open, rolling hills to the E. Incidentally, the only tavern in Bickleton is called the "Bluebird". (JDa, GW)

S: all year  E: 100-2200'
H: FW BF DC
Map: DLA 25:C 5

# Locke, Rowland lakes

F - 16

The highway along the Columbia River (SR 14) provides access to two lakes adjacent to the river which support large flocks of waterfowl in winter, numbers of other waterbirds and landbirds at all times of the year.

**Locke Lake** is located at milepost 69.5. It is small and divided into two parts by SR 14. The southern half hosts flocks of ducks during the winter. In migration, warblers and other passerines can be found in the oak forest at the base of a large cliff. Canyon Wrens nest here and Golden Eagles are seen at times. The gravel road W of the lake leads up Burdoin Mountain through oak woodlands with turkeys, Say's Phoebe, Western Bluebirds and Lesser Goldfinches. An old growth fir forest caps this mountain, with Spotted Owls reported from

there. The view from this road of the Columbia River Gorge is breathtaking and worth the drive.

**Rowland Lake** is at milepost 71 on SR 14. It is formed by a railroad fill across a bay on the Columbia River and divided into two parts by the highway. It is used by wintering waterfowl. Lewis' Woodpeckers are common and Ospreys nest on the channel marker in the river at the W end of the lake. The hillside N of the lake supports Canyon Wrens, Ash-throated Flycatchers and Western Kingbirds. The road past the Department of Wildlife access area goes through a rocky grassland interspersed with oaks and pines. California Quail are found along the lower part of the road and Mountain Quail and turkeys occur further uphill. (WC)

**BENTON COUNTY**

S: all year  E: 380'
H: FW DG WM FL
Maps: DLA 39:B 5-6

# West Richland

F - 17

In addition to farmlands and to vast areas of desert shrub, especially on the Hanford Reservation, the immediate Tri-Cities area has urban habitats and one of the more important waterfowl areas in eastern Washington easily accessible. Go W out of Richland on Van Giesen St and continue to W Richland on SR 224. After crossing the Yakima River, continue another 1.4 miles and turn right on Grosscup Blvd. Continue on this road, follow signs to the so-called Twin Bridges. Just after crossing the bridges the road branches: the left fork is Snively Rd, the right is Grosscup Rd, which is the shortest and can be checked first. After passing the few farm houses, scan the fields

to the left and marshy area on the right. Returning to Snively Rd, look for waterfowl on the Yakima River and smaller birds along its shores. Snively Rd is about 3.8 miles long and brings you to SR 240, which continues NW through the Hanford Reservation or back in a SE direction to Richland. Of the two roads, Snively Rd usually offers the best birding, although at first glance it may seem an unlikely area. It passes through grassy fields, often partially flooded for irrigation, fairly extensive marshy areas, some brush and sagebrush areas, and riparian habitats along the Yakima River. This area is particularly good during spring, when American Avocets, Long-billed Curlews,

125

Wilson's Phalaropes and other shorebirds are here, but is also interesting during other seasons. In fall and winter, the area attracts large numbers of ducks, though these lands are all leased for hunting which makes birding difficult. The bird list for this general area includes 22 species of waterfowl, 12 of hawks, 17 of shorebirds and many other species, including an impressive array of passerines, some resident and some as migrants and winter visitors. Gallinaceous residents of the Yakima Valley reportedly include Gray Partridges and Northern Bobwhites. (BW)

---

# Yakima River mouth

S: Sept-May    E: 380'
H: FW ST PG
Maps: DLA 39:B-C 6-8

F - 18

Thousands of ducks and geese winter in the Tri-Cities area. Near the N end of Richland, Newcomer St runs E from George Washington Way, the main N-S artery in Richland, to the Columbia River. Hundreds of Mallards, American Wigeon and Canada Geese may be seen from the Richland shore and especially that part accessible from Newcomer St. Birds roost on an island, and the shallow channel between the island and shore is often crowded with waterfowl and occasional loons and grebes. Brushy areas around the parks attract passerines. A few miles farther S downriver, Lee Blvd leads into Howard Amon Park at the shoreline and which offers small birds in winter. From the point here, a back road leads S past the Rivershore Motor Inn and out to Columbia Point. However, this "point" may be more readily reached just N of the Yakima River bridge and it offers access to other lands in the Yakima delta. Continuing S on WA 240 (an extension of George Washington Way), cross the Yakima River to the access road (first right hand turn) to Columbia Park, bordering the S shore of the Columbia River for about 4 miles. The delta of the Yakima is mostly closed to hunting and its waters in season dotted with numerous waterfowl.

In the fall, when the river flow is controlled by upstream dams, the extensive mud flats of the Yakima delta offer some of the best birding in south-central Washington, particularly for birders addicted to shorebirds. Columbia Park offers additional shoreline for waterfowl viewing as well as Columbia Park Island and the Audubon Natural Area, both of which include brushy areas and Russian olive trees which attract to wintering land birds. The park lawns attract grazing wigeon and coots.

Overnight camping (fee) is possible. At the E end of the park, US 12 crosses the Columbia and continues through Pasco toward Walla Walla. Just before crossing the Snake River, a road going toward the right leads to Sacajawea State Park at the confluence of the Snake and Columbia Rivers. Immediately across the Snake, the McNary NWR is worth a visit (See I-1, I-2).

Sacajawea Park, SE of Pasco, has lawns, trees and shoreline habitats on two rivers. Adjacent marshy areas and fields are accessible. The museum in the park offers a chance to retreat from severe weather. Overnight camping is possible at Hood Park, just E of Burbank. (BW)

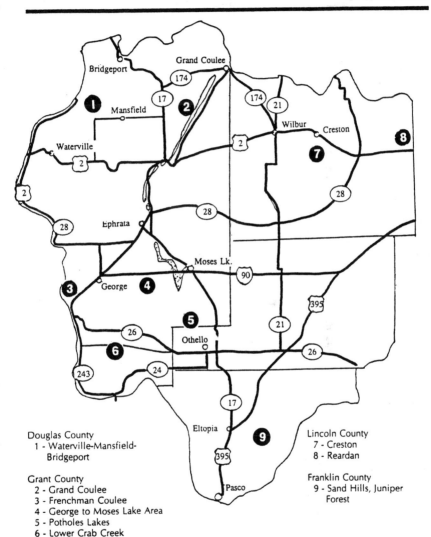

Douglas County
  1 - Waterville-Mansfield-
    Bridgeport

Grant County
  2 - Grand Coulee
  3 - Frenchman Coulee
  4 - George to Moses Lake Area
  5 - Potholes Lakes
  6 - Lower Crab Creek

Lincoln County
  7 - Creston
  8 - Reardan

Franklin County
  9 - Sand Hills, Juniper
    Forest

S: April-June, Jan-Feb    E: 1400-2200'
H: FW RW DG SD FL
Maps: DLA 83:C-D 6-8; 84-85:A-D 1-5

# Waterville-Mansfield-Bridgeport

G - 1

Habitats from sagebrush desert and wheat farms to riparian edge and freshwater lakes and marshes created by massive irrigation projects of the Grand Coulee era present an abundance of birds in many birding areas in this region. The open, wind-swept plateau above and east of the Columbia River is an interesting area for birds. In spring, large numbers of Horned Larks, sparrows, Loggerhead Shrikes, hawks and kingbirds may be seen along the roads in the open country in early morning before traffic has disturbed them.

Thousands of Sandhill Cranes pass through this area during spring migration, usually concentrating near **St. Andrews.** This locality is also known for Long-eared Owls nesting in riparian habitat (may be closed to entry). Sage Grouse may be found south of Hwy 174, 4-5 miles E of Leahy, and they have been reported about 3 miles SW of Leahy, also. In 1990 a Sage Grouse lek was E of Jameson Lake, reached via Jameson Lake Access Rd, going E on Rd 5 NE for a short distance where the road loops around a hill. Other Sage Grouse displayed on the N side of Rd 6 NE (St Andrews W Rd) about 2-3 miles W of St Andrews.

**Jameson Lake,** W of St. Andrews, is reached from US Hwy 12 via the road N through Moses Coulee or S from Mansfield (the roads do not connect). The lake is about 1 mile long, surrounded by sagebrush covered hills, farms and high cliffs which rise almost vertically on the W side, and it has an impressive colony of Cliff Swallows. Canyon Wrens may be heard, and Canada Geese nest hundreds of feet above the lake. Marshy areas have large numbers of blackbirds and other species. Jameson Lake may have crowds of fishermen and lots of outboard motor noise in May-June. It is also a good area for rattlesnakes. Ducks, hawks, Poorwills, Say's Phoebes, and Lark and Brewer's sparrows also nest here.

In winter, birding along the secondary roads between these towns when fields are snow-covered can turn up small flocks of Gray Partridges, Horned Larks, Gray-crowned Rosy Finches, Snow Buntings and Lapland Longspurs along the road margins. Sharp-tailed Grouse are frequently observed feeding on willow buds along the **Foster Creek canyon** south of Bridgeport. Tree Sparrows should also be looked for in the area. When considering this trip, first check the weather and avoid winter storms. County roads run N/S and E/W. Driving N and E or S and W between Waterville and Bridgeport, look for loose flocks of birds. In Bridgeport itself, Bohemian Waxwings may be seen in winter. (RFr, G&WH, RM, MT, BT, TW, GW)

S: April-June   E: 1200-1600'
H: FW RW DG SD ST FL
Maps: DLA 69-70:A-B 4-5; 84-85:A-D 4-8

Grand Coulee Dam water storage has filled depressions in the coulee and formed a series of lakes in the ancient river bed hundreds of feet below the level of the Columbia plateau. The abundance of water has attracted a rich flora and fauna. Go SW from Grand Coulee town on WA 155, along Banks Lake for about 23 miles. At Coulee City, turn W and then S on WA 17. It is about 40 miles to Soap Lake. **Banks Lake** often has birds found usually along the coast, especially during the fall and winter. Sea ducks are regular, jaegers are possible. Large numbers of Herring Gulls winter on the lake, if areas of open water persist, and Glaucous Gulls are sometimes seen with them. The road up Northrup Canyon leaves the highway just N of Steamboat Rock and climbs to several different habitat types. Large colonies of Cliff Swallows can be seen along the lake. Below **Dry Falls Dam,** W of Coulee City, are lakes formed by the rising water table. There is a small parking lot on the S side of the Dry Falls Dam. The rocky island in the lake opposite has a nesting colony of Ring-billed and California gulls. A walk up the rocky east side of the parking lot will show a good variety of waterfowl, Wilson's Phalaropes, and other birds in the marshy lake below. At the Dry Falls overlook in summer you can often look White-throated Swifts eyeball to eyeball as they skim along the top of the impressive escarpment. In winter, look for Gray-crowned Rosy Finches which roost in the cliffs.

At **Sun Lakes,** state park roads go through the riparian groves and lots of birds are seen. A very good bird walk from mid-May to mid-June: park in the lot across the road from the campground, walk up the road to Deep Lake a mile or so. The road follows the stream which you cross between the parking lot and the stable. See waterfowl, raptors (Red-tails nest on the cliffs), swallows, Common Ravens, Black-billed Magpies, Rock Wrens, vireos, warblers and Yellow-breasted Chats, Yellow-headed Blackbird, Northern Oriole, Western Tanager, Lazuli Bunting, Lark Sparrow and others.

**Lake Lenore** has great birding potential around the shore and the hillsides above. Barrow's Goldeneyes nest here. The area can be good in winter, with Gray-crowned Rosy Finches using crevices in the cliffs for roosting, and many freshwater and coastal marine ducks and other waterbirds present. Migrant shorebirds may be seen at the N end of Soap Lake. Tent camping is not too good in this area. Sun Lakes SP, 4-4.5 miles SW of Coulee City is a possibility but may be crowded in summer. There are a number of areas, however, for campers or trailers. About 3 miles S of Soap Lake on SR 17, a large canal parallels the road. In the summer, flocks of Eared Grebes, Wilson's Phalaropes and many ducks are possible. As in many similar spots with these habitats, be alert for rattlesnakes and take care not to brush ticks off sagebrush onto your clothes. (BJ, DP, BT, TW)

## Frenchman Coulee

S: April-Sept   E: 1000'
H: DG SD PG
Maps: DLA 68:D 1

G - 3

Take exit 143 off I-90 E from Vantage at the top of the plateau, cross under I-90, and go to the small "oasis" of Frenchman Springs - a few houses surrounded by trees. Migrants concentrate in such a place, and with luck you may find the trees alive with birds during April-May and August-September. Birds often bathe and drink in the irrigation ditch that runs through the trees. People live here, so please stay out of their yards; the birds are visible from the road. Snipe, teals and blackbirds are common in the small marsh here, and sagebrush birds occur all around the oasis. Nighthawks and Lark Sparrows move in after breeding. Continue on the road, which heads down toward the Columbia River along the S side of Frenchman Coulee. Stop at overlooks along the cliffs for thrilling views of White-throated Swifts slicing the air at eye level, with smaller, accompanying Violet-green Swallows appearing hardly to move by comparison. Red-tailed Hawks, Kestrels, Rock Doves, Say's Phoebes and Rock Wrens breed in the cliffs, and Sage Sparrows can be seen on the flats closer to the river. The colorful basalt cliffs are merely magnificent. (DP)

## George to Moses Lake area

S: April-June   E: 500-1000'
H: FW RW SD
Maps: DLA 52-53:A 1-7; 68-69:B-D 1-7

G - 4

Department of Wildlife WRAs provide access into a number of good habitats throughout this aregion.

**Quincy WRA:** From I-90 between Vantage and Moses Lake, take a Quincy exit 149 or 151 to WA Hwy 281 and turn left on Rd 3-NW or 5-NW. This leads to an area of striking, towering cliffs, some 600 feet high, which drop precipitously to the Columbia River and down to intermediate benches above the river. The entire area is cut by numerous lesser side coulees in which seepage and water from irrigation drainage have now filled over 25 small lakes.

**Winchester WRA:** Access to the S end of Winchester Lake is from the N frontage road (from Dodson and Adams Rds) 11 miles E of George and 14 miles W of Moses Lake. Other points of entry are from county Rd 5-NW between Rds G-NW and H-NW (east-west roads are designated by numbers, and the north-south roads by letters). The lake can also be reached by traveling N on Rd E-NW to 3-NW, then W to a parking lot on the E side of the lake. The lake, in a shallow depression in the generally flat terrain, borders on the the rich, irrigated farmlands of the Columbia Basin irrigation project and the rolling sandy country to the W and S. The water is bordered by a narrow margin of cattails, willows, rushes and some wetland grasses, while the remainder of the land supports typical Great Basin desert cover of sagebrush, rabbitbrush and bunchgrass. As many as 17 species of ducks may be found on the lake, with 11 known to nest here. Mallards, Cinnamon Teal and Blue-winged teal are common; and Northern Pintails, Gadwalls, American Wigeon and Green-winged Teal are also present. Great Basin Canada Geese nest here, and Lesser Canada Geese may be seen during the spring and fall migrations. Common Snipe, Mourning Dove and over 100 more species of birds are known to the area. Big spectacular birds seen include Golden Eagles, White Pelicans and Sandhill Cranes.

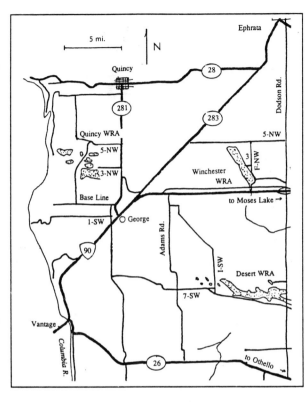

**Desert WRA:** This area includes a portion of the vast, low, rolling sand dune, marsh and sagebrush country W of Moses Lake and S of I- 90. The big wasteways and drainage canals of the area have created channels through the dunes as their waters drain through the Potholes area. Great numbers of waterfowl are found here, with species composition much the same as at Winchester WRA. From I-90 take exit 164 (15 miles E of George, 10 miles W of Moses Lake) S on the Dodson Rd and watch all along its length, especially at ponds and ditches. At the first ponds S of the freeway

there should be many ducks, including courting Ruddies right next to the road in May and June, Redheads and numerous dabblers, Black Terns and possibly Black-necked Stilts. All along this road there are Pied-billed Grebes and coots, a few Forster's and Caspian Terns, very large colonies of Yellow-headed and Red-winged blackbirds and a sample smattering of sagebrush birds. Long-billed Curlews at times feed in plowed fields along here. Proceed to the first crossroad ("8.8 SW") and turn in either direction. To the W there are ponds N of the road with nesting avocets, stilts and Wilson's Phalaropes, and other shorebirds in migration. Just W of these ponds are numerous Burrowing Owl burrows and juveniles are readily seen in season on fenceposts and farm equipment beside the road. Be careful at marshes during the breeding season, as many of these birds nest on the marsh edge, and they may easily be disturbed if you linger in any one spot. An alternative route is to travel E from Dodson Rd on 8.8 SW and look to the N for a good-sized lake which is part of Frenchman Hills Wasteway. This lake throngs with ducks and often has good numbers of gulls, terns and may have shorebirds roosting at its W end. Recently it has been visited in summer by up to 50 White Pelicans which may also be seen on the reservoirs nearby. Farther E along the same road is a T junction; take the

left fork, heading E to O'Sullivan Dam at the S end of Potholes Reservoir. This big lake is often good for water birds, and in the fall there are many shorebirds near the boat-launching area at the SW end of the reservoir (watch for signs as you approach from the W).

**Gloyd Seeps WRA:** Go N from Moses Lake on Stratford Rd, then left on a Wildlife Department road 1 mi N of the Crab Creek bridge, or 2 mi N of the bridge, then go left on county Rd 12-NE, 14-NE or 16-NE to the road end. Brushy scablands slope from the

irrigated farmlands to the E of Crab Creek, which flows over bare rock in some places and through salt grass flats in others. Golden Eagles have nested in this area. In early spring, look for White Pelicans adjacent to the Wildlife Dept. farm 1 mi N of the Crab Creek bridge. Great Basin Canada Geese nest here, and avocets may also.

**Potholes WRA:** Exit I-90 at Hiawatha Rd (exit 169) about 8 miles W of Moses Lake. Drive E along the frontage road for 2.5 miles on the S side of I-90, turn S on Rd D.5. Except during high water, you can drive this road to its end (keep taking righthand forks) near an island rookery with Black-crowned Night-Herons, Great Blue Herons, Great Egrets (at S end of Rd D.5 and on NE arm of Potholes Reservoir), and Double-crested Cormorants. Hundreds of American White Pelicans visit this area in summer. Migrant shorebird possibilities are good, along with nesting Killdeers, Spotted Sandpipers, Wilson's Phalaropes, American Avocets and Black-necked Stilts. Shorebirds are often present along Crab Creek where it drains into the reservoir. This is prime country for canoeing and kayaking to reach more bird areas.

**Moses Lake:** Clark's Grebes may be seen during the nesting season by looking S from the E end of the I-90 causeway crossing Moses Lake as well as from waterfront locations in the city. Western Grebes and many other waterbirds are here also. (GG, G&WH, EH, BJ, PM, DP, BT, TW)

---

S: April-June   E: 700-1100'
H: FW RW SD FL
Maps: DLA 53:A 6-7

# Potholes Lakes

G - 5

This interesting biological area consists of the **Columbia NWR** and state **Lava** and **Goose Lake WRAs.** Mainly dry sagebrush desert with basalt cliffs and scattered small lakes, it is enclosed by intensively irrigated farmland. The lakes have nesting waterfowl and are very important for wintering waterfowl. The few sedge marshes provide nesting sites for Spotted Sandpipers, Wilson's Phalaropes and American Avocets. Cattail marshes offer Soras and Virginia Rails, Marsh Wrens, and Yellow-headed and Red-winged blackbirds. Typical birds of the open desert include Red-tailed Hawks, Common Nighthawks, ravens, Black-billed Magpies, Sage Thrashers, Horned Larks, Loggerhead Shrikes, Western Meadowlarks, and Sage and Lark sparrows. The cliffs provide nesting sites for American Kestrels, Great Horned Owls, Say's Phoebes, Cliff Swallows, Rock and Canyon wrens (the last species uncommon), as well as Red-tailed Hawks and ravens. Along Crab Creek and wherever water seeps through from the Potholes Canal there are willow thickets, and these are inhabited by Eastern Kingbirds, Ash-throated Flycatchers (rare), Yellow-breasted Chats and Northern Orioles. Black-crowned Night- Herons roost along the Potholes Canal S of Potholes Reservoir. Ring-billed Gulls and Caspian Terns nest in the region. Commonly observed mammals

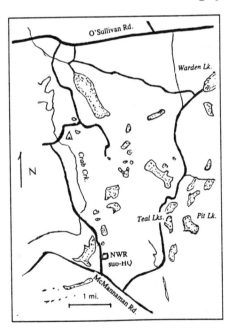

are muskrat, yellow-bellied marmot, Washington ground squirrel, black-tailed jackrabbit and mountain cottontail. Badgers are also present. There are still a number of beavers and coyotes (camp overnight and listen at dusk), and at night you can find deer mice and Great Basin pocket mice are common along the roads. Rattlesnakes are plentiful, so watch out! They prefer the cliffs but may be encountered anywhere. Other common reptiles are gopher snakes and racers.

A local map can be obtained at the NWR headquarters in Othello or sub-headquarters on the refuge. A good sampling can be made from a loop tour. From I-90 exit 164 go S on the Dodson Rd to O'Sullivan Rd, then E just past O'Sullivan Dam, turn S onto an improved gravel road (a map may be obtainable at a stand here). Go S, crossing the Potholes Canal, for about 2.5 miles, past Scabrock Lake, down to a small camp area (with marsh across road). Park, go down W side to the creek, in riparian brush and trees. Nesting specialties here are Yellow breasted Chat and Ash-throated Flycatcher, along with many others, and migrants abound at times. Farther S, just N of where this road crosses Crab Creek again, there are cliffs bordering a wash to the W. This is a good spot to look for Canyon Wrens, and hawks and owls roost in the cliffs and can sometimes be flushed. Continuing S past the sub-headquarters (Canyon Wrens on the cliff across the road) at McMannaman Lake, it is about 0.7 mile to where you turn left (E) onto the McMannaman Rd. Badgers have been seen to the S of this intersection. At about 0.5 mile turn left (NE) at a gravel road marked "Public Fishing Area". (Othello is about 5 miles farther SE on McMannaman Rd). About 4 miles along this road there are sage flats where Sage Thrashers and Sage Sparrows are likely in spring. Next are the S and N Teal lakes (campsite) and then access to top of the Potholes Canal dike to Pit Lake. Further N, take the second road to the right

(E) after you cross a cattleguard (about 3.5 miles from the bridge over the Potholes Canal at Pit Lake), which leads to the S end of Warden Lake. This is a good spot for ducks, shorebirds (including avocets) and Forster's Terns. Stay away from shorebird nesting areas in spring, as these are limited and the birds need maximum protection. Just N of the side road to Warden Lake - or 1 mile S of the O'Sullivan Rd (7-SE) if coming from the N - near a cattle guard is a good spot to stop and listen for Sage Thrashers and also Sage, Brewer's and Lark sparrows. Habitat along the road to Warden Lake is also good for these species. During migrations, Sandhill Cranes pass through in great numbers, usually in late April and in September. In addition to breeding ducks, many other ducks and Canada Geese move through in large numbers. A variety of shorebirds, Forster's and Black terns, and many passerines that do not nest in the area can be found. Birds of dark, dense coniferous forests like Golden-crowned Kinglets may be seen below your eye level, foraging in sagebrush during migration.

Some parts of the refuge are closed to vehicle entry, and during hunting season some areas are completely closed off to visitors. Check with refuge headquarters (Monday-Friday, 9:00-4:30, P.O. Drawer F, Othello 99344) for special regulations. At the NWR headquarters you can obtain bird lists, maps and information on fishing. Primitive campgrounds exist on the refuge and state WRAs; but no drinking water is available. There is an improved campground at Potholes State Park at the W end of O'Sullivan Dam where Clark's Grebe can be seen in the Reservoir and shorebird migrants are readily observed. The round trip outlined above makes an easy one-day trip of about 35-50 miles, depending on side trips taken. (RF, BJ, PM, TW)

# Lower Crab Creek

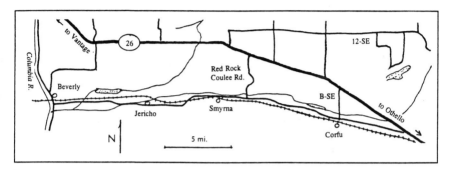

This impressive valley can be reached from SR 243 on the E side of the Columbia River, driving to just N of where Crab Creek empties into the river. Just S of the road to Beverly, a paved road leads E along the N side of the creek, changing to gravel fairly soon. You can continue on to WA 26 at the E end of the road or drive N out of the valley at Corfu or E at Smyrna, both roads leading to WA 26. If coming from the E on WA 26, watch for the turnoff to Corfu, 14.2 miles W of Othello. At this junction there is a large willow grove, excellent for many species of passerine birds during migration. The many small ponds in the valley are likely to be full of waterbirds in season, though birding may not be really worthwhile in the fall-winter hunting season when there are many duck- and Chukar-hunters and dogs and the birds are very wary. All the common dabbling ducks of central Washington can be seen, especially in migration, and a few of the deeper ponds hold goldeneyes, Buffleheads and other divers. With the right water levels, shorebirds are present in small numbers in spring and fall. Other marsh birds are becoming more common as irrigation water seeps increasingly into the many depressions. Avocets and Wilson's

Phalaropes nest on an alkaline pond on the S side of the road, about 4-5 miles E of WA 243. Some species of the desert birds are common here, including Chukars (especially where the road runs nearer the cliffs of the Saddle Mountains), Loggerhead Shrikes and Western Meadowlarks. Scaled Quail have been seen along Crab Creek hillsides, near Beverly. This rare, introduced species is reported by the game department to inhabit the desert areas in Yakima County, Kittitas, Grant and Franklin Counties. A few pairs of Long-billed Curlews and Burrowing Owls may be found in the grassy areas on the E end of the road, along with colonies of Washington ground squirrels in the early spring. Raptors are as common here as anywhere in this desert region, and include Red-tailed Hawks, Kestrels and Prairie Falcons. Large flocks of blackbirds (check for Rusty Blackbirds, which are quite rare) and Starlings winter at the feed lot at Smyrna. The grain fields there may have flocks of Tree and White-crowned sparrows. A few Loggerhead Shrikes spend the winter in the area, and they may be compared directly with more common Northern Shrikes. During some winters Short-eared Owls are abundant, and numbers of Rough-legged Hawks also winter here.

If driving to or from Othello, check the ponds (especially one 10.2 miles W of Othello) on the main road between there and the Corfu turnoff. These can be excellent in spring and early summer for breeding shorebirds (Killdeer, Spotted Sandpiper, Wilson's Phalarope and American Avocet - the latter especially in a tiny pond 1.3 miles W of Othello on the N side of the road) and ducks (Mallard, Gadwall, Pintail, all three species of teal, American Wigeon, Shoveler, Redhead, Lesser Scaup and Ruddy Duck). An area of grassland E of the road that runs N from Corfu may have Long-billed Curlews in it. Camping is possible along Crab Creek (much of the area is in the Crab Creek WRA), though there are no marked facilities. There are motels in Vantage and Othello. The Wanapum Dam is a must-see during July and August when sockeye and chinook salmon are running, passing through the fish ladders and visible at close range in the fish-viewing room. Forster's Terns may be seen foraging along the Columbia River here. (DP, TW)

S: April-May   E: 2000'
H: FW RW DG SD FL
Maps: DLA 86:B-C 4

## Creston

G - 7

In between fields and pastures converted from the native grasslands and sagebrush there are remnants of these habitats, creeks and potholes supporting much interesting birdlife. During migrations large numbers of many species pass through. Scanning areas with stands of sagebrush south of Creston may reward you with a Sage Grouse sighting. Drive S from the W end of Creston (between several grain elevators) on a the Creston South Rd which heads SW and soon curves to the S and eventually becomes gravel. Stop at Sinking Creek for riparian birds; although many typical species are absent from this isolated stand of trees, it should be interesting in migration. Flocks of migrating Horned Larks and Lapland Longspurs may be seen early in the spring. Later, Long-billed Curlews and Horned Larks are found in the fields in this area. Short-eared Owls, Western Meadowlarks, Savannah and Vesper sparrows are common. Sage Thrashers, Brewer's Sparrows and Burrowing Owls may be found in remnant sagebrush.

Displaying Sharp-tailed Grouse have been recorded recently in fields along the Creston South Rd, about 8-10 miles S of Creston.

The ponds throughout this area are good for shorebirds (including avocets) in migration and ducks in summer. Columbian ground squirrels occupy piles of rock along the road, and white-tailed jackrabbits can be flushed from under the sagebrush. Tiger and long-toed salamanders and Great Plains spadefoots breed in the ponds, wildflowers carpet the ground and the countryside turns beautiful during the spring. The area gets brown, dry and dusty as summer progresses, and most of the animals close up shop by July. A road goes S into sagebrush country. It becomes narrow and bumpy, but it allows access to scenic wild areas and eventually reaches a paved road many miles to the S. (PM, DP, MT)

S: April-Sept   E: 2500'
H: FW RW FL
Maps: DLA 88:C 1-2

# Reardan

G - 8

Reardan is about 20 miles W of Spokane on US 2. Turn N on SR 231 and almost immediately you will see marshy ponds on both sides of the road. Going N there is a one-lane shoulder, going S there is virtually none: be very careful if you stop. Park N of the ponds and walk back along the road and around the ponds - obey private property signs. These ponds are very good for many species of ducks and marsh birds, including Black Terns, from April to August. By early

fall the water level falls low enough to expose mudflats and these attract migrating shorebirds; in fact, this is one of the best spots for shorebirds in eastern Washington. Along with the more common species, others such as Solitary, Baird's and Semipalmated sandpipers regularly occur. Piping Plover, Ruff, Hudsonian Godwit and White-rumped Sandpiper have also been seen. (DP, DPe)

## FRANKLIN COUNTY

S: April-June   E: 1000'
H: DG SD FL
Maps: DLA 39:A-C 8; 40:A-B 1-2; 53:D 8; 54:C-D 1-2

# Sand Hills, Juniper Forest

G - 9

An ecosystem unique in Washington is the juniper forest, an interesting and unusual habitat with six of state's most extensive western juniper stands, which also comprise then northernmost juniper forest in the U.S., combined with an area of active sand dunes, up to 120' in height, northeast of the junction of the Columbia and Snake rivers. This 7,140 acre dune and shrub-steppe area is in the heart of Washington's Ferruginous Hawk population (reportedly 10 nests). It is relatively unexplored by birders, and it has interesting potential - one of the state's few records of Scaled Quail came from here in the 1970s. Other animals recorded here include Ord's kangaroo rat and pygmy rabbit.

To see Ferruginous Hawks displaying, come in March or April when the wildflowers also enliven the dunes. This area involves hiking - bring water, boots, wind and sun

protection. Avoid the area in summer as the heat can be stifling and the birds mostly gone.

From the center of Pasco, go E on Pasco-Kahlotus Rd 24 miles to the Snake River Rd. After 3.5 twisty miles, leave the pavement and go left on the gravel East Blackman Rd 2.4 miles to the Joy Rd. Go 2 miles on Joy Rd (Rybzinski Rd in DeLorme WAG) past Juniper Dunes Ranch to road-end. Cross private land on a well-defined trail, taking care to close stock gates that you may open to get by. Pay attention when crossing the dunes to avoid getting lost. Juniper groves are scattered through the area. Another access is by exiting SR 395 about 5 miles NE of Eltopia and going E on the Blanton Rd. At about 2.5 miles turn S on the Gertler Rd for 3 miles, then E on Blackman Ridge Rd for about 2 miles and finally S about 2 miles to the dead end of Joy Rd. (FC, AS)

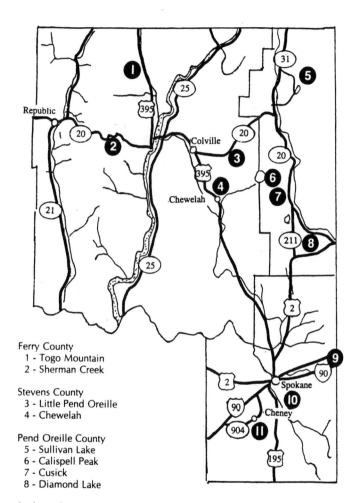

Ferry County
  1 - Togo Mountain
  2 - Sherman Creek

Stevens County
  3 - Little Pend Oreille
  4 - Chewelah

Pend Oreille County
  5 - Sullivan Lake
  6 - Calispell Peak
  7 - Cusick
  8 - Diamond Lake

Spokane County
  9 - Newman Lake Area
  10 - Iller Creek
  11 - Turnbull National
      Wildlife Refuge

S: July-Oct  E: 5000-6000'
H: DC BF
Maps: DLA 117:A-B 5-7

## Togo Mountain

H - 1

Mountains north of the Columbia River offer a variety of forest types and other habitats below them. Birders, however, are often interested in species utilizing the forests, including grouse, owls, woodpeckers and "northern finches". Follow US 395 3.3 miles N from Orient. Turn W onto Little Boulder Rd and watch for the righthand fork at about 1 mile. Continue along Little Boulder Rd for approximately 8 more miles to a small parking area along the south side of the road about one-half mile beyond the "Road not maintained beyond this point" sign.

Park and hike an old overgrown road which runs N from the parking area for about 3 miles to the summit of Togo Mountain. Traditionally, the larch- and Douglas fir-covered south-facing slopes here have been perhaps the best area in eastern Washington during September for Blue and Spruce grouse. The grouse are encountered most often along seep areas. Other area specialties include Black-backed and Three-toed woodpeckers and White-winged Crossbill (the latter is irregularly common). (BWh)

S: May-July  E: 1200-5600'
H: FW WC DC RW WM ST FL
Maps: DLA 116-117:C-D 3-6

## Sherman Creek

H - 2

As SR 20 crosses the county there are many promising possibilities, though finding a place to pull off the often-busy road is not always easy. Some of the best habitat is the higher mountain area of Sherman Pass. Birds like Three-toed and Black-backed woodpeckers (at a large burn), finches, crossbills, Spruce Grouse and others are likely. Boreal Owls have recently been

found nesting at high elevations here. The Sherman Creek WRA on the W shore of Roosevelt Lake (which is the Columbia River made into a lake) is another area where introduced Turkeys may be seen. Bobolinks are reported during the summer at the N end of Curlew Lake, 5 miles N of Republic. Ospreys are seen along the Sanpoil River, S from Republic, in summer. (TW)

## Little Pend Oreille

S: May-July   E: 3000'
H: FW WC DC RW WM ST
Maps: DLA 118:C-D 3-5

H - 3

Many opportunities await birders exploring the northeastern part of the state. Stevens County has many lakes and streams, forests and open habitats and bird species recorded range from northern forest birds to nesting eastern passerines. The Little Pend Oreille WRA lies in the midst of a great birding area. There are opportunities in almost all directions from this high plateau crossed by logging roads. Lakes, marshes and bogs are scattered all through the spruce, larch and lodgepole pine forests. About 18 miles NE of Colville on WA 20 is one possible side trip: a side road off to the NW follows a small stream for about a mile and then rejoins WA 20. Summer birds include American Redstart, Northern Waterthrush, Common Yellowthroat, Gray Catbird, Vaux's Swift and Common Snipe. Ospreys nest near some of the many small lakes in the region. The center of birding activity has been around Middleport. Lake Gillette is about 1 mile to the SW. Barred and Flammulated owls have been found here in recent years. Three-toed Woodpeckers range through the spruces. Blue and Spruce grouse are fairly common

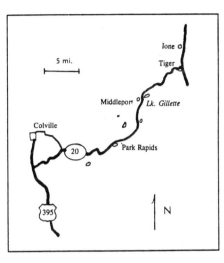

residents throughout this region. Turkeys are reportedly successfully introduced above the Colville River Valley and the E shore of Roosevelt Lake. (BJ, DP, DPe, TW)

## Chewelah

S: all year  E:1700-5700'
H: FW WC DC BF RW WM ST FL
Maps: DLA 104:B-C 2-3

H - 4

The area around Chewelah includes a wide variety of habitats and birds. W from the caution light in Chewelah on Main St, marshes and ponds have many breeding waterbirds and migrants. Bobolinks may be here in hay fields, and also to the E of town and also about 3 miles up Sand Canyon Rd

(off Hwy 395 N of town). Turkeys are possible in open and mixed-habitats along the Addy-Gifford Rd, the Orin-Rice Rd, and the Gifford-Rice Rd. Northern Waterthrushes may be found at a bog about two miles N of a sawmill at Arden. (EH, JN)

More species of breeding land birds can be found in this part of the state than anywhere else, with the juxtaposition of dry and wet coniferous forests, large stands of aspens and cottonwoods, open meadows, and a fair range of elevations which can be traversed in a short period of time.

S: June-Aug   E: 1900-6000'
H: FW WC DC BF RW WM ST
Maps: DLA 119:A-C 5-8

## Sullivan Lake

H - 5

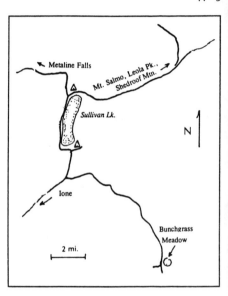

The area can be entered from SR 31 at Ione or Metaline Falls. If coming from Ione, watch for the Harvey Creek Rd which turns off to the right about 6 miles from town. This road runs E and S about 8 miles to Bunchgrass Meadow. This is one of Washington's few known localities for moose at present, and there are Three-toed Woodpeckers in the trees and Lincoln's Sparrows in the moist thickets. Watch for scaled-off bark as evidence of the woodpeckers' presence. There are campgrounds at the N and S ends of Sullivan Lake and surrounding streams are excellent for birds of riparian woodland, including many warblers such as Nashville, Yellow and Wilson's, Northern Waterthrush and American Redstart. Black-chinned Hummingbirds and Ovenbirds have been seen here. Birds of the coniferous forest are the dominant species and include warblers, many woodpeckers, flycatchers, nuthatches, thrushes and chickadees. Four species of chickadees can be found here in a single day: the Black-capped in deciduous growth, Chestnut-backed in lowland Douglas fir and red-cedar forests, and Mountain and Boreal in the montane forest stands. From the N end of the lake, the Sullivan Creek Rd leads E into the Salmo Mountains. About 10 miles up this road, past three campgrounds, you have a choice of good roads to take: Leola Peak, Shedroof Mountain and Salmo Mountain are high peaks with boreal species better represented than anywhere else in Washington. Three-toed woodpeckers, Boreal Chickadees and Pine Grosbeaks are

here; Goshawks and Spruce Grouse are further possibilities. White-crowned Sparrows nest in the scrubby vegetation in the higher part of Salmo Mountain, one of their few breeding sites E of the Cascades in the state. Boreal Owls and White-winged Crossbills are found in these mountains. The northeastern counties of the state are especially fine for owls. Barred Owls nest here (and in a large number of places from Pend Oreille County west to Whatcom and

142

Skagit counties). Boreal Owls have recently been found nesting in the area, also. Several state records of Hawk Owls come from the NE region, and there is an old record of the Great Gray Owl from Bunchgrass Meadow. Pygmy-owls are common, and by imitating their call you can often attract hordes of small birds to close range. This is also an excellent area for mammals. Caribou occur on Salmo Mt; white-tailed and mule deer apportion the deciduous and coniferous forests between them, and red squirrels chatter and yellow pine chipmunks seem to "whist" from every patch of woods. The redtail chipmunk, considered a separate species but almost inseparable in the field from the yellow pine, occurs on the higher peaks in this area. Columbian ground

squirrels live in colonies in the meadows, pikas live in rock slides, beavers in ponds, and large carnivores are more likely to be seen in this largely uninhabited region than elsewhere in Washington.

Another very good site for many of the same species found at Sullivan Lake is Big Meadow Lake, about 6 miles on a well-marked road W of Ione. At the lake take the trail around to the S side. Barred Owl, Red-naped Sapsucker, Northern Waterthrush and American Redstart are regular here. In 1990 broods of Bufflehead and Common Goldeneye, both rare nesters in the state, as well as of the much more common Barrow's Goldeneye, were present on the lake. (PM, DP, DPe, TW)

---

S: June-July   E: 1800-6000'
H: FW DC BF RW ST FL
Maps: DLA 105:A-B 5-6

## Calispell Peak

H - 6

About 3.5 miles N of Cusick (or 25.5 miles S of Tiger) look for Tacoma Creek Rd (Air Force Survival School sign, milepost 415 or SR 20), turn W onto a gravel road about 8 miles to the Calispell Peak Rd and go about 3.5 miles on this. Stop at a clearing on the left side of the road (there may be a 20' muddy stretch just before the clearing which is impassable for some vehicles). Just past the cattle guard is a one-time nesting site of Three-toed Woodpeckers. Park off the road,

hike through the clearing and climb over fallen logs to a large beaver-dammed swamp about 100' beyond the clearing. Look for Spruce Grouse, Pygmy-Owls, Northern Waterthrushes, and Black-capped, Mountain and Chestnut-backed chickadees, and Townsend's Solitaires which nest regularly in this general area. And Black-backed Woodpeckers should also be watched for. (DPe, TW)

---

S: May-July   E: 1500'
H: RW ST FL
Maps: DLA 105:B 6

## Cusick

H - 7

At Cusick, turn W off SR 20 just N of the bridge. Within a short distance of SR 20, look for Bobolinks in the hay fields on both sides of the road. Along SR 20, Catbirds and

Veeries can often be found along the streams in the willows, along with many other riparian species. (TW)

## Diamond Lake

S: May-July   E: 2000'
H: FW DC BF RW ST FL
Maps: DLA 105:C-D 6-7

H - 8

About 12-13 miles S of Cusick via SR 20 and SR211, in the area between SR 211, US 2 and Diamond Lake, listen at night in late May to early July for the soft, ventriloqual "boop" of Flammulated Owls in the mixed woods along beaver ponds and streams. On the upper exposed hills, Poorwills are common. Lazuli Buntings, American Redstarts and many other species of deciduous woods and coniferous forests and edge habitats are common. (DPe)

## SPOKANE COUNTY

Among birding opportunities in Spokane County are three which give a diverse sampling of habitats and corresponding bird species. Newman Lake has remnants of grasslands, Iller Creek hillside forest, Turnbull wetlands and others.

## Newman Lake area

S: May-July   E: 2000'
H: RW DG ST FL
Maps: DLA 89:C 8

H - 9

Go E about 15 miles from Spokane on SR 290. Between this road and I-90 are roads running N-S, including the Starr Rd and Idaho Rd. Driving these and connecting crossroads, generally between the railroad tracks on either end. While many birds may be found in the area, it is known mainly for being the only recent nesting location of the Upland Sandpiper in Washington: they may be extirpated now. Careful scanning of the fields left as natural grassland (now being developed) may find this species, and Gray Partridge, Grasshopper Sparrow and other birds. Extending your coverage in any direction will expand habitat variety. A road map of the Spokane County area is almost a requisite. (TW)

## Iller Creek

S: May-June   E: 2300-3600'
H: WC DC BF ST
Maps: DLA 89:C-D 6

H - 10

Along Iller Creek and the ridges of the Browne's Mountain complex are compressed a number of the habitat types found in eastern Washington. Because of the varied habitat, the area along the creek offers some of the best passerine birding in the eastern half of the state and certainly in Spokane County. Although best from mid-May

144

through June, birding holds up quite well through the heat of summer. Of the thrushes, vireos and warblers normally recorded for eastern Washington, all are commonly found in the area except Northern Waterthrush and Common Yellowthroat (one record each). Although the Iller Creek drainage is in private ownership and has in the past been subjected to logging activity, it has also been traditionally open to public use.

To reach Iller Creek, exit I-90 at the Argonne interchange (Exit 287) and proceed S 3.5 miles along Argonne and then Dishman-Mica Rd to Schafer Rd. Turn right and go 0.9 mile to 44th Ave; turn right (W) and go 0.2 mile to Farr Rd; turn left (S) and go 0.3 mile to Holman Rd; turn right and proceed 0.4 mile past the last homes and park in the turnout at the top of a rise from which the drainage can be viewed. Look for Calliope Hummingbird, Orange-crowned Warbler and Yellow-breasted Chat in the buckbrush on the W side of the road and Lazuli Bunting and perhaps Black-headed Grosbeak along the slopes of the creek below. Begin hiking the road as it drops to and then follows the W side of Iller Creek for about another half mile. As you move along the alder-, maple- and cottonwood-lined lower stretches the following species are often found: Red-naped Sapsucker, Willow and Dusky flycatchers, Black-capped Chickadee,

House Wren, Gray Catbird, Swainson's Thrush and Veery, Red-eyed and Warbling vireos, Nashville, Yellow, MacGillivray's and Wilson's warblers, American Redstart, Brown-headed Cowbird, Rufous-sided Towhee, Dark-eyed Junco and Chipping, Fox and Song sparrows. Beyond this section, as one works upstream, the road eventually becomes a narrow jeep track and finally a trail as it ascends the drainage about two miles to top out in an old burn cradled between Krell Hill and Big Rock. Here the ponderosa pine and cottonwood are replaced by western hemlock, Douglas-fir, grand fir and western larch. Birds common along this portion include Ruffed Grouse, Hammond's Flycatcher, Mountain and Chestnut-backed (winter) chickadees, Red-breasted Nuthatch, Winter Wren, both Golden-crowned and Ruby-crowned kinglets, Yellow-rumped, Townsend's and Nashville warblers, Western Tanager and Red Crossbill. In the burn area, American Kestrel, Pileated and Lewis' woodpeckers and Brown Creeper have nested, and in the rocky outcrop to the east, Rock Wrens are regularly found. Additionally, Olive-sided Flycatchers can be heard calling along the north face of the ridge. Raptors commonly seen along the drainage are Sharp-shinned and Red-tailed hawks and Northern Harriers. Barred Owls have occurred here, and a rare Black-throated Green Warbler was seen here, too. (BWh)

---

S: April-Nov   E: 2000'
H: FW DC BF DG ST
Maps: DLA 72-73:A-B 3-5

## Turnbull National Wildlife Refuge

H - 11

Look for the NWR "flying goose" sign on the main street of Cheney, SW of the main business section. Follow this and drive S on the Cheney-Plaza Rd for about 4 miles. The main road into the refuge is well-marked. Maps of the refuge can be obtained on weekdays or by writing in advance (Rt 3, Box 107, Cheney WA 99004). A nature trail proceeds to **Kepple Lake** from the NWR

headquarters, and anywhere along it or on the main road through the refuge is good. A very interesting and different area is **Stubblefield Lake,** for which permission must be obtained to visit. Most of the refuge is a ponderosa pine parkland, with scattered aspen groves and thickets of roses and red-osier dogwood, serviceberry and other shrubs. In the pine areas many bird species characteristic of the western dry coniferous forest may be found, including Hairy Woodpecker, Western Wood-Pewee, Mountain Chickadee, Pygmy Nuthatch, Cassin's Finch, Red Crossbill and Chipping Sparrow. For a completely different avifauna, make stops at several of the moist and shady aspen groves where Ruffed Grouse, Red-naped Sapsucker, Downy Woodpecker, Willow Flycatcher, Black-capped Chickadee, White-breasted Nuthatch, House Wren, Gray Catbird, Veery, Red-eyed Vireo, Yellow Warbler, American Redstart and more may be found. Note that this is a typical list from an eastern deciduous forest. In addition, Black-chinned Hummingbirds are recorded from Turnbull, and Least Flycatchers are possible in the aspens. Most of the common waterfowl of the west nest here, including Canada Goose, Mallard, Blue-winged and Green-winged teal, Redhead, Ruddy Duck and many other less common species can be seen. Small flocks of Tundra Swans come through the refuge during migration, along with many other species. Other marsh birds found here include Pied-billed Grebe, Sora, Virginia Rail, American Coot, Common Snipe, Spotted Sandpiper, Black Tern, Marsh Wren, Common Yellowthroat and Yellow-headed and Red-winged blackbirds. The native bunchgrass prairies around Stubblefield Lake are a remnant of once more extensive grasslands and support Gray Partridges, Western Meadowlarks, and Grasshopper and Vesper sparrows. The lake itself can be very good for ducks and shorebirds during migration, and the hawthorn groves around it equally good for migrant landbirds. A pair of Long-eared

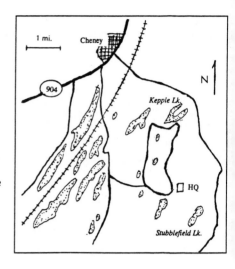

Owls has nested in the grove just to the S end of the lake. The refuge is a good habitat for mammals, also: coyote, Columbian ground squirrel, yellow pine chipmunk, red squirrel, white-tail deer, badger and long-tailed weasel. In May and June, the open spaces among the pines are carpeted with an astonishing collection of wildflowers. No camping is allowed on the refuge, but accommodations can be found at some of the nearby (touristy) lakes or in Cheney. Refuge personnel are available on weekdays to suggest spots for bird-finding. June is the best month overall, when nesting is at its peak, but May and September are good for migrants in general, and April, October and November for waterfowl migration. (DP)

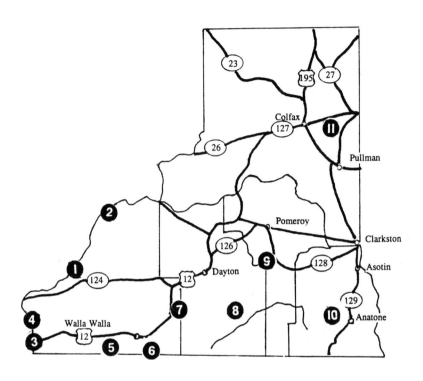

Walla Walla County
  1 - Fish Hook Park
  2 - Monumental Dam area
  3 - Walla Walla River delta
  4 - McNary NWR, WRA
  5 - Touchet-Louden area
  6 - Mill Creek area
  7 - Lewis Peak/Coppei Creek

Columbia County
  8 - Western Blue Mountains

Columbia-Garfield-Asotin
  counties
  9 - Dayton-Asotin

Asotin County
  10 - Eastern Blue Mountains

Whitman County
  11 - Kamiak Butte

S: November-March    E: 450'
H: FW PG
Maps: Walla Walla; DLA 40:B 2

# Fish Hook Park

I - 1

A well-planted Corps of Engineers park area has good numbers of wintering owls: Barn, Great Horned, Long-eared, Western Screech and Northern Saw-whet owls roost here from November through February. Great Horned Owls in this area prey on just about anything, including Canada Geese, Mallards, pheasants, Red-tailed Hawks, coots and skunks. In November, thousands of Mallards gather on the river in the evenings. Trumpeter Swans and Rusty Blackbirds are among other species recorded here during the winter. Fish Hook Park can be reached from the Tri-Cities by taking Hwy 12 and, just past the Snake River Bridge, turning left onto Hwy 124, proceeding E for 14.2 miles, turning left onto Fish Hook Rd for 4 miles. The gate at the park entrance will be closed any time after September. Park here without blocking the road, cross the fence and proceed into the park. During the winter months the owls roost in the clumps of pines scattered about the park. Please approach the roosting areas quietly and avoid spooking the birds. (MD)

S: all year   E: 500'
H: FW DG PG
Maps: DLA 41:A 5; 54:D 4

# Monumental Dam area

I - 2

The Monumental Dam in northern Walla Walla County can be reached from the N by taking SR 395 to Connell, turning E on SR 260 to Kahlotus, turning S on Pasco-Kahlotus Rd for 0.5 mile and then left onto Devil's Canyon Rd. This canyon has such desert birds as Chukar, Prairie Falcon, Canyon and Rock wrens, 6 species of sparrows and, in winter, Gray-crowned Rosy Finch. In the evenings, Barn and Great Horned owls can be seen and heard. Drive down the canyon road to Lower Monumental Dam; do not cross the dam but turn right and drive 3 miles to Wind Dust Park and a picnic facility. Though there is great potential here for spring and fall rarities, November-February is also an important season because of the presence of wintering owls. In recent years pines in this little park have hosted as many as 15 Long-eared Owls, along with Barn and Great Horned owls. Care and caution are necessary in this owl haven. Please do not spook or alarm the roosting

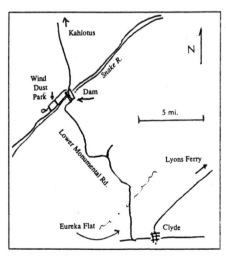

birds which can be found in most of the pines during the winter. All roads to this area are paved. Winter temperatures can be very cold but weather sunny. Summers are HOT! There are many more people than birds in the summer, but poorwills are possible. Return to the dam and drive across it. In winter check all the gulls - Glaucous is possible.

To reach this area from Walla Walla take Hwy 125 N. At 0.5 miles N of the state penitentiary turn left onto Harvey Shaw Rd.

After going under Hwy 124, this becomes Ayer Rd. Take Ayer Rd to Clyde. Clyde, on Eureka Flat, is the best chance in winter for finding Lapland Longspurs and Snow Buntings among thousands of Horned Larks. At Clyde, turn left, go 0.5 miles to Lower Monumental Rd which goes to the dam. Watch for Short-eared Owls and Gray Partridge (and rattlesnakes in summer) along this road. In winter, Gyrfalcons are possible, attracted to large numbers of Mallards and wigeon. (MD)

---

S: all year   E: 360'
H: FW RW
Maps: DLA 40:D 1-2

# Walla Walla River delta

I - 3

The Walla Walla River delta area can be an exceptionally rich area for waterfowl and shorebirds, depending on Army Corps of Engineers' management of water levels at McNary Dam downstream. Formed by soil deposited into the Columbia River by the Walla Walla River, the area continues to grow. It has been covered by birders only for the last few years and exciting new records are always possible.

Several sites are worth exploring close to the junction of Hwys US 12 and SR 730:

**Wallula Habitat Management Area** is reached by driving 0.2 mile N of the Walla Walla River bridge on Hwy 12, then turning E. Make an immediate left and proceed along a gravel road to an overlook of the first lake. This part of the unit does not allow hunting. Waterfowl numbers in spring and fall can be impressive. Further along the road are areas reserved for hunting.

**North Delta** is reached 0.3 mile N of the Walla Walla River bridge. Turn W onto a gravel spur and park near the railroad tracks. From the tracks, views of the delta allow distant observation of shorebirds, waterfowl, gulls and terns. It is not difficult to wade the channel and traverse the mudflats if water levels are low, though the mud is slippery and knee-high boots or canvas wading shoes

are recommended. If no mud is visible this is probably not worth the effort. When water levels are favorable, shorebird numbers and variety can great and include Semipalmated, Baird's and Pectoral sandpipers. Parasitic Jaegers appear to be regular, harassing the many terns in late summer. Peregrine, Ruddy Turnstone, Red Knot, Stilt Sandpiper (50 at once on one occasion!), Sharp-tailed Sandpiper, Red Phalarope and Northern Waterthrush are among other species recorded here.

**South Delta** is reached by going W 0.4 mile from the highway junction to the first paved turnoff towards the water. Good views of the southern part of the delta can be had from the grain complex here. Waterfowl numbers, especially in early spring can be exciting: many Greater Scaup, Canvasbacks and Redheads.

**"Shorebird Overlook"**, 0.2 mile E of the junction on Hwy 730 on the N side of the highway, provides views down onto a lake which in the fall often attracts many shorebirds, including Stilt Sandpiper. Another overlook is reached by traveling toward Pasco on Hwy 12 and turning E 0.2 miles after crossing the Walla Walla River. Turn left on the first gravel road and go to a small parking lot overlooking a lake which is closed to hunting and good for waterfowl.

Another interesting spot is reached by taking Hwy 730 toward Oregon. Just before entering Oregon there high basalt cliffs on the E side of the highway. In spring and summer there is a colony of White-throated Swifts here, along with Canyon and Rock wrens and rattlesnakes. Look from wide spots along the highway or you can hike up the trail near two rocks called the Twin Sisters or Twin Captains. Gray-crowned Rosy Finches sometimes roost in old Cliff Swallow nests here in winter. (DHe, AS, BW)

---

S: all year   E: 360'
H: FW SD FL
Maps: DLA 40:C-D 1

## McNary NWR, WRA

I - 5

McNary refuge lies along SR 395, E and SE of Burbank. The 3200 acre refuge, mostly sloughs backed up from McNary Dam, is best covered by automobile. It is a feeding and resting area for migrating and wintering waterfowl and also provides nesting habitat for many birds. When the area does not freeze over, numbers are fairly constant from November until spring. Twenty-five species of waterfowl visit annually including Tundra Swans in October. In spring, Lesser Scaup, Buffleheads, Canvasbacks, Redheads, goldeneyes and Ring-necked Ducks can be seen, along with Mallards, Pintails, wigeon, Gadwalls, Shovelers and teals. Shorebirds like American Avocet, Long-billed Curlew and Killdeer nest here. White Pelicans are regular in migration and sometimes spend the winter. Songbirds, found in vegetation along the refuge impoundments and along the bank of the river, include Yellow-headed Blackbird, Northern Oriole and many more. Burrowing Owls also nest here. (MC, PM, TW)

---

S: all year   E: 500'
H: FL
Maps: DLA 40:D 3

## Touchet-Louden area

I - 5

The portion of the Walla Walla River Valley that lies E of Touchet and US 12 and the Washington-Oregon state line is being farmed almost exclusively for the production of alfalfa seed. These fields provide excellent habitat for small rodents which in turn provide a food source for birds of prey. On a drive through the area in winter it is not uncommon to count over 100 hawks, most observed easily without leaving your vehicle. Red-tailed and Rough-legged hawks and Northern Harriers are most common; one or more Prairie Falcons can usually be found as well. The number of birds present in this area offers an excellent opportunity to compare species and various plumages.

During the spring and summer months the Rough-legs are replaced by Swainson's Hawks. Both Red-tailed and Swainson's hawks breed in the valley and nest of both species are common in the trees growing along the Walla Walla River as well as elsewhere in the valley. In late summer, look for areas where the alfalfa is being harvested. Adults as well as juvenile birds concentrate around these fields, feeding on the rodents exposed by the operations. A number of roads cover the area and no specific route need be followed. Turn S off Hwy 12 at a small diner located in the town of Touchet. Continue S through Touchet and across the Walla Walla River. In the summer "bee crossing" signs warn motorists to drive slowly to protect honey bees the growers breed to pollinate their alfalfa. At the disposal transfer site either turn E or continue straight ahead. Explore the secondary roads while watching for hawks. The roads in the area are laid out on a grid: a couple of turns will bring you back to Hwy 12. (DHe)

---

## Mill Creek Road

S: May-Aug   E: 1000-6000'
H: DC ST BF
Maps: DLA 41:D 6-7

I - 6

Follow US 12 to the E side of Walla Walla. Turn right at the Corps of Engineers sign. Go straight ahead for about 1 intersection. This road is Mill Creek Rd (but no signs) - watch for a sign for Rooks Park, which is about 0.6 miles up Mill Creek Rd and has proved to have good birding in the spring. Goshawk, Osprey, Barred Owl and Vaux's Swift have been recorded here. Walla Walla County's first Swamp Sparrow was found here in 1987. Cross the footbridge over Mill Creek for the best birding.

Farther up Mill Creek Rd, Dippers, Winter Wren, Hermit Thrush, MacGillivray's and Yellow warblers may be seen along the road. Eleven miles up Mill Creek, at Kooskooskie, the road turns to gravel: this is the Washington-Oregon state line. Continue up this road 17 miles to the junction with . Forest Service Rd 64, which is an unimproved road that eventually leads to Dayton. It is impassable, however, from November to mid-July, and during wet weather is suitable only for 4-wheel drive vehicles. Current road conditions are available at Forest Service offices in Walla Walla and Pomeroy. From the junction of FS roads 65 and 64 travel N on Rd 64; the Washington State line is 5 miles. Travel another 3.6 miles to Table Rock Lookout. This fire lookout is open during the summer and offers one of the most spectacular views in the northern Blue Mountains. At this point either return to Walla Walla over the same route or continue another 25 miles N on Rd 64 to Dayton.

Hairy and Downy woodpeckers, Clark's Nutcrackers and Steller's Jays are common. Check the stands of Engelmann spruce for Three-toed and stands of lodgepole pine for Black-backed woodpeckers. Boreal Owls have been found along the Washington-Oregon border in the fall, and Barred Owls have been reported in this area as well. The area is also a good place to find accipiters, including Northern Goshawks. (DHe)

The Blue Mountains appear to be Washington's "woodpecker heaven", with all species on the state list present here. In addition, there are Flammulated Owls, Mountain Quail and Turkeys. Green-tailed Towhees are much sought here, in their only known nesting area in Washington, and Rocky Mountain species such as Broad-tailed Hummingbird are to be anticipated. Road maps of the Blue Mountains are essential, and because roads may not be cleared of snow until midsummer, local inquiry is advised. We recommend a Forest Service map (available at ranger stations in Walla Walla or Pomeroy).

S: May-Nov/all yr. E: 2000-4880'
H: WC DC RW DG FL
Maps: DLA 41:C-D 7-8

# Lewis Peak, Coppei Creek

I - 7

Two good birding areas in the W Blue Mountains offer both regional specialties and a variety of other interesting species covering a good range of habitats and elevation. One area, Lewis Peak, is open May-November; the other, Coppei Creek, is accessible all year.

Drive E from Walla Walla on Hwy 12. After about 8 miles you pass through small town of Dixie, and 2 miles further you come to a large grain elevator on the E side of the highway (this area shown as Minnick on some maps). This elevator, covered with graffiti, has "Stella" painted on its S side. Turn E on the "Stella" side of the elevator and cross the old railroad bed. The road then forks (see below).

**Lewis Peak.** At the fork, take the righthand road: this is the Lewis Peak Rd. Along the road watch for Gray Partridge, Mountain and Western bluebirds, Vesper Sparrow, wapiti (elk) and black bear. The road enters conifers at about 5.7 miles. Much of the land is private and posted: please stay on the road. AT 8.5 miles there is a three-road fork. Park here, lock the car and walk up the road on the right to walk the rest of the way to Lewis Peak. Watch and listen for White-throated Swift, Three-toed Woodpecker, Gray Jay, Solitary Vireo, Green-tailed Towhee, Pine Grosbeak (winter only), Red Crossbill. The peak is bisected by the Columbia County boundary. Most of the

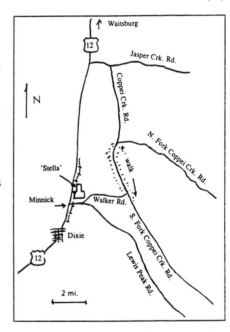

land is private and luckily open to the public. This is the highest point in Walla Walla County and the only area in which to find Pine Grosbeak, Gray Jay and Green-tailed Towhee (has nested just off the SW side of the peak). Lewis Peak is just 3 miles W of Skyline Rd where Boreal Owls were discovered in fall of 1987. Beware of wood ticks during the summer.

**Coppei Creek.** At the fork just past "Stella" and the old railroad bed, take the left hand road which is the Walker Rd. Go over and down the hill until you reach the South Fork of Coppei Creek Rd. Park the car at this junction and walk N along the road. Early morning visits from early May through late June will encounter Gray Catbird, Red-eyed Vireo, American Redstart, Yellow-breasted Chat, 5 other warblers, Black-headed Grosbeak and Lazuli Bunting. Ruffed Grouse, Gray Partridge and Golden Eagle are also possible. Many interesting reports have recently come from this stretch of Coppei Creek (between Walker Rd junction and the North Fork junction) at different seasons, and include Band-tailed Pigeon, Black-throated Green Warbler and White-throated Sparrow. The area, with the N-S orientation of the stream, along the W side of the Blue Mountains, acts as a migrant trap with interesting potential.

After walking to the junction (with the North Fork), return to the car and drive S down the S Fork of Coppei Creek. The road is 5.7 miles long and ends where the creek flows across it. Stop here and park. Northern Goshawk, Northern Pygmy Owl, Pileated Woodpecker, Winter Wren, Townsend's Solitaire and Townsend's Warbler may be seen. Return to the car and drive back to the N Fork of Coppei Creek, watching along the way for Eastern Kingbirds, Western Bluebirds and Say's Phoebes (spring and summer).

The North Fork of Coppei Creek Rd is dirt/gravel and in good shape. It is on this road that you will climb up into the Blue Mountains. Birds to watch and listen for are Northern Saw-whet Owl (nests), Red-naped Sapsucker, Veery, Swainson's Thrush and Varied Thrush. During the winter, the Coppei Creek drainage has large flocks of Robins, Bohemian Waxwings, White-crowned Sparrows and forest birds like nuthatches, 3 species of chickadees, and Brown Creepers. The upper reaches of North Coppei are closed in the winter. (MD)

S: July-Aug   E: 1600-6000'
H: DC RW WM ST
Maps: DLA 42:B-D 2-4

# Western Blue Mountains

I - 8

Edmiston campground is SE of Dayton. Watch for Williamson's Sapsucker, Wild Turkey and many other species. At Godman Springs, 5 miles uphill from Edmiston campground, Three-toed Woodpeckers and Pine Grosbeaks are possible. Look for woodpecker activity at old forest-fire burns. Flammulated Owls have been recorded in the past at Stayawhile Springs, about 5 miles SW of Godman Springs. The W.T. Wooten WRA is reached from US 12, exiting at Marengo, then going up the Tucannon River for about 15 miles. There are multitudes of woodpeckers. Mountain Quail and Turkeys reported here and up roads and trails in the area. Bighorn sheep may be watched for above the Tucannon River on Cummings Ridge. (EH, DPe)

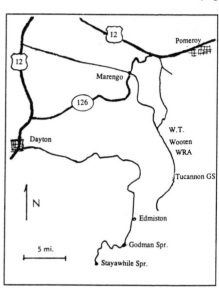

S: May-July   E: 1500-2000'
H: FW RW DG ST FL
Maps: DLA 42-43:A-B 1-8

# Dayton-Asotin

I - 9

While traveling around the Blue Mountains between Walla Walla and Asotin, many low elevation areas can be sampled. During the nesting season, these areas can have dense populations of many species. Wooded Lewis and Clark State Park, between Waitsburg and Dayton has Mourning Dove, Western Screech-Owl, Black-billed Magpie, Gray Catbird, Veery, vireos, Yellow-breasted Chat and Fox Sparrow and others. Along the Snake River, Golden Eagles and Ferruginous Hawks might be expected. Mountain Quail and Gray Partridges are reportedly present in suitable habitats. (DPe, TW)

## Eastern Blue Mountains

S: July-Aug  E: 2000-5500'
H: DC RW WM ST
Maps: DLA 43:B-D 5-8

I - 10

The Asotin WRA is about 12 miles up Asotin Creek from the town of Asotin on the E slope of the Blue Mountains. While travelling through this area, keep a watch for Mountain Quail, not a sure thing for birders anywhere in the state. Going from Asotin through Cloverland, Wenatchee Guard Station is attained. At present this is the one of the few localities where Green-tailed Towhees occur in the state. Uphill, if the roads are OK, you can reach Wickiup Springs, where there are Williamson's Sapsuckers, Goshawks and Blue Grouse. Field Springs State Park is reached from Asotin via Anatone. This is another woodpecker paradise and camping site.

This area of Washington is special in that some of the fauna has close affinities with Rocky Mountain forms. The Golden-mantled ground squirrel and Gray Jay subspecies here, for example, are much more similar to those found in Colorado's Rocky Mountain National Park than to other races occurring in other parts of Washington. (EH, DPe)

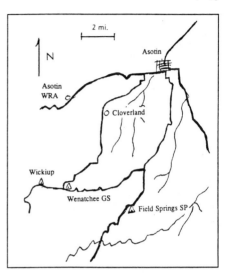

## Kamiak Butte

S: May-July  E: 2000-3700'
H: DC BF
Maps: DLA 57:A-B 7-8

I - 11

Kamiak Butte, rising above the bare, dry Palouse Hills, has a its cover of coniferous and deciduous trees, and hence is an island of unique habitat. Drive N about 11.5 miles from Pullman on WA 27 (about 2.5 miles S of Palouse). About 0.3 mile N of Fallon, drive W. Follow signs to Kamiak Butte County Park, about 1 mile W (on FugateRd), then about 0.5 mile S. N. Pygmy-Owl, Great Horned Owl, Calliope Hummingbird, Pygmy, Red- breasted and White-breasted nuthatches and Red Crossbill are typical species. Several vagrant eastern warblers have been found here in June. (PM, DPe, JW)

Common names are from The Audubon Society Field Guide to North American Mammals, by John O. Whitaker, Jr, Alfred A. Knopf, 1980. See that book for scientific names and additional information.
(* - species most likely to be seen.)

## Marsupials

Virginia Opossum, Farmland and mixed woodland. Local west of the Cascades, where introduced. Frequently seen as a road kill.

## Insectivores

Masked Shrew. Moist forest and meadows in mountains. Northern one-third of state.

*Vagrant Shrew. Moist meadows and brushy areas.

Dusky Shrew. All habitats but driest ones. Throughout except Columbia Basin and southeast.

Preble's Shrew. Wet areas in Blue Mountains.

Water Shrew. Streams and ponds in mountains.

Pacific Water Shrew. Marshes, bogs and swamps west of the Cascades.

Trowbridge's Shrew. Coniferous forest in Cascades and west.

Merriam's Shrew. Sagebrush in Columbia Basin.

Pygmy Shrew. Variety of habitats in extreme northeast corner.

Shrew-mole. Moist forest and meadows west of Cascades. Often found dead.

Townsend's Mole. Moist forest and meadows west of the Cascades. Mounds conspicuous.

Coast Mole. All habitats in western lowlands, the Cascades, and Yakima Valley and Walla Walla region. Mounds conspicuous in moist areas.

## Bats

*Myotis. Eight species of similar habits, some of them difficult to distinguish. Little Brown, Yuma and California virtually throughout the state. Long-eared and Long-legged in western lowlands, Cascades and Blue Mountains. Keen's on the Olympic Peninsula. Small-footed occurs east of the Cascades, where it roosts in crevices in basalt cliffs. Fringed found in southeast corner. Most Myotis species roost in caves or old buildings, less often under tree bark.

Silver-haired Bat. Forested areas. Roosts in trees.

Western Pipistrelle. Near water in southeast along the Snake and Columbia rivers. Roosts in crevices.

Big Brown Bat. Wooded areas. Roosts in caves, crevices and buildings.

Hoary Bat. Wooded areas. Roosts in trees.

Townsend's Big-eared Bat. Variety of habitats, local. Roosts in caves, crevices and old buildings.

Pallid Bat. Open areas of Columbia Basin. Roosts in caves and cliff crevices.

## Lagomorphs

*Pika. Talus slopes in Cascades and northeast mountains.

Pygmy Rabbit. Sagebrush of central Columbia Basin. Very low numbers.

*Eastern Cottontail. Thickets locally west of Cascades and around Pullman. Introduced from eastern North America.

*Nuttall's Cottontail. Sagebrush of Columbia Basin.

*European Rabbit. Thickets and meadows on San Juan Island and nearby islands, where introduced from Europe. Formerly abundant, much reduced as of this writing.

*Snowshoe Hare. Forests and thickets in mountains and western lowlands.

White-tailed Jack Rabbit. Grassland on periphery of Columbia Basin. Low numbers.

*Black-tailed Jack Rabbit. Sagebrush of Columbia Basin. Formerly common; populations now low.

## Rodents

Mountain Beaver. Moist thickets and forest in Cascades and west. Burrow openings often seen.

*Least Chipmunk. Sagebrush in narrow zone from Kittitas and Douglas counties southward.

*Yellow-pine Chipmunk. Ponderosa pine zone east of Cascades and subalpine zone in all mountains. In more open areas than Townsend's.

*Townsend's Chipmunk. Coniferous forest and brush from the Cascades west. Occurs in dense forest between the pine and subalpine populations of Yellow-pine Chipmunk.

Red-tailed Chipmunk. Coniferous forest and talus slopes of mountains in extreme northeast corner. Difficult to distinguish from Yellow-pine, usually occurs at higher elevations.

Woodchuck. Open areas in far northeastern corner; only a few records.

*Yellow-bellied Marmot. Open rocky areas east of Cascades, from pineland through sagebrush.

*Hoary Marmot. Talus slopes and meadows high in Cascades.

*Olympic Marmot. Talus slopes and meadows high in Olympics.

*Townsend's Ground Squirrel. Grassland and sagebrush in Yakima Valley from Ellensburg south, only west of the Columbia River. Active for a few months in early spring.

*Washington Ground Squirrel. Sagebrush east and south of the Columbia River. Active for a few months in early spring.

*Columbian Ground Squirrel. Meadows and grasslands from Hart's Pass east around eastern third of state, peripheral to sagebrush region.

*California Ground Squirrel. Grassy fields, oak groves and valleys from Ellensburg southward on lower east side of Cascades, also locally along Columbia and Cowlitz rivers west of Cascades.

*Golden-mantled Ground Squirrel. Wooded and open rocky areas in northeastern and Blue Mountains.

*Cascade Golden-mantled Ground Squirrel. Wooded and open rocky areas in Cascades. Probably a well-marked subspecies of the previous species.

*Gray Squirrel. City parks and yards in the Seattle area and in urban Pierce County. Introduced from the east.

Western Gray Squirrel. Local in oak woodland on lower east side of the southern Cascades and from Tacoma southward. Much reduced in numbers.

*Fox Squirrel. Asotin and along Okanogan Creek near Okanogan. Introduced from east.

*Red Squirrel. Forested areas east of Lake Chelan in northern third and in Blue Mountains.

*Douglas' Squirrel. Coniferous forest from Cascades west. Contacts Red Squirrel locally in north Cascades, with some hydridization.

Northern Flying Squirrel. Coniferous and mixed forest.

Northern Pocket Gopher. Most open habitats in Cascades and east. Pattern of winter tunnels obvious after snow melts.

Western Pocket Gopher. Open meadows from Olympics and Tacoma south.

Great Basin Pocket Mouse. Sagebrush of Columbia Basin. Tracks and burrow openings conspicuous in sandy areas.

Ord's Kangaroo Rat. Sandy sagebrush in Benton, Franklin and Walla Walla counties.

Beaver. Ponds, lakes, slow streams and rivers. Most ponds along stream courses were formed by Beavers.

Western Harvest Mouse. Grassland and sagebrush, usually near water, east of Cascades. Often lives in old blackbird nests.

Deer Mouse. All habitats, open to forested, sagebrush to subalpine.

Northern Grasshopper Mouse. Sandy grassland and sagebrush of Columbia Basin.

Bushy-tailed Woodrat. Local in rock piles and cliffs, most common in Columbia Basin. Characteristic white urine stains on cliffs.

Southern Red-backed Vole. Coniferous forest in Cascades and east.

Western Red-backed Vole. Coniferous forest west of Cascades.

Heather Vole. Meadows and forests in high mountains.

Meadow Vole. Wet meadows in northeast mountains and locally in central Columbia Basin.

*Montane Vole. Grassland at base of Cascades and from Spokane south in Palouse country. Populations cyclic, very variable in numbers.

*Townsend's Vole. Wet meadows west of Cascades. Populations cyclic, very variable in numbers. Runway systems often obvious.

Long-tailed Vole. Wet areas throughout, mostly in mountains.

Creeping Vole. All habitats, especially grassy meadows, Cascades and west.

Water Vole. Marshes, streams and wet meadows in Cascades, Blue Mountains and extreme northeast corner.

Sagebrush Vole. Sagebrush of Columbia Basin.

*Muskrat. Marshes, ponds and slow streams throughout.

Northern Bog Lemming. Alpine meadows in North Cascades and extreme northeast.

Black Rat. Vicinity of human habitations, also nearby forest and brush. Introduced from Old World.

*Norway Rat. Urban areas, especially around water, sometimes penetrating into countryside. Introduced from Old World.

*House Mouse. Near human habitations but may be away from them in all habitats. Introduced from Old World.

Western Jumping Mouse. Meadows and thickets near streams in mountains of northeast and southeast corners.

Pacific Jumping Mouse. Meadows in coniferous forests in the Cascades and west.

*Porcupine. Forested areas but wanders far into open.

Nutria. Marshes. Escaped from fur farms in Puget Sound lowlands and Nespelem area.

---

## Carnivores

*Coyote. Open areas, woodland and forest, lowlands (including urban areas) to high in mountains.

Gray Wolf. Recently found in North Cascades National Park, possible outside park. Very low numbers.

Red Fox. Native populations in mountains, also introduced into western lowlands from east.

Black Bear. Wooded areas.

Grizzly Bear. Recent sightings in North Cascades National Park in Whatcom and Okanogan counties. Possible elsewhere.

*Raccoon. Many habitats, including urban, especially near water.

Marten. Coniferous forest.

Fisher. Mixed forests of Cascades and Olympics, reintroduced after local extinction.

Ermine. Wooded areas.

*Long-tailed Weasel. All habitats; near water in dry regions. Road-killed males common in spring.

Mink. At or near fresh water.

Wolverine. Occasionally wanders into mountains from north.

Badger. Sagebrush, grassland and open pineland east of Cascades. Burrow openings are conspicuous.

Western Spotted Skunk. Most habitats west of Cascades and in southeast corner. Much rarer than Striped Skunk.

Striped Skunk. Brushy and open country. Frequent as a road kill.

*River Otter. Fresh and salt water. Some groups may migrate seasonally between freshwater and marine habitats.

Sea Otter. Recently reintroduced on north coast, where found near offshore kelp beds. Most otters seen along the coast, and all seen along shorelines east of Cape Flattery, are River Otters.

Mountain Lion. Forested areas, still widespread but extremely unlikely to be seen.

Lynx. Forested areas in Cascades and eastern mountains.

Bobcat. Most habitats.

Northern Fur Seal. Usually well offshore, especially during spring migration. Only females and young have been recorded as far south as Washington.

*Northern Sea Lion. Coast and inland marine waters, especially rocky areas where they may haul out. No breeding sites. Numbers decreasing.

*California Sea Lion. Coast, and inland marine waters. Especially hauled out in rocky areas, but widespread in deeper waters. Visitor from farther south, increasing recently and hauling out on islands, docks and buoys. Approaching "pest" status in the eyes of some.

*Harbor Seal. Common in marine waters along coast, and in protected waters, even up lower Columbia River. Hauls out on sand beaches, rocks, docks and log rafts.

Northern Elephant Seal. Occasional offshore and deeper protected waters. Increasing.

Caribou. Small herd migrated into coniferous forest of northeast in past. Present status unknown.

Pronghorn. Open hillsides in Yakima and Kittitas counties. Introduced from Oregon.

*Mountain Goat. Alpine and subalpine slopes of Cascades south to Mount St. Helens and Mount Adams, also introduced into Olympics; migrates downward in winter. Few in mountains of northeast corner.

Bighorn Sheep. Rocky slopes with scattered trees. Virtually extirpated in eastern Washington, then reintroduced on east slope of Cascades, Blue Mountains and northeast mountains.

---

### Artiodactyls

*Elk. Forest and meadows of all mountainous regions, migrating from lowlands to subalpine zone. Extirpated and reintroduced in many areas, with only the native form in the Olympics having persisted. Increasing in Cascades.

*Mule Deer. Most habitats from sagebrush to subalpine zone, open to forest. From Cascades west the tail is black (the "black-tailed deer"), from the east slopes and eastward it is white at base ("mule deer"); intermediates can be seen near Cascade passes.

*White-tailed Deer. Wooded areas in northeast, also introduced in Blue Mountains and an isolated population near mouth of Columbia River.

Moose. Forested areas near water, a few in northeast corner and a few have turned up in Whatcom and Skagit counties.

## Cetaceans

The following list includes all species recorded to date. Killer Whale, Harbor Porpoise and Dall's Porpoise are relatively widespread in protected waters and Minke Whale is seen with some frequency in San Juan Islands waters and eastern Strait of Juan de Fuca. Killer Whale, Harbor Porpoise and Gray Whale are regularly seen from shore either along the outer coast or inland waters. Other asterisked species have been seen with some regularity well offshore.

Baird's Beaked Whale, *Berardius bairdi.*
Pacific Beaked Whale, *Mesoplodon stejnegeri.*
Hubbs' Beaked Whale, *Mesoplodon carlhubbsi.*
Goose-beaked Whale, *Ziphius cavirostris.*
Sperm Whale, *Physeter catodon.*
Pygmy Sperm Whale, *Kogia breviceps.*
Striped Dolphin, *Stenella coeruleoalba.*
Common Dolphin, *Delphinus delphis.*
*Right Whale Dolphin, *Lissodelphis borealis.*
*Pacific White-sided Dolphin, *Lagenorhynchus obliquidens.*
False Killer Whale, *Pseudorca crassidens.*
*Killer Whale, *Orcinus orca.*
*Grampus, *Grampus griseus.*
Short-finned Blackfish, *Globicephala macrorhyncha.*
*Harbor Porpoise, *Phocoena phocoena.*
*Dall's Porpoise, *Phocoenoides dalli.*
*Gray Whale, *Eschrichtius robustus.*
Finback Whale, *Balaenoptera physalus.*
Sei Whale, *Balaenoptera borealis.*
Minke Whale, *Balaenoptera acutorostrata.*
Blue Whale, *Balaenoptera musculus.*
Humpback Whale, *Megaptera novaeangliae.*
Right Whale, *Balaena glacialis.*

161

Common names from Amphibians & Reptiles of the Pacific Northwest, by R.A. Nussbaum, E.D. Brodie, Jr. and R.M. Storm, University Press of Idaho, 1983. See that book for scientific names and additional information. (* - species most likely to be seen.)

Amphibians appear to be decreasing in many areas. Reports of rare species should be sent to Non-game Section, Washington Department of Wildlife, 600 N Capitol Way, Olympia WA 98501-1091.

### Salamanders

Northwestern Salamander. In and near ponds in forest, most easily found in spring. East slope of Cascades to coast.

*Long-toed Salamander. Usually near water, most easily found in spring. Throughout except lowest parts of Columbia Basin.

Tiger Salamander. Larvae in ponds and lakes, adults may be far from permanent water in sagebrush/grassland. East of Cascades.

Pacific Giant Salamander. In and near streams and mountain lakes in coniferous forest, adults usually underground. East slope of Cascades to coast.

Cope's Giant Salamander. Olympic Peninsula and southwest part of state. Uncommon.

Olympic Salamander. In streams and seeps in forest. Olympic Peninsula and coast inland to Lewis and Skamania counties.

*Roughskin Newt. In and near ponds where often visible; adults often cross roads. East

slope of Cascades to coast, eastern steppe, semidesert.

*Ensatina. In forest, under and in logs. West of Cascades.

Dunn's Salamander. In forest, near water, usually associated with rocks. Pacific, western Lewis, Wahkiakum and Cowlitz counties.

Larch Mountain Salamander. Moist talus slopes, usually near waterfalls, most easily found in spring. A few localities just north of Columbia River in Skamania County.

Van Dyke's Salamander. In moist areas, under logs and talus. Local in mountains and lowlands of Olympic Peninsula and Pierce County south.

*Western Redback Salamander. In coniferous forest, under and in logs. West of Cascade crest.

### Frogs

Tailed Frog. In and near mountain streams, most easily found at night. East slope of the Cascades (in Chelan Co.) to coast, also Blue Mountains.

Great Basin Spadefoot. Sagebrush/grassland, most easily found in spring when breeding in ponds. Columbia Basin.

*Western Toad. All habitats except sagebrush, usually near water. Not in central Columbia Basin. Black tadpoles form aggregations in mountain lakes.

Woodhouse's Toad. Drier areas, breeding in quiet water bodies. Southern border of state from eastern Klickitat to Whitman County.

*Pacific Treefrog. Almost ubiquitous (but not in trees!), usually near water, throughout.

*Red-legged Frog. Near or in ponds, mostly in forest. West of Cascade crest.

*Cascade Frog. In ponds and slow streams. Cascades and Olympics mostly above 3,000 feet.

Spotted Frog. In ponds and slow streams, except in sagebrush. Throughout state (virtually extirpated in west) except lower parts of Columbia Basin.

Wood Frog. Near ponds and lakes. Sight record from northeast corner needs specimen confirmation.

*Northern Leopard Frog. Ponds and slow streams. Potholes Reservoir S to southern border from Klickitat to Asotin County; also introduced in Pend Oreille, Spokane and Okanogan counties.

*Bullfrog. In ponds and lakes. Introduced widely, especially west of Cascades.

Green Frog. In ponds and lakes. Introduced to Toad Lake, Whatcom County; Gillette Lake, Stevens County; and locally in King County.

## Turtles

Snapping Turtle. Present in King and Pierce counties, presumably released captives.

Western Pond Turtle. In ponds and slow streams, may be seen basking. Very local in King, Pierce, Thurston, Clallam, Skamania and Klickitat counties.

*Painted Turtle. In ponds and lakes, may be seen basking. Throughout east of the Cascades and local, probably introduced, from Puget Sound southward.

Green Turtle. Rarely found beached on outer coast in winter.

Loggerhead Turtle. Rarely found beached on outer coast in winter.

Leatherback Turtle. Uncommon off the coast, very rarely near shore or in Strait of Juan de Fuca.

## Lizards

*Sagebrush Lizard. Sagebrush. Columbia Basin.

*Western Fence Lizard. On and near rocks and logs, usually in open woodland. East slope of Cascades and Blue Mountains; also local around southern Puget Sound.

*Side-blotched Lizard. Sagebrush. Lower parts of Columbia Basin.

*Short-horned Lizard. Sagebrush and grassland. Columbia Basin.

Western Skink. Sagebrush, grassland, dry woodland, often near water; secretive. East of Cascades.

*Northern Alligator Lizard. Forest and edge, often around logs. East slope of the Cascades to coast; also locally in northeast.

Southern Alligator Lizard. Pine and oak woodland. Lower E slope of Cascades from Ellensburg south.

## Snakes

Rubber Boa. Forest and pine and oak woodland. Throughout except Columbia Basin, rare and local west.

Ringneck Snake. Oak-pine and riparian woodland, open rocky or brushy areas, hidden during day. Southern border from Cowlitz to Whitman County and north almost to Ellensburg.

Sharptail Snake. Forest or woodland, usually in moist areas, hidden during day. Very local: Gravelly Lake, Pierce County (still present?), Lyle, Klickitat County; and more numerous in Kittitas County.

*Racer. Sagebrush, grassland, and open woodland. East of Cascades, also very local west.

Striped Whipsnake. Sagebrush. South part of Columbia Basin.

*Gopher Snake. Sagebrush, grassland, open woodland. East of Cascades, local around southern Puget Sound.

California Mountain Kingsnake. Oak woodland. Klickitat and Skamania counties along Columbia River, one record in eastern Yakima County.

*Common Garter Snake. Most habitats except sagebrush, often near water and always near it in dry areas. Throughout.

*Western Terrestrial Garter Snake. Most habitats except sagebrush. Usually near water, including salt water. Occurs throughout but less common west of Cascades.

*Northwestern Garter Snake. Most habitats except driest ones. Cascades to coast.

Night Snake. Sagebrush, under rocks in day. Lower part of Columbia Basin, Cascades lower E slope.

*Western Rattlesnake. Sagebrush and grassland, lower edge of ponderosa pine woodland. East of Cascades, usually below 2,500 feet elevation.

## REPORT SIGHTINGS OF UNUSUAL BIRDS

1) Take photographs if possible, AND

2) Write up thorough description of what you saw (see suggested form, next page) right away, BEFORE consulting field guides AND

3) Contact any local observers you know of for a supporting identification (have them write-up descriptions, also) AND

4) Contact a member of the Washington Bird Records Committee as soon as possible:
Kevin Aanerud, Seattle (206) 523-6195,
Ben Feltner, Seattle (206) 767-9937,
Eugene Hunn, Seattle (206) 524-8112,
Phil Mattocks, Ellensberg (509) 962-2191,
Dennis Paulson, Seattle (206) 528-1382,
Jeff Skriletz, Olympia (206) 357-7607,
Bob Sundstrom, Seattle (206) 634-1909,
Bill Tweit, Olympia (206) 754-7098, OR

Contact nearest member of the Washington Ornithological Society or known bird experts of local Audubon Societies and ask them to contact others, OR

5) If none of these people can be reached, leave details with the Seattle Rare Bird Alert (206) 526-8266.

### Where to send reports of unusual birds

Send thorough written descriptions and copies of photographs to Phil Mattocks, Secretary, Washington Bird Records Committee, 915 E 3rd Ave, Ellensburg WA 98926. Evenings (509) 962-2191. OR to Bill Tweit, Regional Editor, American Birds, POB 1271, Olympia WA 98507-1271. Evenings (206) 754-7098. **Also send reports of seasonal occurrences of birds** to Bill Tweit, Regional Editor, American Birds, POB 1271, Olympia WA 98507-1271. Evenings (206) 754-7098.

## RECORDED BIRD REPORTS, "HOT LINES"

Washington Rare Bird Alert (Seattle Audubon Society) (206) 526-8266

Vancouver Rare Bird Alert (Vancouver Natural History Society) (604) 737-9910

Victoria Rare Bird Alert (Victoria Natural History Society) (604) 478-8534

## Documentation of an Extraordinary Sight Record

### Washington Bird Records Committee

1. Species_____ 2. Number_____

3. Location_____

_____

4. Date_____ 5. Time bird seen_____to_____

6. Name of observer completing this form_____

7. Description of size, shape, and plumage. Describe in detail all parts of the
   bird, including the beak and feet. Please mention more than just the diagnostic
   characters, yet include only what was actually observed in the field.
   Use additional sheets if necessary.

8. Description of voice or call, if heard.

9. Description of behavior.

10. Habitat - general and specific.

11. Distance to the bird.

12. Optical equipment used (incl. binoculars, telescopes, cameras).

13. Light (sky condition, amount of light on bird, position of sun).

14. Similarly appearing species which are eliminated by items 7, 8, and 9. Explain.

15. Previous experience with this species and similarly appearing species.

16. Other Observers.

17. Field guides, other books, articles, and advice consulted, and how did these influence this description?

18. Were field notes about the observation written— during the observation, immediately after, later, or not at all?

19. Signature_____ 20. Date_____

21. Address_____
    _____
    _____

    Copies of this form will be sent to the Secretary of the Bird Records Committee (currently, Phil Mattocks, 915 E. Third Ave., Ellensburg, WA 98926), and to the appropriate Regional Editor for American Birds. Thank you.

Feb 1989

## BIRDING REFERENCES, INFORMATION

BOOKS:

In addition to the well-known field guides by the National Geographic Society, Peterson, Robbins, Pough and Hoffman, there are other references for Washington.

Jewett, S.A., W.P. Taylor, W.T. Shaw and J.W. Aldrich. 1953. **Birds of Washington State,** University of Washington Press, Seattle.

Campbell, R.W., N.K. Dawe, I. McTaggart-Cowan, J.M. Cooper, G.W. Kaiser, and M.C.E. McNall. 1990. **The Birds of British Columbia. Vols. 1 & 2.** Royal B.C. Museum/Can. Wildl. Serv.

Cannings, R.A., R.J. Cannings and S.G. Cannings. 1987. **Birds of the Okanagan Valley, British Columbia.** Royal B.C. Museum.

Godfrey, W.E. 1986. **The Birds of Canada.** (Revised edition), National Museum of Canada Bulletin 203, Ottawa. *Excellent for field marks, measurements, habitats and distribution. Almost a "must".*

JOURNALS:

Valuable and essential if one wants to keep current with field ornithology, these publications supplement field guides which cannot keep up with ever-changing occurrences, ranges and newly determined field marks.

**American Birds,** 950 Third Ave., New York NY 10022. *Five issues per year published by the National Society and includes the annual Christmas Bird Count, summaries of migration, nesting and winter seasons for all of North America.*

**Western Birds,** P.O. Box 595, Coronado CA 92118. *A quarterly journal of Western Field Ornithologists, dealing chiefly with identification, distribution and occurrences in western North America.*

**Birding,** American Birding Association, POB 6599, Colorado Springs CO 80934. *Includes articles on identification, where to find birds in many parts of the world, contacts for birders. ABA also publishes a helpful monthly newsletter,* **Winging It,** *for ABA members.*

**Washington Birds,** journal of the Washington Ornithological Society, POB 85786, Seattle WA 98145, and newsletter, **WOSNEWS,** *provides valuable information, bird news and contacts.*

In addition, the **Auk,** published by the American Ornithologists' Union; the **Condor,** published by the Cooper Ornithological Society; the **Wilson Bulletin,** published by the Wilson Ornithological Society; and the **Northwestern Naturalist** (formerly **Murrelet**) published by the Society for Northwest Vertebrate Biology, also include articles of interest to this region.

BIRDING GUIDES:

Butler, Z. and K. Marsh, 1983. **Birding in Southcentral Washington.** Washington. Yakima Valley Audubon Society, Yakima.

Ennor, H.R. 1991. **Birds of the Tri-Cities and vicinity.** Lower Columbia Basin Audubon Society.

Evanich, J.E., Jr. 1990. **Birder's guide to Oregon.** Portland Audubon Society.

Hunn, E.S., 1982. **Birding in Seattle and King County: Site guide and annotated list.** Trailside Series, Seattle Audubon Society, Seattle.

Lewis, M.G. and F.A. Sharpe. 1987. **Birding in the San Juan Islands.** The Mountaineers, Seattle.

Mark, D.M., 1978. **Where to find birds in British Columbia.** Kestrel Press, New Westminster.

Taylor, K. 1984. **A birder's guide to Vancouver Island.** Keith Taylor, Victoria.

Vancouver Natural History Society. 1993. **A bird watching guide to the Vancouver area, British Columbia,** Cavendish Books, Vancouver.

ATLASES:

**Washington Atlas and Gazetteer. 1988.** DeLorme Mapping Company, Freeport, Maine. *Invaluable and virtually essential for covering the state. Nearly perfect maps include topography, back-country roads.*

Speich, S.M. and T.R. Wahl. 1989. **Catalog of Washington Seabird Colonies.** Colonies. U.S. Fish Wildl. Serv. Biol. Rep. 88(6). *Maps and most recent published data on seabirds nesting in marine areas.*

171